French Peasant Fascism

French Peasant Fascism

Henry Dorgères's

Greenshirts

and the

Crises of

French

Agriculture,

1929–1939

ROBERT O. PAXTON

NEW YORK   OXFORD   •   OXFORD UNIVERSITY PRESS   1997

Oxford University Press

Oxford   New York
Athens   Auckland   Bangkok   Bogota   Bombay   Buenos Aires
Calcutta   Cape Town   Dar es Salaam   Delhi   Florence   Hong Kong
Istanbul   Karachi   Kuala Lumpur   Madras   Madrid   Melbourne
Mexico City   Nairobi   Paris   Singapore   Taipei   Tokyo   Toronto   Warsaw

and associated companies in
Berlin   Ibadan

Copyright © 1997 by Oxford University Press, Inc.

Published by Oxford University Press, Inc.
198 Madison Avenue, New York, New York 10016

Oxford is a registered trademark of Oxford University Press

Library of Congress Cataloging-in-Publication Data
Paxton, Robert O.
French peasant fascism : Henry Dorgères's Greenshirts and the
crises of French agriculture, 1929–1939 / Robert O. Paxton.
p.   cm.
Includes bibliographical references and index.
ISBN 0-19-511188-5; 0-19-511189-3 (pbk.)
1. Peasantry—France—Political activity—History—20th century.
2. Fascism—France—History—20th century.   3. Dorgères, Henry,
1897–1985.   4. Fascists—France—Biography.   5. France—Politics and
government—1914–1940.   I. Title.
HD1536.F8P385   1997
320.53'3'08863—dc21   96-46864

Frontispiece photo: A peasant demonstration protesting the judicial sale of cattle
for back taxes in Quimper on 1 February 1936. Reprinted with permission.

1 3 5 7 9 8 6 4 2

Printed in the United States of America
on acid-free paper

ACKNOWLEDGMENTS

HENRY DORGÈRES, the main rightwing peasant agitator of 1930s France, was a conspicuous figure in his day, but I had great difficulty finding substantial traces of him and his movement on paper. Many public archives were closed, private ones were rare, and even when the documents lay before me, the police or prefectoral agents who wrote them seemed poorly attuned to the peasants they were describing. Few of Dorgères's principal followers were still alive to give me their eye-witness testimony.

Such an accumulation of obstacles makes me particularly grateful to the many people who helped me to get around them. I hope I have included them all here. The unwillingness of a few people to let me see the archives they supervise encourages me to think that these matters are still capable of arousing passion.

I wish to thank, first, the then Director-General of the Archives de France, M. Jean Favier; the then head of the Section Contemporaine of the Archives Nationales, Mme. Chantal de Tourtier Bonazzi; and her successor, Mme. Paule René-Bazin. They helped me to navigate the complicated process of gaining access to French public archives of the 1930s. I was able to work usefully in the departmental archives of the Aisne, Bouches-du-Rhône, Calvados, Charente-Maritime, Corrèze, Côtes d'Armor, Eure, Eure-et-Loir, Finistère, Ille-et-Vilaine, Loir-et-Cher, Loire-Atlantique, Oise, Pas-de-Calais, Seine-Maritime, Seine-et-Marne, Seine-et-Oise, and Somme. Almost all the *directeurs des services d'archives* of these departments and their staffs assisted me efficiently and courteously.

A few local archivists went far beyond their normal duties to aid my project. I am particularly grateful to Daniel Collet, archivist at the Archives Départementales du Finistère, who guided me to precious papers and interviews. Alain Droguet, *directeur* of the Archives Départementales des Côtes-d'Armor; Eliane Carouge of the Eure; and Guy Quincy of the Corrèze were also outstandingly helpful. Corentin Renot, mayor of Pleuven, let me consult his town's archives.

A number of other persons helped me locate local materials. Mme. Dominique Arnould, archivist of the Chambre d'Agriculture of the Aisne, and Christian Bougeard, in the Côtes-d'Armor, offered me both hospitality and local knowledge. I am also indebted to Jean-Pierre Le Crom in the Loire-Atlantique, Jacqueline Sainclivier and David Bensassoun in the Ille-et-Vilaine, Gabriel Désert in the Calvados, Yves Le Maner in the Pas-de-Calais, and Julien Papp in the Eure. Dominique Lerch made available his documentation about Joseph Bilger's Bauernbund in Alsace, and Freddy Raphael and Mme. Geneviève Herberich-Marx shared their deep knowledge of Alsatian politics.

Mme. Mireille Tanguy-Prigent and Mme. Michel Geistdorfer in the Finistère let me see materials from, respectively, their father and husband, well-known opponents of Dorgères.

Several authors of *mémoires de maitrise* generously brought me their work and discussed their findings: Clément Lépine, "La Naissance du mouvement Dorgériste," Université de Paris Nord, Paris XIII, 1992–93; Nicolas Varin, "Dorgères et le dorgérisme en Picardie," Université de Paris I, Panthéon Sorbonne, 1993–94; Jean-Luc Allais, "Dorgères et ses hommes: la Défense Paysanne en Basse-Normandie," Université de Caen, 1992–93; and José Arnoux, "Milieux ruraux et urbains dans le Pas-de-Calais dans la tourmente nationaliste de l'entre deux guerres: le Dorgérisme et le P.S.F.," Université Charles De Gaulle, Lille III, 1990–91.

The following persons were willing to talk to me about Dorgères or his major lieutenants: Joseph Argouarc'h, René Bourrigaud, Jean-Louis Chalony, Mme. Louis Divanac'h, Robert Fiche, Mme. Poriel (daughter of Joseph Divanac'h), Jean Suplice, and Raymond Triboulet.

I received valuable scholarly assistance from Gilles Postel-Vinay, Isabelle Boussard, Patrick Fridenson, Michel Cépède, Gilbert Garrier, and John T. S. Keeler. Pascal Ory, this subject's trailblazer, gave me crucial initial encouragement.

Justice Minister Robert Badinter granted permission to consult Dorgères's trial records. Ezra Suleiman, Jean-Noel Jeanneney, and Louis Joxe helped me to obtain permission to see Dorgères's Ministry of the Interior file, and Antoine Prost helped me over a momentary difficulty in the Loir-et-Cher. Jean-Paul Brunet kindly helped me to gain access to the archives of the Prefecture of Police.

At the Musée Henri Queuille at Neuvic d'Ussel (Corrèze), where the papers of the longest-serving minister of agriculture of the Third and Fourth Republics are housed, Marcel Barbanceys, *conservateur,* and Jean Chastrusse, *directeur des archives,* received me with enthusiasm, although the Queuille archives are richer for the postwar period than for the 1930s. The librarian of the Ecole d'Agriculture at Beauvais let me consult a valuable *mémoire* on the agricultural strikes of 1936. Mlle. Isabelle Richefort, of the Service d'Archives at the Ministry of Agriculture, gave me access to the valuable clipping file of Michel Augé-Laribé (no interwar minister left any archives). Mlle. Monique Genay let me use the library of the Assemblée des Présidents des Chambres d'Agriculture. I also thank M. Bruno Jourdan for permission to consult the papers of André Tardieu, the peasants' favorite minister of agriculture between the wars, in the Archives Nationales. I also thank Denis Lefèvre and the Office Universitaire de Recherches Socialistes for access to the clipping file of Michel Cépède.

Emmanuel Le Roy Ladurie let me read the manuscript of the autobiography that his father was reworking right up to his death, but he has not been willing to open his father's important archive to any scholar.

Financial support from the German Marshall Fund of the United States and Columbia University permitted me to take some time off from teaching and administrative duties to pursue this subject in Paris and in the archives of eighteen rural French departments. Finally, but certainly not least, Sarah Plimpton gave wise editorial advice and encouragement over the years.

None of these helpers and friends is in any way responsible for the way in which I have interpreted this material or for any errors, which are entirely my responsibility.

CONTENTS

ABBREVIATIONS

AGPB   Association Générale des Producteurs de Blé (wheat growers' association)

APPCA   Assemblée Permanente des Présidents des Chambres d'Agriculture

CA   chambre d'agriculture

CAP   Comité d'Action Paysanne

CDP   comité de défense paysanne

CGB   Confédération Générale des Planteurs de Betteraves (sugar beet planters' association)

CGPT   Confédération Générale des Paysans-travailleurs (peasant union affiliated with the CGT)

CGT   Confédération Générale du Travail (principal labor union)

CGV   Confédération Générale des Vignerons (vintners' association)

CNAA   Confédération Nationale des Associations Agricoles

CNP   Confédération Nationale Paysanne

COC   Commission d'Organisation Corporative (agency that constructed the Peasant Corporation)

CROC   commission régionale d'organisation corporative (local branch of COC)

FNSEA   Fédération Nationale des Syndicats d'Exploitants Agricoles

JAC   Jeunesse Agricole Chrétienne (Catholic young farmers' association)

PAO   Progrès agricole de l'ouest (Dorgères's main weekly newspaper)

PAPF   Parti Agraire et Paysan Français

PCO   Le Paysan du Centre-ouest (Dorgères's weekly newspaper in the Loire Valley)
RPF   Ralliement du Peuple Français (Gaullist party)
SA   syndicat agricole
SADP   Syndicat Agricole de Défense Paysanne
SDP   syndicat de défense paysanne
SFIO   Section Française de l'Internationale Ouvrière (French Socialist Party)
UNSA   Union Nationale des Syndicats Agricoles

Units of Measurement

hectare 2.5 acres
kilo 2.2 pounds
quintal 100 kilos (220 pounds)

French Peasant Fascism

INTRODUCTION

In Search of Henry Dorgères

.

HENRY DORGÈRES WAS THE leading rightwing agrarian agitator in rural France between the two world wars. *Haut les fourches! (Raise Your Pitchforks!)* was the title he chose for the book of memoirs and exhortation published in 1935,[1] and the phrase became his trademark.[2] It captured perfectly the truculence and earthy physicality of Dorgères's message, which summoned French farmers to take their own destinies in hand, by violence if necessary.

But Dorgères never wielded a pitchfork himself. He was born Henri-Auguste D'Halluin, the son of a modest butcher in the Nord; he took the pen name of Henry Dorgères at the age of twenty-nine, after he had become established as a journalist for a farmers' newspaper in Brittany. As Pierre Barral, an historian of French agriculture, put it, he was "better at ranting than at planting."[3] He had an empathetic grasp of the grievances and resentments of the most inarticulate French farmers in the 1930s, however, and he had a genius for putting them into words.

By the end of 1935, at his peak, Dorgères had put together what he claimed was the most vigorous and authentic peasant movement in France. He commanded a little press empire of farmers' newspapers, the strongest of which were *Le Progrès agricole de l'Ouest* in Brittany and *Le Paysan du Centre-Ouest* in the Loire Valley. He was reaching for national coverage with the weekly *Le Cri du sol* and the monthly *La Voix du paysan,*[4] both published in Paris. His network of *comités de défense paysanne* aspired to organize every rural commune in France, although, in practice, they succeeded mostly in the north and west. Some of the most vigorous also published local newspapers.[5] An action squad of young men, the

Greenshirts, with its own monthly, *Haut les fourches,* stood ready to guard meetings and undertake raids against strikers or other enemies of agriculture. At the summit, the Comité Central (later Syndicat Agricole) de Défense Paysanne, with offices in Paris, oversaw the whole operation.

Looking back in 1943, Dorgères claimed that his organizations had enrolled a half million members on the eve of the war, and that even though other farmers' organizations might have more members, his, being more highly motivated, was "by far the strongest [peasant] organisation in the country."[6] But it was as an orator capable of stirring thousands of farmers to action that Dorgères was best known to the French public. Some of his gatherings were the biggest political meetings ever seen in rural France.[7]

Many descriptions of the orator Dorgères survive. Paul Marion, future Vichy propaganda chief (1941–44), covered, for the illustrated weekly *Vu,* Dorgères's campaign for a parliamentary seat at Blois in March 1935. Marion admired "his bull neck, his round and sturdy back," a contrast to his "delicate profile of a Caesar or of a Virgilian shepherd," the whole harmonized by "the solid jaw." When Dorgères spoke in the high-columned grain market in Blois, the Halle aux Grains, Marion imagined the lofty building transformed into a "cathedral of peasant heresy."[8] In this "rustic and religious setting," wrote Marion, Dorgères was a modern-day Savanarola, reducing to silence the absurd leftwing teachers and officials who tried to refute him: "His voice beat the walls again and again, persuasive and firm, rhythmic as a Greek chorus. . . . He never missed a beat."[9]

Raymond Triboulet, who worked for Dorgères as a journalist in the late 1930s—then joined the underground movement *Ceux de la Résistance* in the German-occupied Calvados and the Gaullist Ralliement du peuple français (RPF) in 1947, taking a cabinet seat in the 1960s—remembered Dorgères's oratory with awe:

> Even peasant crowds, calm by nature, were transported outside themselves by this flow of astonishing rapidity, this voice which grew ever stronger and higher. These long phrases, shouted all in one breath, provoked a crescendo of physical exaltation in the crowd gathered in vast meadows as far as one could see.[10]

From a hostile perspective, *La Voix socialiste* of La Rochelle portrayed him with "swollen veins, face contorted. . . . He bellowed at you enough to make the dead tremble."[11]

Dorgères's stentorian, gesticulating style has vanished from public oratory, and the vast open-air meetings for which it was suited have been redirected from politics to rock music. Dorgérist speeches were meant to be seen and heard across seas of spectators, whom the orator hoped to transform into participants in a ritual communion. This style might have worked on radio (though Dorgères never, as far as I know, had access to that medium). It would have seemed ridiculously exaggerated in television's more intimate, face-to-face exchange—for Dorgères as for most of the other great oratorical demagogues of the 1930s.

But Dorgères is interesting for more than what his oratory shows us about public space and about styles of communication in the French countryside before television. Perhaps the last city-bred propagandist to be accepted as their leader by significant numbers of French peasants, Dorgères helped promote four major contemporary developments in French rural society and culture.

First, he helped replace rural notables by authentic farmers as leaders of the increasingly inclusive network of agrarian organizations that, even today, forces the French nation to pay attention to its agriculture. Second, he gave a powerful impulse to the old dream of agrarian unity, although it was others who eventually overcame the Third Republic's wearisome division of farmers' organizations into two clans, republican and clerical: Vichy's Corporation Paysanne, and then, after World War II, today's FNSEA.[12] Third, Dorgères mounted the most serious peasant revolt against the parliamentary Republic since the *chouannerie* of the 1790s, and he let the conservative farmers of northern and western France taste the forbidden fruit of direct action. Finally, he helped force the French nation to confront the question of its rural-urban balance. For Dorgères (in agreement with most rural notables of his era), a large population of family farmers was indispensable to French prosperity, independence, virtue and identity. Even today—as France surges ahead with its breakneck transformation, within forty years, from a half-peasant nation to the world's second largest agricultural exporter (based on the high-tech productivity of 5% of its population), the latest and fastest rural revolution of any industrialized country—many French city dwellers, most of whom have never heard of Dorgères, agree.

Preaching an authoritarian, corporatist state in the 1930s, by violent overthrow of the Republic if necessary, Dorgères was squarely in the "magnetic field"[13] of the fascist experiments that looked so successful in that decade. If anyone was in a position to detach large numbers of French peasants from the Republic and create a French form of rural fascism in the 1930s, it was Henry Dorgères.

Today, surviving followers of Dorgères and their families reject indignantly any suggestion that they were fascist. As we shall see, however, Dorgères himself accepted the label, at least for a time in 1934. It is true that he later rejected all foreign models: "neither fascism nor communism."[14] Labeling, however, can be a sterile exercise, and in any event, Dorgérism was the French rural variant of the extreme right of that decade. The strength or weakness of such a movement is an important issue, for it was in the countryside that both Mussolini and Hitler won their first mass following, and it was angry farmers who provided their first mass constituency. Yet, so far, every student of fascism in France has ignored the countryside. Given the salience of angry farmers in the success of fascism elsewhere and the importance of the peasantry in French society, that is a crippling omission. This book starts from the premise that the countryside is the most rewarding setting within which to study the potential and the limits of French fascism in the 1930s.

As for the private Henri-Auguste D'Halluin behind the orator, we shall never be able to know him. Dorgères's accounts of himself were devoted entirely to the public persona, and they were distorted by bombast and exaggeration. I was able to find only a handful of Dorgères's personal letters. Six letters were seized by the police when Dorgères was under surveillance by sucessive French goverments as a major danger to the state in 1933–35.[15] Some of Dorgères's followers showed me a few scraps of personal correspondance dating from after World War II, and I have seen one letter he wrote to a historian near the end of his life. None of Dorgères's own papers seem to have survived his forlorn death in the Paris suburb of Antony (Hauts-de-Seine) on 22 January 1985.[16] When the old man died, his audience reduced to the other habitués of the Le Bouchon bar in Antony, one can imagine the arrival of a brisk cleaning squad who threw out his effects and papers. What was, for Dorgères, the accumulated witness of a lifetime's work, and for historians a precious source, was to them only trash.

We are limited to a study of the public person, and for that we must draw together several disparate and imperfect sources: Dorgères's own inflated accounts (including two postwar autobiographies),[17] cross-checked as carefully as possible with meager and sometimes erroneous reports by journalists and police agents, and the fading recollections of a few eye-witnesses, both pro and con.

My search for Dorgères and his movement in departmental archives across northern and western France was a frustrating one. I did not know, when I began what I thought would be a modest project, how hard it would be to find material in French archives, public or private, concerning how previously inarticulate small farmers gathered and expressed their grievances in the 1930s. The powerful elite organizations that had already structured French agriculture—the farmers' associations (syndicats agricoles) and the specialized associations that lobbied for single products like wheat, wine, or sugar beets—are much better documented, of course.

The first problem was that the prefectoral reports and police records for the 1930s were still classified in the early 1990s. What the late Henri Michel had criticized a quarter century earlier as "the anachronistic fifty-year rule for the consultation of public archives"[18] had in the meantime become, in practice if not in law, a sixty-year rule.[19] It was possible for a scholar to obtain an exemption *(dérogation)* from this rule for the purpose of scholarly research, and Director-General Jean Favier of the Archives de France and his staff graciouly supported my requests for that purpose throughout the years I worked on this project.

Even with their support, however, access to departmental archives was not assured. The originating agency *(service versant)*—the prefect himself, in the case of prefectoral and police reports—had to give his assent. The task sometimes took more than a year and several visits: one visit to discover what dossiers had to be consulted and then, if the prefect and both the local and national archival authorities all gave their authorization after considering the possible objections of local citizens, another visit to consult them. If an additional relevant box turned up during the consultation, new permissions were required. Local archives were closed to me in two departments. In one, the prefect's rotation to another post turned things around; nothing availed in the other. In contrast, many departmental archivists not only welcomed me but also seemed pleased to assist with my project. I learned that in archival matters the Napoleonic state gives way to local option.

Access to the documents, however, was not my only problem. French archives are generally quite thin for the 1930s. Deliberate destruction on the eve of the German occupation of Paris,[20] German pillage,[21] accidental destruction from battles,[22] Allied bombing,[23] administrative decisions,[24] and sheer mischance[25] have made the 1930s the most thinly documented decade of the entire Third Republic.

Finally, when at long last what remains of the archives were laid out on my desk, I could see that French police and prefectoral officials were far less prepared in the 1930s to analyze peasants' rebellions than workers' rebellions. They rarely indicated in their reports whether, say, the crowds who blocked the sale of an indebted farmer's property, occupied some prefecture, or roughed up some deputy were smallholders, renters, or sharecroppers—or, indeed, anything precise about their socioeconomic status. In the absence of mass arrests or deaths within the rural crowd, we do not have the kind of data that enabled historians like George Rudé and Jacques Rougerie to provide a sociological profile of urban crowds between 1789 and 1871.

The fundamental problem, however, was cultural. Third Republic officialdom was simply not attuned to the language and concerns of the lower levels of the peasantry they were expected to govern. As Dorgères always maintained, the *classe paysanne* was simply outside the ken of most of the Third Republic's bureaucrats.

The Dorgérist movement itself left almost no documents, except its newspapers. The authentic farmers who ran it lived in an oral culture, in explicit rejection of the written culture of the French republican school system and bureaucracy. I had the privilege to meet a few of them or their families and reminisce over a glass of strong Breton *poiré*. Some of them had photographs or even a few brief notes from Dorgères in his declining years. If any of them had a real archive, he or she did not want to reveal it. As we have seen, Dorgères's own papers do not seem to have survived, nor have I been able to locate his two sons. As for the rural notables who made common cause with Dorgères for a while in the middle 1930s, I was not able to find any important private archive that can be consulted today.[26]

On reflection, the very poverty of its documentation, both by its own leaders and by the state, tells us something important about Dorgérism. It was less a solid organization than a truculent mood of rebellion and self-help among angry farmers, who were learning that they could expect neither their traditional leaders nor the French state to deal with their problems. Poor documentation also confirmed that small farmers were indeed the disinherited of the Third Republic, neither listened to nor understood by public authorities.

In view of Dorgérism's relative formlessness, it began to seem a poor strategy to treat it unthinkingly as an analogy of, say, a political party, a labor union, or an economic pressure group and to describe its institutions and programs from the top down. As an alternative strategy, I have studied local cases of Dorgérist action, concrete expressions of its cultural particularity. I had two reasons for proceeding in this way. There was, first, my conviction that movements of the radical Right—fascism and its emulators—are better studied as political behavior than as creed. Second, this localist approach fits the decentralized nature of the *comités de défense paysanne*. They tended to express some concerted village purpose rather than to reflect some central initiative.

Thus this book treats Dorgérism more as behavior than as rhetoric. Specifically it presents five different types of Dorgérist action (Chapter 3). We examine first the market-day rally—Dorgères's technique for giving a voice to hitherto mute peasants who felt despised and unrepresented by both the Republic and by the traditional French rural leadership. Next come campaigns to limit the state's invasion of peasants' lives through social security and other forms of social and economic intervention. Third and fourth are Dorgérist actions against communism in rural settings:

against farm workers' strikes and against strikes in factories that processed farm products. Finally, we examine the Greenshirts' efforts to organize the market for certain cash crops whose dispersed small producers felt defenseless against concentrated buyers.

Dorgères and his followers understood these actions as epic narratives, designed to be told and retold in peasants' rallies, enhanced by a little dramatic heightening. They functioned as exemplary theatrical scenarios designed to encourage laggards and furnish a vicarious solidarity to the isolated and powerless. At a minimum, these scenarios of rural protest are diverting enough and today unfamiliar enough to be worth recounting in detail. I also hope in these stories to "penetrate deeply enough into detail to discover something more than detail,"[27] for they show us something of French rural sociability in the twilight of the era in which the countryside was far more densely populated and more distinct from urban life than it is today. So we shall use Dorgères's narratives for a purpose different than his: to identify those openings in 1930s French rural society in which Dorgérism found room to develop a following.

I have taken particular pains to clarify the relations between Dorgérism and the traditional agricultural organizations and rural notables of the time (Chapter 4). It does not suffice to study a movement like Dorgères's Greenshirts in isolation. The activist Far Right of the twentieth century has been successful to the degree that it has been able to obtain the assistance, or at least the complicity, of established conservative elites.

But before we can get down to the grass roots, we need to make two detours. Chapter 1 examines the multiple stresses that made many French peasants angry and frustrated enough to listen to Dorgères in the 1930s. Chapter 2 recounts Dorgères's beginnings and the foundation of his movement, as best they can be reconstituted now.

one

. . .

THE TRIPLE CRISIS OF THE FRENCH PEASANTRY, 1929–39

DURING A LONG DECADE that began in the late 1920s, the men and women who drew their living from agriculture in France faced very hard times. Peasants always face hard times, and they always feel that city people care little and understand less about them. But the crisis of the 1930s went beyond the recurring insecurities—illness, bad weather, poor harvests—that peasants have always taken for granted as part of their lot. This crisis, which seemed to threaten the French family farm with extinction, had three dimensions.

First, the economic dimension of the peasant crisis of the 1930s—during the Great Depression—was an ever-deepening decline of farm prices that lasted so long and plunged so low that even the most diligent efforts could barely keep a family alive. Second, the cultural dimension of this crisis was the low esteem for peasant life, values, and needs that seemed to permeate the Third Republic. Schools, films, literature, and the popular press were devoted, or so it seemed to farm families, to making the peasants' children feel contempt for their way of life. They lured the best young people away to the cities and emptied the villages in a disheartening "rural exodus."

The third dimension concerned politics: it might be called a crisis of representation. There seemed to be no leader or institution in the French Third Republic with sufficient concern, comprehension, or will to devote public attention to the peasants' plight. Public policy on both the Left and the Right seemed overwhelmingly committed to cheap bread from abroad and at whatever cost to the future of independent small farmers. There was not even a thinker or writer who could give French peasants the dignity of understanding that what was happening to them was not the result of sloth, stupidity, or moral failure. No account of peasants' anger in the 1930s is complete without consideration of all three parts of the crisis, and we take them up one by one.

The Depression

The Great Depression of the 1930s hit agriculture before it affected the other branches of the economy. The prices farmers received for their products began a long slide in the late 1920s. This was a worldwide phenomenon, and its roots went back into the last third of the nineteenth century. First came the creation of a worldwide market in foodstuffs in the 1870s and 1880s, as the railroad and the steamship put cheap grain from the plains of Russia, Australia, and the Americas on the tables of every city on earth. After that revolution had occurred, French farmers began to confront a choice that has not been fully resolved even today: they must either produce cheaper or better foodstuffs than their foreign competitors or shelter behind the walls of an autarkic economic fortress.

A more immediate root of the agricultural depression in Europe was the economic dislocations caused by World War I. During the 1914–18 conflict, European farmers put down the plough and took up the sword. Their young men were in uniform; their horses had been requisitioned by the artillery; their fields were being sown with lead. The belligerent countries of Europe were forced to import food and to abandon their prewar agricultural exports. New producers rushed into the breach. Vast new areas were put to grain and animal production in Canada, Argentina, Australia, and in what was to become the dust bowl of the dry central plains of the United States. When the war ended, these producers had no intention of giving up their new markets, even though European agricultural production soon returned to prewar levels and even exceeded them. The result was overproduction, a flooded market, and a worldwide downward spiral of farm prices.

Wheat—cheap to grow and cheap to transport by the new mechanized techniques—was at the center of these trends. Almost every French farmer grew some wheat, specialization then being far less complete than it is today. Wheat still occupied five million hectares (eleven million acres) in France, 24% of the country's cultivatable land. French agriculture, despite its inefficiencies, was a formidable engine for the production of wheat. With 2% of the world's population, France produced 7% of the world's wheat in 1929.[1]

Wherever agriculture touched hearts, as well as pocketbooks, there was a mystique about wheat, and nowhere more so than in France. Wheat marked the turning seasons; it was the symbol of regeneration, "our sacred plant."[2] "Wheat forms the basis of the farmers' whole mental world," commented one rural agricultural official in 1934.[3] So it is with wheat that we begin the account of the French peasants' Depression agonies.

Within France itself, cultivators had gradually, unevenly but steadily, increased their yields over the years by using improved strains and increasing quantities of fertilizer. Because France had an exceptionally large proportion of small family farmers who invested little and clung to traditional ways, French wheat productivity per acre remained among the lowest in Europe. Certain areas of extensive wheat cultivation, however, particularly the Paris basin and the northern plains, kept abreast of the latest techniques. The war-damaged farmlands of northeastern France received massive reinvestment and became more productive than ever.[4] These high-yield farms carried French wheat productivity steadily upward in the 1920s, even as many small farms continued to produce small quantities by the inefficient old methods. Thus France continued its paradoxical role as both an exporter and an importer of wheat. In poor years, between the wars, France still had to import wheat; in good years, France produced more than enough for its own use and more than it could export in a glutted market.

French wheat growers also faced a declining internal market, for reasons more specific to their own country. As French consumers enriched their diet with other foods, they ate less bread. The French government and the wheat producers' association, the Association Générale des Producteurs de Blé (AGPB), tried to reverse this trend. But their various measures—improving quality, requiring millers to use techniques that consumed larger quantities of wheat for each unit of flour *(taux de blutage)*, and keeping foreign wheat out of French bread—had the effect of sweeping against the tide. Zero French population growth made the steady shrinkage of domestic wheat consumption even more apparent. No wonder so many peasant leaders were passionate natalists.

Add to these structural factors the accident of perfect weather for maximum wheat harvests for two seasons in a row. The harvests of 1932 and 1933 were the most abundant in French agricultural history. Far from being good news, this meant a collapse of wheat prices even within the protected French market. In the middle 1930s, France (like the United States and other large wheat-producing countries) was drowning in surplus grain.

The price of wheat in France eroded steadily through the late 1920s, prosperous years for everyone except farmers. Wheat prices had reached their postwar peak in 1926:

1926	198 francs per quintal
1927	166
1928	161
1929	150
1930	147[5]

These prices were already far below the 300 francs per quintal[6] that farm spokesmen thought were necessary to make rural life attractive enough to stem the rural exodus.[7] And even these inadequate prices were not to last. After a slight improvement in 1931, the bottom dropped out of the price of wheat in France. In several weeks after August 1932, it fell from 160 francs to 100–110 francs per quintal. The government's effort to defend a minimum price or 115 francs per quintal in July 1933 failed. It dropped to 80 francs in 1934, and averaged 70 francs in 1935.[8] Many farmers sold their wheat in 1935 for 55 francs per quintal, if they could sell it at all. At that moment, when they did not yet know that the bottom had been reached, many farmers, large and small, thought they were going to be driven from the land.

A report from the prefect of the Haute-Garonne is graphic. At the Halle aux Grains in Toulouse, he wrote the Ministry of the Interior on 17 October 1933, that once again that week no one was buying wheat.[9] There were many weeks like this all over France between 1932 and 1935. Big farmers could store their wheat and wait, living uneasily on their savings. But small farmers, lacking storage facilities and faced with urgent bills, usually had to sell at once. Either they could not sell their grain at all or they had to give it up for less than they had spent to grow it. Then they could not find the few francs needed to pay their bills for seed and fertilizer, to pay the rent *(fermages* or *baux)* if they leased their land (as so many did), and to buy a few indispensable items of personal consumption. First they cut back purchases; then they went into debt to the fertilizer merchant or the landlord.[10]

"Farmers' debt . . . is the drama of our time," Deputy Edouard Barthe, chief representative of the winegrowers, told the Chamber of Deputies on the last day of 1935. "It is probably the greatest threat to social peace; it imperils the very life of our country."[11] Gilles Postel-Vinay has calculated that the increased peasant debt of the 1930s was lighter than that of the previous agricultural depression of the 1880s because the wartime profits and inflation of 1914–18 had permitted the liquidation of previous debt.[12] But the new debt of the 1930s was "crisis debt" rather than the "investment debt" of optimistic periods of modernization,[13] and it was resented all the more bitterly after the debt-free 1920s. When the French state chose this difficult moment to collect more taxes, to extract social security contributions for a farm's one or two hired hands, and during the Popular Front to extend such urban benefits to farm workers as the forty-hour week and paid vacations, these added costs were the last straw. The situation was particularly embittering for young farmers, who after returning from the war had taken out loans to get started. We find these angry war veterans especially numerous in the ranks of Dorgérism.

Peasants' anger reached the boiling point by late 1933. "I implore you, calm down our countryside," former Premier Joseph Caillaux wrote from his retirement in the Sarthe to Agriculture Minister Henri Queuille on 18 May 1934. "It is already boiling over. Don't stir it up any further."[14] Feelings were to grow even more tense in 1935.

In 1935, as they contemplated the pittance they received for wheat, some farmers imagined that they might simply use it as currency. On the Far Left, Renaud Jean, the Communist deputy of the Lot-et-Garonne and the main peasant spokesman in the French Communist party, proposed that peasants pay their taxes in wheat at the price set (but not enforced) at 115 francs per quintal in July 1933. Similar ideas spread on the Far Right, as was not unusual in peasant matters. In the Eure-et-Loir, the Parti Agraire held a banquet in March 1935, payable in wheat.[15] In June, Dorgères proposed the payment of farm rents in kind, according to a scale set by a mixed arbitration committee.[16] In some areas where it had been a traditional practice, farmers were allowed to exchange wheat for flour. The Norman farmers' leader, Jacques Le Roy Ladurie, both scholarly and inflammatory as usual, recalled that members of the Convention of 1793 had been paid in wheat[17]—a refreshing idea for peasants who had both wheat and contempt for parliamentarians in abundant supply.

There were many ways for a wheat farmer to go bankrupt in those years. Valentin Salvaudon, whose refusal to pay social security for his workers had set off Dorgères's first mass obstruction of a judicial sale in June 1933 (see Chapter 3), lost his farm in the following season because he had bought up his neighbors' wheat, expecting a price recovery that never arrived. Others lost their farms to creditors: the bank, the state, or a landlord. Sales of farms for debt were as vivid a part of Depression folklore in France as in the American dust bowl as described by John Steinbeck or Erskine Caldwell.

Parliament was not idle during the wheat crisis. It tried actively to remedy the situation. Indeed, some said it was too active. Thirteen French governments held power during the four years between January 1932 and

January 1936, and each new ministry felt obliged to give the impression of boldly tackling the wheat price collapse. During the nearly five years between December 1929 and March 1934, successive French governments passed six laws and thirty-nine decrees and issued thirty-one arrêtés and two avis concerning the wheat market[18]—and the lawmaking continued after that. These measures took official France (though not village France, in its everyday reality) from a nearly free market through a cycle of different experiments with state intervention, interpersed with one period of return to the free market.

Turning the import-export valves was the main device French governments traditionally used to stabilize French agricultural prices. So it was to the regulation of international trade that they first turned when an abundant wheat harvest accelerated the price decline in 1929. They did so all the more readily since they tended to blame the crisis on foreigners' overproduction.[19] The import duty on wheat went up to 50 francs per quintal in 1929 and to an unheard-of 80 francs per quintal in 1930, effectively excluding foreign wheat from the French market. It had been 7 francs before World War I and 18 francs in the early 1920s—lower, in fact, taking inflation into account.[20] André Tardieu, prime minister in 1929 and again in 1930 and minister of agriculture in 1931, was particularly active. His law of 1 December 1929 strengthened the government's power to raise agricultural import duties by decree without recourse to parliament (the padlock law, *la loi du cadenas*). It also established subsidies *(ristournes)* on wheat exports, limits on the proportion of foreign wheat that French flour could contain, and restrictions on temporary admission *(admission temporaire)*.[21]

Tardieu also put an end to the negotiation of Commercial Treaties, by which France had agreed during the 1920s to accept agricultural imports from countries like Spain and Italy in return for export possibilities for French industry—a typical example, according to peasant spokesmen like Dorgères, of the French Republic's readiness to sacrifice French agriculture to industry.[22]

Tardieu's most striking invention was the application of quotas *(contingentement)* to the total amount of certain products imported. This step got him into trouble with the United States, but Tardieu was remembered with particular fondness by peasant activists. Dorgères considered him to be the best minister of agriculture since Jules Méline in the 1880s, and Dorgères in no way lessened his admiration when Tardieu became a powerful advocate for a more authoritarian form of republic in the mid-1930s.

When regulating international trade did not stop the decline of wheat prices, French governments began to try to influence the internal farm economy. First, in 1930–31 came modest measures to sop up the excess by encouraging and subsidizing storage; carryover of stocks to a later year *(report)*; and alternative uses *(dénaturation)*, that is, turning wheat into animal feed or distilling it into alcohol.[23] After the moderate Left had won the elections of 1932, Edouard Daladier took the bold step in July 1933 of setting a minimum price for wheat of 115 francs per quintal.[24] The minimum price system was further strengthened on 28 December 1933,[25] including a tax of 3 francs per quintal on wheat to generate the funds needed to pay the costs of the state's intervention in the agricultural economy.

Because Daladier's experiments produced more inequity than price stabilization (small farmers were constrained to sell quickly to "speculators" at prices lower than the minimum), the more conservative Pierre-Etienne Flandin moved back toward market freedom (28 December 1934, the fifth law on wheat). Thereafter, wheat prices fell even more freely, and the farmers who had complained about state regulations now complained bitterly about the free market.

Reversing course sharply again in the summer of 1936, the Popular Front undertook state management of the entire wheat market of France, through the famous (or infamous) National Wheat Office (Office National Interprofessionel du Blé) of August 1936.[26] By this time, wheat prices had finally turned upward again on their own (largely by long-term self-correction of the market and low harvests), and the Third Republic's cycle of major wheat legislation came to an end.

The French government spent large sums on its various attempts to bolster wheat prices. As of 30 June 1935, on the debit side of the budget was the sum of 946 million francs for intervention in the wheat market.[27] From 1 January to 31 October 1935, "supporting the wheat market" was the largest item among treasury expenses, at 1,700,000,000 francs, coming just ahead of national defense (1,170,000,000 francs).[28]

These actions failed to reverse the collapse of wheat prices. The first measures of storage, carryover *(report)*, and alternative usage were too feeble, and, in any case, most poor peasants didn't have access to storage facilities; those who did worried about the mountain of wheat they had accumulated. The price-fixing of 1933 didn't work, partly because the state lacked sufficiently coercive administrative machinery for market supervision, partly because small peasants desparate for cash sold anyway, below the minimum. The grain wholesalers and millers (the "speculators" denounced by Dorgères) were delighted to oblige. Flandin's return to the free market in December 1934 did not work because the huge "overhang" of previously stocked wheat exerted an exceptional downward pressure on prices.

If the 1936 Wheat Office seemed to work better than previous measures, this was partly because the market was beginning to correct itself anyway. Somewhat surprisingly, in view of their opposition to the Popular Front and their lack of rapport with Prime Minister Léon Blum and his minister of agriculture, the gentleman farmer Georges Monnet[29]—the conservative agrarian organizations preferred to work with the Wheat Office than to fight it.[30] But the farmers were calmer by then because prices had already begun to recover, and they were well represented in its councils—even though it was not run entirely by the agricultural profession as they would have preferred but was "interprofessional," including representatives of the milling and baking industries, grain traders, and consumers.

Not only did the successive governments' blizzard of laws and decrees not help, but also they did not even earn the gratitude of the wheat growers. Government policy changed too often and acted too little or too late while at the same time setting up vast systems of paperwork that infuriated and burdened the wheat growers. The best-informed and most intelligent spokesmen for the wheat growers—such as Pierre Hallé, the brilliant and energetic secretary-general of the wheat producers' powerful pressure group, the General Wheat Growers' Association (Association Générale des Producteurs de Blé, AGPB)—eventually drew negative conclusions about democratic government itself. Publicly, Hallé doubted that the parliamentary system had either the expertise or the authority to manage a market. He thought that the professional associations, like his own AGPB, should organize the wheat market within a corporatist system in which real authority lay with the producers. Privately, he went much further. He wrote to André Tardieu, for example, on 22 August 1936, agreeing with the former prime minister that the present regime in France was "intolerable and unfixable. . . . That is why we must throw it down." For Hallé, by the time the Popular Front was in power, the only solution was a mass movement capable of swaying the public by emotion, since "reason doesn't work any more."[31]

It is not surprising, therefore, given this cultivated expert's sweeping rejection of democracy in general and the French Republic in particular, that Hallé was willing to appear often on the same platform with Dorgères, a man whose company he would not have ordinarily sought. For example, Hallé was one of the speakers at the giant rally in Rouen on 17 September 1935, when Dorgères, who had just been sentenced for advocating a tax strike, was putting into motion the Peasant Front's plan to bring about a giant peasant boycott of the entire French economy and the French state.[32]

Even experts like Pierre Hallé were not sure what they wanted, however. They had no more conclusive answers than the parliamentarians. When he was disillusioned by the malfunctioning of the minimum price established in July 1933, Hallé recommended a "progressive return to the free market," while at the same time demanding "the reinforcement of the state authorities charged with applying the regulations concerning wheat."[33] Then, after successive forms of state intervention had failed, Hallé shifted away from both the market and state authority to a nonstatist form of corporatism, "professional organization."

Hallé recognized that there were several possible economic models. France could throw open its doors to the world wheat market and enjoy cheap bread at depressed world prices. He admitted that bread was cheaper in countries like Britain and Belgium, which imported cheap foreign wheat, than in protectionist France.[34] But that course meant the destruction of many family farms and the deliberate sacrifice of a large part of the French rural community. Like his mentor André Tardieu, Hallé believed passionately that French moral and social survival depended on retaining a large population of family farmers, even though they were unable to produce food at world market prices. Economic efficiency meant less to him than social and moral good: a France "in balance" (*équilibre* was a ubiquitous word among conservative political and economic commentators from Jules Méline to Philippe Pétain). A "balanced economy" meant cities and industries no more powerful than a large, healthy rural population.

For those less well educated than Pierre Hallé, it was even easier to become obsessed by the tragedy of the wheat glut. For ignorant small farmers unable to sell their wheat, the trouble was not vast economic forces but evil people. The uneducated farmer's list of personal enemies included the huge milling companies, which put many small millers out of business and encouraged the import of cheap wheat by ship, such as the immense Grands Moulins de Paris built just after World War I. There were also fraudulent dealers, speculators, and "international finance." Some of the large milling companies and international wheat dealers were tempting targets.

Dorgères never missed an opportunity to blame peasants' sufferings on the big international wheat broker Louis Louis-Dreyfus, whom he loved to call King Two Louis *(le roi deux Louis)*. Dorgères and his followers never stopped believing that a lot of foreign wheat was entering France because of the fraudulent operations of brokers such as Louis-Dreyfus, abetted by ill-conceived government programs like temporary admission and covered by corrupt politicians. Louis-Dreyfus was a rural demagogue's dream target: wealthy, a powerful force in the international wheat trade, and the bearer of a name so resonant that the most un-abashed barnyard anti-Semite would not dare dream it up. No wonder Dorgères shifted his message in December 1932 from social security to wheat prices.[35]

If the Great Depression had delivered a knockout blow to wheat alone, the calculating French peasant would have quickly shifted to other prod-ucts. Indeed, this occurred. Far from staying mired in timeless custom, French peasants have always responded rationally and quickly to market opportunities—and they did so in the 1930s. They turned their energies most often to milk, meat, and vegetables; sometimes to flax or tobacco; and, where geography permitted, to wine. But the Depression also affected all the other cash crops, at different times and according to different factors. Sooner or later in the 1930s, every one of the alternative cash crops suffered a price collapse. All of French agriculture seemed stricken by some inexorable doom.

Wine came after wheat in economic and emotional importance. The production of these two crops affected so many French families that many (including Dorgères) called them "electoral crops": their fate got politi-cians elected and governments overthrown, and they could not be ig-nored. In addition to its economic importance as the support of a million and a half vintners *(vignerons)*[36]—one French family in six[37]—wine, like wheat, enjoyed a special mystique in France. Wine and bread, declared André Tardieu in a speech opening the Conférence Internationale du Vin on 7 March 1932, are the "culminating expressions of material and spiri-tual civilization."[38] "The prolonged consumption of wine," affirmed M. de Mirepoix, president of the wine producers' association (la Confédéra-tion Générale des Vignerons, CGV), to the Conseil National Économique on 1 December 1930, "has certainly contributed to the formation and the development of the fundamental qualities of the French race: cordiality, frankness, gaity, wit, good taste—which set it so profoundly apart from people who drink a lot of beer."[39]

The severe problems faced by producers of wine between the wars, like those of wheat growers, had their roots in the last quarter of the nineteenth century. First had come the scourge of *Phylloxera,* an American plant louse introduced accidentally into France in the 1860s, which de-stroyed more than half of the vineyards in the 1870s and 1880s and reduced French wine production by two-thirds. A solution had been found by grafting new vines onto resistant roots of the American wild grape. But the cost of replanting, along with new facilities for transporting wine by rail, gave an advantage to new industrial-scale vineyards that stretched for miles along the Mediterranean coast. Soon, by the early

1900s, the market overflowed with cheap wine. After the 1907 revolt of struggling small *vignerons* in the south, so massive it had required the intervention of troops, the winegrowers accepted a regulated market of a kind that the dispersed and individualistic wheat growers were incapable of matching, though they sometimes envied it.

The Great Depression did not spare the French wine producers, in spite of their organized market. The acreage devoted to wine production in Algeria, where grapes had first been planted while French production was reduced by the *Phylloxera* epidemic, almost tripled between the wars, to the rage of the Midi.[40] Within metropolitan France, while acreage remained constant, yields crept upward as techniques improved. At the same time, French wine consumption leveled off, while Prohibition in the United States—an insult from which American-French relations have never recovered—closed a once-important market from 1919 until 1933. Then the perfect harvest weather of 1933 produced the biggest grape crop in French agricultural history. "Wine production," concluded an agricultural official in 1939, "is in the process of destroying itself by its own excesses."[41]

The French state had long been tracing, for tax purposes, the quantity of wine produced and sold. During the overproduction crisis of the early twentieth century, it began also to regulate quality and to balance the wine market by purchasing the excess for distillation. In the 1930s, it turned to the regulation of production. Increasingly minute provisions concerning exactly what could be planted, irrigated, stocked, distilled, or sold[42] culminated in the Wine Statute *(statut du vin)* of 30 July 1935. This sweeping regulation amounted, according to one agricultural expert, to "a beautiful example of a guided economy."[43]

It restricted imports, limited new plantations, banned some inferior strains of grape, penalized an emphasis on sheer quantity, and reached the ultimate blasphemy: the uprooting of some vineyards. About 56,000 hectares (123,200 acres) of vines were actually pulled up in 1935–36, about a third of the amount foreseen.[44] Producers of wines of high quality were further protected by reinforced restrictions on the right to use regional labels *(appellations d'origine)*. Whereas earlier legislation (1919) had left it to the courts to enforce regional labels, a new Comité National des Appellations d'Origine des Vins et des Eaux-de-Vie (1935) enforced much more detailed restrictions on the kinds and qualities of wines that could use these coveted restricted labels, *appelations contrôlées*. The state's ultimate safety valve was an expensive program of distilling all the excess wine into industrial alcohol.[45]

But wine figures little in our story of Dorgères. I wondered why his movement did not profit from the stresses of the Great Depression and the labor troubles of 1936–37 in the wine country. The Midi in general had been fixed politically on the Left by long tradition. More specifically, the "wine producers had long been subjected to discipline by the supervision of their wines by the tax bureau" (l'Administration des Contributions Indirectes).[46] One gets the impression also, from reading accounts of the ritualized forms taken by regular labor conflict in the southern vineyards since the early 1900s, that the southern vineyard workers' strikes of the Popular Front era were not the shocking novelty the farmhands' strikes were to the farmers of the north and west. For a combination of reasons, Dorgérism found almost no political space in the southern wine country.

In the Loire Valley, in contrast, Dorgères did well among winegrowers. The Loire wine producers took positions contrary to those of the Midi in all things. The less sunny Loire Valley depended on *chaptalisation*—the addition of some sugar in the fermentation process to raise the alcoholic content, a technique that the Midi was always trying to ban. The Loire Valley, which was always complaining about southern overproduction, was the only wine-producing region where Dorgères found a substantial following.

Meat and milk were at the opposite pole from wine, with its elaborate organization and regional concentration. The former were produced by a mass of individualistic small farmers all over France. These products were more important, proportionally, for small farmers than for large ones.[47] More and more small farmers had turned to raising a few animals in the 1920s, for meadows required smaller investments in labor and fertilizer than grain, and increased consumption after World War I made meat and milk profitable. Whereas French families had traditionally eaten meat two or three times a week, the war introduced every soldier to a small daily meat ration, and many of them continued to eat meat daily afterward.[48] Then the Great Depression burst this little bubble of prosperity. Cattle raisers were overextended, and meat was the first thing a consumer might give up when belts had to be tightened—and no one bought a new belt, either.

To make matters worse, an outbreak of bovine tuberculosis in the 1930s gave the British a pretext to stop all imports of French meat. Cheap frozen meat from abroad, however, which had gained a foothold in France to feed soldiers during World War I, remained a subject of peasants' fears even after the government swore it had been excluded by postwar tariffs. Imports of frozen meat radicalized farmers everywhere in Europe: the construction of a frozen meat plant in Altona played a major role in the Nazis' success in nearby Schleswig-Holstein. The vulnerable cattle raisers of the poorer soils there (the *Geest*) gave the Nazis some of their highest percentages in all of Germany; indeed, Schleswig-Holstein was the only German state to give the Nazis an outright majority in free parliamentary elections, in July 1932.[49] Dorgères knew that frozen meat was a good theme in the cattle-growing regions of northern and western France, and he used it to good effect.[50] Some leading Dorgérists in the Seine-Inférieure and the Calvados, whom we meet more directly later, were distressed animal raisers.

Milk was one of the last of the farmers' cash products to collapse in the French Depression, and for a time it became the last lifeboat for many small family farms. Milk had become "country cottage's treasury":[51] 78% of French milk in 1934 came from small producers.[52] But although the consumption of dairy products had increased in France since World War I, milk itself was not yet important in the French diet. Indeed, until the 1920s milk had been, for many cattle growers, an unsalable waste product. Even in the 1930s the average daily consumption in France of a quarter of a liter of milk per day was the lowest in Europe.[53] Overproduction, poor sanitation, and consumer suspicion and indifference dropped prices by the spring of 1934 more than 75% below prewar levels,[54] and they kept going down. It was the final blow for many small French farmers.

The collapse of milk prices was particularly wounding because it exposed the weakness of peasants. The myriad small milk producers were defenseless against the powerful middlemen who bought their milk, often representatives of large regional buyers (such as Gervais, in Normandy), even sometimes of big international firms like Nestlé. Regions where dairy farmers were hard hit were often ripe in the 1930s for Dorgérism: for example, the Guérande peninsula near Nantes; the Bray region of coastal Normandy; and the coastal meadowlands near Isigny, near the future Normandy landing beaches in 1944. One successful Far Right peasant organization in Alsace, Josef Bilger's Bauernbund, was built around a milk cooperative. Still other milk-producing areas generated local forms of rightwing peasant radicalism like the Entente Paysanne, which flourished in the Charentes before Dorgères came on the scene.

Beet sugar had always been the most regulated and managed of French agricultural projects from its beginnings as Napoleon's high-tech response in 1811 to the unavailability of Antillean cane sugar during the British blockade. Sugar remained an affair of state. Since cane sugar cost less to produce, beet sugar survived in western Europe only with various forms of state aid: protective tariffs, export subsidies, and (after these had been outlawed by the Brussels Convention of 1902) systems of government purchase of excess production for distillation into alcohol. Under these circumstances, French sugar refining had long been highly concentrated in a few large firms.

The sugar beet growers (mostly big farmers in the northern plains) followed suit by becoming the most solidly organized producers of agricultural products. The National Confederation of Beetroot Producers (Confédération Générale des Planteurs de Betteraves, CGB), formed in 1921,[55] soon chose to strike a bargain with the refiners rather than to fight them. Successive efforts to negotiate quantities and prices culminated in the agreement of May 1931, which provided for annual negotiation of production quotas, prices, storage of the surplus, and propaganda in favor of sugar consumption. The state kept the system going by buying the surplus sugar beet production for distillation into alcohol, although when the amount tripled between 1930 and 1933 the state set a ceiling of 2,300,000 hectoliters on the amount of beetroot alcohol it would buy at full market price.[56] The state also set up an Arbitration Commission in August 1935 [57] to settle differences between the growers and the refiners. Another act of the same day gave state authority to the contracts negotiated between growers and refiners. By 1935 the production and refinement of beet sugar was thus regulated by negotiation between professional organizations, underwritten by state authority. Some enthusiasts for corporatism saw this arrangement as a trial run for autonomous, professional self-administration in action.[58]

Not even this highly structured market system allayed the fear and anger of sugar beet growers during the Depression. Even this elite group of big farmers included a few prominent followers of Dorgères, such as Pierre Leclercq, second president of the CGB (1942–55) and prewar president of the Dorgérist Comité de Défense Paysanne (CDP) of the Pas-de-Calais, a "shock trooper" with a "fiery temperament."[59] Dorgérisme had little utility for the sugar beet planters as a weapon against state reductions in distillation quotas or against intransigent refiners; but when their vital wage laborers—planters, thinners, weeders, and diggers—went out on strike in 1936 and 1937, the Greenshirts could be useful. The Comité de Défense Paysanne grew rapidly in the Pas-de-Calais in 1937, and Pierre Leclercq organized actions against striking agricultural laborers, as in the Cambrésis in June 1937.[60]

The producers of vegetables and fruit for urban markets (maraîchers and primeuristes) were a particularly vulnerable group, because they were divided among a host of small individual producers, were poorly organized, and were subject to drastic price fluctuations, as well as labor problems. The Great Depression hit them hard through the shutdown of international trade. The export of potatoes, cauliflower, and strawberries, which kept whole sections of Brittany alive, were badly damaged when Britain reduced its agricultural imports, especially after the adoption of Imperial Preference at the Ottawa Conference of 1932. Since the growers were often close to cities, their work force was subject to socialist influences. The market gardeners of the Paris region concluded a collective contract with their employees during the strike wave of the summer of 1936 and then found themselves financially pinched the following fall. As we shall see, the market gardeners were among Dorgères's most eager followers, not only in Brittany where he was generally well received, but also in the Paris basin and even in the otherwise inhospitable Midi. Vegetable growers in the lower Rhône Valley—the melon growers of Cavaillon and market gardeners around Avignon—became Dorgères's main islands of support in a largely indifferent south.

Then there were cash crops like flax to which some small farmers in the north and the Seine-Maritime turned for substitute cash income in hard times. Flax could compete with imports from the USSR only with government subsidies, however. These were increased in the late 1920s, but even so, flax was in difficulty even before the crash of 1929. The issue of whether to import flax from the USSR was easily politicized. Like many agricultural producers, flax growers wanted state help but not outside interference. Out of that inner conflict came many expressions of frustrated and inarticulate anger, some that could take the form of direct action. At Tréguier, in Brittany, a peasant direct action group (Dorgères was not directly involved) expelled strikers from a linen mill in February 1937 and established patrols for the "peasants to maintain order themselves."[61]

Last, but certainly not least, came the *bouilleurs de cru*: the "home brewers" of hard cider of the northern apple and pear country whose right to operate home stills was deeply rooted in local particularism and resistance to state regulation. The *bouilleurs de cru* had never recovered from the blow struck by the French state in 1916: they were forbidden as a war measure to practice their traditional distillation at home (alcohol having become an ingredient of armaments). The right to distill was partially restored in 1923 but was subject to vexatious taxation and licensing requirements. Throughout the interwar period, the home brewers fought in vain for complete liberty to distill at their pleasure. The Great Depression reduced this significant cash source for a multitude of small farmers and inflamed their previous allergy to taxes, to government paperwork, and to the inspectors who—according to the horror stories common in *bouilleur* propaganda—invaded their domiciles when only their wives were home.

Therefore the apple and pear cider country of Normandy was one of Dorgères's most fertile recruiting grounds. Dorgères's truculence and love for a fight suited the *bouilleurs'* rebellious spirit perfectly. They furnished some of his most fervent supporters, such as Abel Néel and others of the Pays d'Auge in upper Normandy. The main farmers' organization of the region, the Association des Agriculteurs du Pays d'Auge, got into trouble for raising a considerable sum—more than 5000 francs—to help Dorgères pay his legal expenses in 1935. But even though the *bouilleurs de cru* provided Dorgères with some of his most faithful followers, even after the war in the 1950s, this effervescence was so widespread and so refractory to any central authority that much of it escaped from Dorgères' control. The leaders of the spectacular *bouilleurs*' rebellion in the Orne—where on 31 March 1935, at Passais, a crowd ceremonially removed the government's seals from their stills and burned them at the War Memorial, "at the foot of the soldier, our brother"—refused to let Abel Néel raise a cheer for Dorgères. Seeing the CDP as a political movement, they indignantly rejected any attempt by "the agitators of the Peasant Front to take over their movement."[62] There was far more peasant anger and taste for direct action in France than Dorgères could harness, for lack of a powerful national party.

Because the worldwide Depression hit agriculture early, farm prices went down when the cost of the items farmers bought remained the same or were even still going up. This produced a classic "scissors crisis" in 1933–35: farmers received less than before when they sold their wheat, wine, milk or steers, but they had to pay the same as before (or perhaps even more than before) for tools, fertilizer, seeds, clothing, and other indispensable cash purchases. Finally, labor costs went up because of social security in 1930 (see Chapter 2) and the new social legislation of 1936. Thus French peasants suffered at a different rhythm and for different reasons than city people. Indeed, the salvation of peasants might well have required sacrifices from urban dwellers, so peasants were even more ready to look to Dorgères's peasant particularism for help than to any urban party or movement.

Some economists have argued that the Great Depression of the 1930s was less cataclysmic for French agriculture than that of the 1880s, both in its length and in its amplitude.[63] Certainly the burden of debt was lighter in the 1930s, and state aid was greater. But the psychological impact of the Depression was stronger in the 1930s. The agricultural crisis of the 1880s had struck especially hard at modernizing big wheat growers and at the winegrowers. It did indeed set off waves of protest and the first major effort to organize the agricultural interest, the gentry-led farmers' associations (the *syndicalisme des ducs*) that followed the legalization of economic organizations in 1884.[64] But a much higher proportion of French peasants had become exposed to world market pressures by the 1930s, and they had more ample means to express their anger in the more democratic politics of the time. Moreover, the experiments with directed economy during World War I had led them to expect more help. Above all, many French farmers of the 1930s were persuaded that the French Republic was making their situation worse. They saw the Depression of 1930 not as a natural catastrophe, to be borne with stoicism, but as a willful sacrifice of their interests by a Republic that listened only to the middle and working classes. For some of them, salvation required a change of political regime.

Thus the Great Depression spread pain and anger throughout all sectors of French agriculture and prepared French farmers to listen to appeals to violence and to city-country antagonism from leaders like Dorgères. But we cannot expect the map of Dorgérism to correspond exactly to the map of peasant pain. Some peasants with little pain followed him, and others in great pain did not. So we must look also at the cultural and political aspects of the crisis that helped define the opportunities available to Dorgères.

A Vanishing Way of Life

French farmers feared in the 1930s that their way of life was dying out. The most conspicuous measure of rural society's decline was the "rural exodus": the departure of sons and daughters who no longer wanted to work on the farm. We have a lot of statistical information about the *exode rural*. Successive censuses after the late nineteenth century reveal a gradual but continuing shift of the French population from rural areas to towns and cities until, in the census of 1931, the fatal threshold was crossed. Thereafter more French people were urban than rural dwellers.[65] Village populations were also aging. It was the young people who were leaving. The countryside was losing its most dynamic element, the progenitors of its future.

The statistics also show, however, that the rural exodus was much slower in France than in the more aggressively industrial and urban parts of Europe, such as Britain, Belgium, and the Rhine and Ruhr valleys of Germany. France remained the most agricultural of the great industrial nations. Within France, moreover, the exodus was slower in the period 1880–1945 than it was to be after World War II. Paradoxically, the rate of rural departure was it at its lowest in the 1930s, when the clamor against it was at its highest. During that Depression decade, some victims of urban unemployment returned to the sanctuary of the family farm.[66] If French defenders of rural society complained more loudly than those in other countries, it was precisely because so many remained to express their feelings.

In emotional terms, however, the pain felt by those aging remnants was no less sharp because the departures were slower. The dry census numbers stood for intense personal disappointments among millions of French rural men and women. Parents discovered that no son or son-in-law wanted to cultivate the fields on which they had lavished a lifetime of care. There were already abandoned villages, the first signs of the slow extinction that was to affect so many rural communities after World War II. First the village store closed and then the café; the baker was replaced by a *dépôt de pain,* where bread baked in a larger town was dropped off. No business could be transacted without visiting the notary or the bank in a larger town. Without young families, the schools closed. The *curé* was replaced by an itinerant priest who visited one Sunday a month. Traditional village festivities ceased to be observed, one by one. The texture of many farm villages would soon become too thin to support a satisfying social life. Suicide, primarily an urban phenomenon in the nineteenth century, was becoming familiar in the countryside in the twentieth.[67]

World War I brought new reasons to leave the farm. Some young men who had seen other worlds refused to return to the slow seasons and the endless drudgery of rural life. Also more young peasants had been killed in the war, proportionally, than other sectors of the population.[68] Many skilled industrial workers and artisans had been given special assignments to armaments factories and had thus been spared the horrors of the trenches. Also middle- and upper-class youths could obtain staff or office assignments (though young combat officers from the middle and upper classes were killed in extremely high numbers). Dorgères helped make the sacrifice of their sons at the front in 1914–18 a central element of the peasants' identity. He often told his rural audiences that their sons had paid an extra blood tax *(impôt de sang),* whereas many townsmen and most workers had been shirkers *(embusqués).* The Unknown Soldier was, by statistical probability, a peasant, the peasants' demagogues told them. Yet, Dorgères would say, the French Republic was now letting its peasant war heroes lose their farms and their dignity.

It was not always easy for rural French people to understand their own fate clearly. The predominant perspective of modern political economy, among Marxists and middle-class liberals alike, held that the decline of small family farming and the growth of industry, commerce, and specialized agribusiness were both good and inevitable. Believers in the benefits of progress considered that the elderly farmers who were watching their villages die around them had no legitimate complaint. They had only to remain silent and fade away. Their consolation was supposed to be that their disappearance would signal the arrival of a better world of urban plenty, excitement, and variety. Their fate was sad, but it was the price of modernity.

It is true that in France important strands of the political leadership—not limited to the reactionary Right—had throughout the nineteenth century consciously sought to distance France from the English economic model and to avoid Britain's complete urbanization and attendant social conflicts and stark individualism. They wanted the social fabric to endure, and that meant maintaining a balance between industry and agriculture. In the 1930s, therefore, there were powerful people in France who believed that the drain of human vitality away from the farms and villages to the cities was more than sad: it was the destruction of France. They considered family agriculture the one remaining healthy part of a corrupt country. For them, the farms and villages of France were the place where prolific families, simple faith and patriotism, and the discipline of hard work still reigned. Without them, France would be frivolous, sterile, cynical, skeptical—and weak. The peasantry as a moral resource had become a stock item of patriotic oratory. Dedicating a war memorial to peasant soldiers in the smallest rural commune of the Ariège in 1935, Marshal Pétain said, "At the darkest hours, it was the calm and firm look of the French peasant that kept my confidence up."[69] The conservative agrarian press often reprinted these remarks in the late 1930s.

Of all the French premiers of the period 1929–39, André Tardieu was certainly the most vigorous apostle of the strengths and virtues of peasant France. France had resisted the Depression longer than the more fragile, overindustrialized, overurbanized states, Tardieu believed, because of its "balance." Industry and commerce were essential to great power status, of course, but without the counterweight of a solid peasantry, they were subject to dizzying business cycles, collapses of purchasing power, and severe social conflicts. France "has always preferred the solid to the colossal," he told an audience at Giromagny (Territoire de Belfort) soon after he had left the Agriculture Ministry (January 1932). It was a strong peasantry that made France a "country with sound money, maintaining its purchasing power and a penchant for paying its debts." It was the "overdeveloped peoples," with their fragile, unbalanced "hypertrophic" economies, that had inflicted "dumping born of desperation" upon France and had finally thrown the stable French economy into a depression.[70] Thus peasants were a resource of economic stability, as well as a bank of moral, familial, and patriotic virtues. Tardieu concluded that France should do what was necessary to remain half agricultural.[71]

Furthermore, French agriculture should be based on family farms that practiced polyculture. Tardieu perceived "an ever more marked contrast between the kinds of cultivation practiced by countries of large-scale production and by peasant nations, whose very existence is bound up with working the land."[72] France should not model its agriculture on what was done on the vast plains of the American Middle West or Argentina or, still less, the Ukraine. There was no one model of "modernization" to which France was bound to adhere. France was special. France was a "peasant nation," and she must protect herself from being denatured.

All the major agricultural pressure groups in 1930s France urged the preservation of the small family farm, even those that represented big planters. The national wheat growers' organization (the AGPB) put it bluntly in a resolution in the spring of 1938: "Protecting the peasant family and keeping it on the land is more than ever the essential precondition of our country's safety and revival."[73] A very large number of peasants and their friends believed this passionately in the 1930s, and many of them believed that something drastic must be done to reverse the decline of the family farm. Dorgères took that sense of urgent need and of the inadequate government response to its logical conclusion: the peasants must act outside the laws of the Republic if necessary to protect their way of life.

Less educated peasants tended to personalize their explanation of the disappearance of their way of life. Some personal enemy must be to blame. In 1930s France, public debate easily slipped into personal invective, as exemplified by the small sticker found in a urinal in Vernon (Eure) in 1936 after Prime Minister Léon Blum had devalued the franc: "Attention: the franc isn't French any more. It is Jewish. Léon Blum has circumcised it."[74]

Many peasants blamed schoolteachers personally for the rural exodus. The virulence of antiteacher feeling among the peasantry is surprising, even though Eugen Weber, following Roger Thabault, prepared us to see primary education as an engine of destruction of traditional local cultures.[75] The Dorgérists cultivated a genuine obsession with teachers as the enemy: agents of urban imperialism, bad shepherds who made farmers' sons and daughters ashamed of their parents' profession and eager to become something else. No other group seemed to arouse the same animosity—not even the creditor, the middleman, or the stereotypical Jew. The cultural enemy was as important to the peasants as the economic enemy, although they were surely linked in a struggle for cultural self-expression. The peasants clearly resented what they believed was the teacher's condescension and the message transmitted by the primary school—implicitly or explicitly—that farming was a lowlier profession[76] than most others and that the ladder of education should lead able and ambitious peasant youths to the city.[77]

Agrarian activists demanded a special curriculum in rural schools that would put agriculture in a positive light and prepare the ablest young peasants to continue their fathers' *métier.* But this development seemed more likely in the "free" (i.e., Catholic) secondary schools and agricultural colleges *(ecoles d'agriculture)* than in the state schools. The private *ecoles d'agriculture* played a major role in the formation and dissemination of agrarian corporatism and social paternalism, and many of the conservative agrarian notables had attended them. Rémy Goussault went to Beauvais, Jacques Le Roy Ladurie to Angers, and so on.

One of the *ecoles d'agriculture* was particularly closely linked to Dorgères: the new school at Le Nivot near Lopérec (Finistère), which had been set up in the 1920s with support from the Office Central des Associations Agricoles du Finistère et des Côtes du Nord ("Landerneau") of the comte de Guébriant. The *ecole d'agriculture* at Le Nivot had the explicit mission of combatting the prejudices of the public school system and forming peasant leaders to fight for agrarian, Catholic values. This moral role was as important as technical training in the latest agricultural methods.[78]

In 1933–34, the director of the *ecole d'agriculture* at Le Nivot, Le Floc'h, corresponded with Dorgères because he was in trouble with the tax bureau. Dorgères, who was trying to assemble a large number of rural tax-payers who were "resolved to let themselves be sold rather than give in,"[79] advised Le Floc'h not to pay. The tax collector threatened to have the school's farm sold by the public authorities. Dorgères organized a mass assembly to block the sale. Le Floc'h was on the platform with Dorgères at Rouen on 22 February 1935 when Dorgères worked the crowd up to a fever pitch over the coming tax strike, and he therefore was among those prosecuted for being an accomplice in that tax strike, along with a half dozen other men close to Dorgères (whom we encounter at one point or another in Chapter 3) such as Mayor Pierre Suplice of Bourg-Dun (Seine-Inférieure) and Mayor Jean Chalony of Pleuven (Finistère).

Le Floc'h was acquitted, but he serves as a striking example of the link between the Dorgérist movement and the passionate resentment of what was perceived as the antirural bias of the public schools. Even though the private *ecoles d'agriculture* required the payment of tuition and therefore served mostly the wealthier part of the agrarian elite, the resentment the rural elite shared with many small farmers toward primary teachers, whom both suspected of teaching their children to have contempt for their parents' way of life, helped unify the peasant constituency.

The Communist party's encouragement of its country schoolteachers to be active political militants added to the sharpness of the conservative attack on them—an attack that culminated in Vichy's high priority for school reform. In many Dorgérist meetings, it was the teacher who rebutted the peasant orator *(apporte la contradiction)* and who received a few bruises for his pains. Dorgères and his associates were often involved in campaigns to get local schoolteachers dismissed, and at times they found the local prefect willing to help. The prefect of the Finistère wanted to have the Communist schoolteacher Signor transferred in January 1935 because his counterdemonstration to a Dorgères speech in Pont-L'Abbé had blown the affair out of proportion and had required a police presence.[80] Dorgères's main lieutenant in the Seine-Maritime, Pierre Suplice, began his public career by trying to get rid of the Communist schoolteacher and organizer Darius Le Corre,[81] and later Suplice found himself fighting strikes of farm workers led by the Communist schoolteacher Gaonac'h.

The *fonctionnaires* were a second enemy of the peasant way of life, according to rural demonology. In the Dorgérist view, there were too many *fonctionnaires;* they lived easy, undemanding lives at the taxpayers' expense. Worse still, they complicated peasants' lives with regulations and paperwork. Worst of all, they invaded the peasants' domiciles to verify that peasants had inscribed their employees in social security payment offices *(caisses)* and that the *bouilleurs de cru* were not violating the law.

A third personalized enemy was the organizer of farm workers' trade unions. Left to themselves, conservative agrarians believed, all those who worked on the soil recognized their common interests, from the greatest landowner to the simplest sharecropper or day laborer. Did they not all share the common table at harvest time? The natural harmony of rural life was threatened only when agitators from the city came with their false message that farm workers were proletarians and that their interests were opposed to those of their employers. Dorgères singled out André Parsal, secretary of the farm workers' union of the Confédération Générale du Travail (CGT), the Fédération de la Terre, for particular vilification during the strikes of 1936–37. Parsal was a "strike-grower" *(gréviculteur),* capable of sowing only conflict, not grain.[82] Or he was "Partsale," a filthy land collectiviser *(sale partageur).*[83]

Yet Dorgères envied the organized Left, even as he hated it. He was constantly urging the peasants to abandon their age-old individualism and to organize as effectively as the workers did. He wanted to emulate the Left's effective organizations. "The peasantry has just as much right to speak as Léon Jouhaux [the trade union leader], or as the bosses," he told a rally at Neufchâtel (Eure) on 13 February 1939.[84] But peasants lacked the powerful organizations of both the workers and the businessmen. Think what they could accomplish if they paid dues like workers.[85]

The problem, according to Dorgères (and many other conservative agrarian leaders in the 1930s), was that the French Republic was systematically damaging rural interests. In their conspiratorial view of French history, the state had deliberately and increasingly sacrificed agriculture to commercial and industrial interests. In some versions this demonized history began with the French Revolution and its legacies of individualism, equal inheritance, and secularism. More often the first major wrong turn was considered to be the Cobden-Chevalier Treaty of 1860, by which France acceded to British proposals for freer trade—the GATT (General Agreement on Tariffs and Trade) of its day. Therafter, and especially under the Republic, the state deliberately sought to keep food prices low, as a favor to industrialists and their workers, without regard for the survival of those who produced the food.

The struggles of the French state against inflation after World War I gave some substance to this view of history in which peasants were the eternal victims. French consumers had been forced to learn to live with inflation, beginning in 1914, after the long century of nearly stable prices, from Napoleon's gold *franc germinal* in 1803 until the beginning of World War I in 1914. Prices of daily necessities had multiplied about five times between 1914 and the restabilization of the franc in 1928. This inflationary wave surged through French society like a slow-moving earthquake: it plunged those with fixed incomes into poverty and opened up opportunities for fortunes for some others. Inflation focused the attention of consumers and governments alike on a struggle against the high cost of living *(la vie chère)*—another phrase resonating with echoes of the revolutionary struggle between the people and hoarders *(accapareurs)* who drove up the price of bread.[86] *La vie chère* recurs everywhere in the economic and political commentary of the interwar period. The prefects, in their weekly or monthly reports, often devoted a paragraph to it.

The trouble was that fighting *la vie chère* had become so ingrained during the inflationary 1920s that it could not be turned off in the 1930s, when the problem had ceased to be inflation and had become depression instead. The orthodox response of governments and economists to the Depression was to search for ways not to stimulate the economy but to make life even cheaper for the unemployed. Deflation was the standard remedy: cure the Depression by cutting costs, as in the famous decree-laws of Pierre Laval in 1935. The Republic thus continued right up to the Popular Front of 1936 to combat *la vie chère* and to try to make bread cheaper instead of trying to increase purchasing power, as Keynesians were to do later.

A government committee against the high cost of living (Commission Contre la Vie Chère), chaired by two eminent leaders from the Left and the Right, Edouard Herriot and André Tardieu, studied ways during 1934–35 to reduce prices.[87] It was self-evident to Senator Henri Chéron that "we all want to take measures to lower the cost of living," as he told the Senate in March 1933, defending his proposal to empower the government to use an emergency law of 19–22 July 1791 to regulate bread and meat prices.[88] From an urban consumer's perspective, the decline of farm prices in the late 1920s and early 1930s was an unquestioned good.

Rural France, however, already had a very different explanation of what keeps an economy prosperous. In 1930, as France was temporarily spared the crash that threw millions out of work in Britain, Germany, and the United States, exponents of a Peasant Republic were sure that French stability came from the solid, enduring purchasing power of prosperous farmers. At the annual Assembly of the Presidents of the Chambres d'Agriculture, 17–18 March 1930, Senator Joseph Faure, introducing Prime Minister Tardieu, observed that France was not like its neighbors. France was escaping massive unemployment because of "the purchasing power of our countryside." Tardieu responded in very similar terms: France escaped the "ills" of its "neighbors" because of the "farmers' purchasing power." In May 1931, as minister of agriculture, he said the same thing at the Paris fair.[89]

As France in turn slipped into the Depression, ruralists could blame it on what seemed to them the Republic's apparent sacrifice of its peasant base. Their calls for the restoration of peasants' purchasing power—a rudimentary forestaste of Keynes—became more and more strident, as farm incomes fell in the 1930s, and more and more widespread, ranging from the cautious senators who sat in the *chambres d'agriculture*[90] through the agrarian party (Parti Agraire et Paysan Français)[91] to the increasingly corporatist and antirepublican Union Nationale des Syndicats Agricoles.[92] Dorgères, too, spoke constantly of the prosperity that a healthy peasantry could bring to the city by its purchases.[93] It did not escape them that Hitler also tried to restore peasants' purchasing power with higher food prices in 1933 (although, in the longer term, Hitler favored rearmament over agriculture).[94] From a peasant's perspective, cutting food prices to help feed the cities was making the peasants alone bear the entire cost of fighting the Depression. "The peasants don't want to bear the whole cost of the struggle against 'la vie chère.' "[95]

Two "moral economies" confronted each other across the urban-rural divide in 1930s France: cheap bread versus a stable peasant economy. The urban moral economy advocated a consumer-based agricultural policy— the cheapest possible food supply, drawn from wherever it could be found in the world at the lowest cost, without regard for the impact of cheap food imports on French farmers. Ruralists wanted a producer-based agricultural policy—a living wage for farmers and the preservation of a large rural population, even if that meant paying more for bread.

The agrarian "moral economy" also assumed that agriculture lives by its own particular economic logic, different from that of commerce and industry. In this perspective, agriculture responds better to cooperative than to competitive market conditions. Indeed, the market (still according to ruralists) functions differently for agriculture than for other commodities, for several reasons. For one thing, demand being inelastic and supply erratic agricultural producers are subject to others both for the price of what they buy and for the price of what they sell. Moreover, peasants, dependent on family labor, calculate how much land to cultivate in terms of the family life cycle rather than in terms of immediate market gain.[96] Social relations in agriculture, too, do not resemble the class conflict of commercial or industrial settings. They display a natural harmony based on common labor and hardship (according to the agrarian perspective) unless outside agitators sow division. The peasant economy, in a word, is specific and unique, responding to its own laws and reasons.

The urban political economy of cheap bread has a long and powerful lineage, drawing from both monarchical and republican roots. It starts with the determination of French monarchs to ensure the food supply of Paris,[97] and it continues with the determination of the revolutionary Republic to keep the counter revolution from starving the cities.[98] Thus when the Left press accused Dorgères of bringing starvation because of his role in the strike of the market gardeners who supplied Paris in October and December 1936, their term of abuse *(affameur)* had echoes of the Committee of Public Safety in 1792–93.[99] But cheap bread remained on the urban agenda when conservatives were in power, too.

The misadventures of Pierre-Etienne Flandin, prime minister from November 1934 to June 1935, were a striking demonstration of that conflict. The new *président du conseil* began his term of office with a step that he thought would evoke unanimous gratitude: he cut bread prices for Christmas. "Cheap bread" seemed a self-evident benefit in the city; in the country, it meant that family farmers would go hungry. The conservative Flandin, probably to his complete astonishment, became through this well-intentioned act the most hated French prime minister in the countryside for the entire decade of the 1930s, even more than the Socialist Léon Blum in 1936. Even the usually docile chambres d'agriculture wrote a bitter public letter to Flandin that accused him of showing disrespect for them and for the whole agricultural profession.[100]

Convinced that the entire Third Republic leadership, from Left to Right, was committed to cheap food from the world market, even if that hastened the extinction of the whole peasant way of life, French agrarians demanded a larger role in setting national policy. As Premier Tardieu had already put it in September 1930, "The organized peasantry within a strengthened State, that will make a stronger France tomorrow."[101] Doubting the future of a Republic that followed other priorities, Tardieu was to become by the middle 1930s the advocate of a new authoritarian and corporatist constitution for France.[102] Many agrarian leaders were to follow a similar itinerary toward cooperation with Dorgères.

A Crisis of Representation

Who would speak for peasants' interests in the bewildering and seemingly insoluble collapse of rural life in the 1930s? Neither elected officials nor appointed bureaucrats nor the traditional agricultural organizations seemed capable of recognizing the problem, let alone finding remedies.

Even though peasants were, according to the census, nearly half the French population, almost none of them were present in the national legislative bodies. Though many deputies and senators claimed to speak for "agriculture," only one parliamentarian called himself a "peasant": Jules Hayaux (senator of the Haute-Saône, 1927–38), who gloried in the nickname "the peasant senator." The distinction was important: "agriculture" was the business of farming, but "peasantry" was a way of life. Even Hayaux, however, was only a make-believe peasant. He was a farmer's son who had been a *lycée* professor until he was elected to the Senate in 1927. The real peasants first had to get rid of the nostalgic intellectuals who usurped the title before authentic, hard-handed farmers could run their own affairs.

Dorgères expected nothing good from parliament. The Chamber of Deputies contained 195 lawyers out of 615 members, he pointed out, and not one real farmer.[103] Parliament was a "cart with 928 horses";[104] no wonder it had "brought the country to ruin."[105] Dorgères and his friends were involved in fistfights with several deputies: Renaud Jean, Communist deputy of the Lot-et-Garonne, in 1936; Robert Mauger, Socialist deputy of the Loir-et-Cher, in 1939;[106] and an unseemly scuffle with the wife of François Cadoret, Radical deputy of the Finistère, in 1933.[107] He quoted with pleasure the cry raised in one county fair *(comice):* "Throw the deputies in the outhouse!"[108] Dorgères did not want to improve the legislature with the addition of some farmers as deputies; he wanted to replace it with three corporate chambers, one of them for the peasantry.

Some parts of French agriculture were better represented in parliament than others. The wine-producing Midi had the energetic and creative Edouard Barthe. But the conservative west could not find anything to respect in parliament. Its agricultural grandees were often city boys who had grown up to occupy all the positions in farmers' organizations without ever having worked a farm. The "typical cacique" of this sort, in some farmers' opinion,[109] was Henri Chéron. This one-time pharmacist's assistant in Lisieux had become a Radical senator for the Calvados, a man skilled in the ways of getting an anticlerical town dweller elected to represent a conservative, predominantly agricultural department.[110] He had sponsored profarm legislation,[111] and he had worked his way up as a board member of the Republican farm credit and insurance associations of the Calvados until he became president of the departmental *chambre d'Agriculture*.

Chéron personifed the radical republicans' efforts to build rural support outward from the country market towns through the *comices* and a network of farmers' credit, insurance, and cooperative associations linked to the Radical-Republicans by the Société d'Encouragement à l'Agriculture.[112] He was "the inescapable representative of the rural village and of the county fair in the parliaments of the Third Republic."[113]

But Chéron was anathema to many of the farmers in the Calvados: he was a townsman who dared speak for the farmers, and he represented the impious Radical party. He could feel his own position, as well as that of radical republicans, threatened when Dorgérist orators made fun of his enormous girth and his flowery oratory and made it risky for him to appear before a farm audience. The election of a real farmer, though a wealthy and educated one, Jacques Le Roy Ladurie, to the presidency of the Calvados Chambre d'Agriculture in 1935—not long before occupied by the corpulent Chéron—was a kind of revolution.[114]

The upper house was full of rural senators, many of them members of their departmental *chambres d'agriculture*. They defended agriculture by their lights, but they were mostly, at best, absentee proprietors of farms that they did not cultivate themselves. A few of the agricultural senators, such as Joseph Faure, had actually run their farms as young men, but it was hardly possible to keep up with a farm and a legislative seat at the same time. The closest most of the agricultural senators came to farming was membership on the board of local farm credit or insurance associations or of a departmental *syndicat agricole*.

Some thought that French farmers would never be properly represented in the French Republic without a separate farmers' party, as in some eastern European countries between the wars, with their Green International, based in Prague. The Parti Agraire et Paysan Français (PAPF) was the most ambitious French attempt to launch one. Whereas Dorgères and the corporatists wanted to do away with parliament, the PAPF found it sufficient to send authentic peasants to the Palais Bourbon. Peasants, stated the first number of a PAPF newspaper, *Le Paysan du Centre-Ouest*, are "the despised and disdained class." They have never thought to "emancipate themselves at election time . . . to have their own candidates, what an audacious move!"[115] The PAPF, formed in 1928, attempted to provide the peasant half of France with peasant deputies. The effort was a failure. One PAPF deputy was elected in 1932 (Louis Guillon, for the Vosges) and eleven in 1936 (including two who had been close to Dorgères: Pierre Mathé, for the Côte d'Or, and Joseph Cadic, for the Morbihan). Another PAPF deputy was elected in a by-election in October 1936 (Jules Radulphe, Calvados).[116] But it had split in February 1936 between Left and Right factions, and it was decapitated by the death of its leader in July 1936.

One problem with the PAPF was that its leader, Gabriel Fleurant, nicknamed "Agricola," was yet another urban intellectual with a romantic attachment to rural life but no calluses on his hands and no mud on his boots. Asked in 1933 about Fleurant Agricola, when the PAPF seemed to be making enough headway to interest the Ministry of the Interior, the subprefect of Dieppe reported to the prefect of the Seine-Maritime that Agricola, "whose bucolic name doesn't manage to make people forget that he wears a lawyer's robes and lives by making deals," had failed to interest the peasants of his department. They wanted "an agrarian policy, yes, but not an agrarian party."[117] The subprefect was quite unfair to the estimable Fleurant Agricola, who did not wear lawyer's robes at all. He was a former teacher who had helped found the sugar beet growers' association in 1921; had worked to build farmers' organizations in the Oise; and had been an editor of *Action agricole,* the weekly paper of the big cultivators of the Paris basin, before forming the Parti Agraire in 1927.[118] But most peasants knew better than to listen to a romantic, intellectual agrarian.

In the final analysis, the French political terrain was already so fully occupied by the traditional Left-Right spectrum that no room was left for professional representation. Indeed, the very idea of representation on which French republicanism rested was that individual citizens elected their representatives without being guided by any guilds or associations or other "intermediary bodies" (as the famous preface to the Le Chapelier law had put it in 1791 in abolishing any kind of economic interest group). The misfit with professional representation was one of the reasons that corporatists like Dorgères rejected the Republic. They wanted to replace parliament's Right-Left division, in their opinion artificial and prone to class conflict, by the representation of professional associations that cut across class lines.

The elections of 1932 put the French government in the hands of a Center-Left majority dominated by the Radical party, anathema to much of the agrarian elite of northwestern France. The Center-Left governments that followed went back to negotiating commercial treaties with other nations, such as Spain and Switzerland, that agreed to import French industrial goods, provided France agreed to import some of their agricultural products. Thus it was these governments that took the blame when agricultural prices fell rapidly in 1933–34. But the parliamentary Right was no more willing to raise agricultural prices than the Left. Indeed the prime minister whom the peasants most hated in the 1930s, as we have seen, was the conservative Flandin, who lowered the price of bread and never consulted the *chambres d'agriculture*.

Many French farmers came to feel in the 1930s that the Third Republic was foreign to them. It stood for a systematic degradation of their relative situation and of their self-respect. The French system of political representation offered no way in which the peasants' moral economy could be effectively advocated as a viable alternative. Dorgères was to make a strong impression on his peasant readers by his simple exercises in parliamentary arithmetic. He counted up forty ministers of agriculture in that "Ali Baba's cave" and hardly any farmers at all.[119]

If parliament seemed barren ground to farmers, perhaps they could look to the administrative state for help. In truth, the French state had been intimately involved in the promotion and protection of certain specialized crops, like sugar beets, since Napoleon. French farmers had no intention of giving up state support. In the 1930s, however, farmers' reactions to state action had become ambiguous. They wanted state help, but they bridled at state interference. Furthermore, the play of politics risked putting the state machinery into the hands of the enemies of agriculture. The better organized and more sophisticated among the French agrarian elite had come to prefer corporatism to direct state regulation: self-administration of agricultural affairs by the farmers' own organizations. For this they needed merely the distant sanction of a night-watchman state.

The unorganized small farmers tended simply to reject state interference in their affairs by the more elemental reaction of violence. Those in the conservative north and west had a long tradition of refractoriness to the state's tax collector, military inscription, schoolteacher, and—for the *bouilleurs de cru*—the inspector who invaded homes to make sure the alembics remained sealed. Their perception of the state's agent as enemy was reinforced after 1930 by the new system of social insurance, with its new network of paperwork and inspectors, and by a plethora of complicated legislation designed to help stem the decline of agricultural prices, none of which seemed to work.

The third and final possible recourse for farmers was their own *syndicats agricoles*. France had a network of agricultural organizations that claimed to speak for farmers and press their views on parliament and the state. Both Tocqueville and Marx have made it harder for us to understand how powerfully organized French agriculture was in the 1930s. Tocqueville arrived, through his study of history, at a powerful image of a rural France stripped of its local voluntary associations, first by a centralizing monarch and then by a Jacobin dictatorship. Marx arrived at a similar image through sociology: the smallholding peasant as individualistic and as refractory to common action as potatoes in a sack. Both images of unorganized or unorganizable French peasants are profoundly misleading. French farmers were extensively and richly organized between the two world wars. They frequented a great variety of fairs *(comices* or *foires),* festivals *(fêtes),* and markets *(marchés);* they belonged to a complicated and overlapping collection of *syndicats, cooperatives, mutuelles,* and insurance and retirement funds *(caisses).*

We can bring some order into the bewildering array of French farmers' organizations in 1930 by arranging them on three grids: chronological, political, and social.[120]

Chronologically, successive strata of agricultural organizations had been laid down by generations of French lawmakers, rather as a river deposits layers of alluvia in its periodic floods. The old layers were never removed; the new layers were simply superimposed on top of them. The earliest form of agricultural association was the learned society. Already in the eighteenth century, great improving landlords like the duc de La Rochefoucauld-Liancourt met with their peers to discuss and propogate the latest technological improvements in farming.

The lineal descendant of these aristocratic learned societies of the Enlightenment was the Société des Agriculteurs de France—the august SAF—founded in 1861 and recognized officially by a decree of Thiers in 1872. The SAF was still active in the 1930s, presided over by the marquis de Vogüé and an executive committee dominated by ancient aristocratic titles—no longer at the forefront of political enlightenment but still keenly interested in technical progress. The SAF's influence was limited not only by snobbery but also by a mainly pedagogical conception of its mission: it disseminated new technology and conservative politics through a handsome review on coated paper (the *Revue des agriculteurs de France*) and correspondence courses.

The other descendant of the aristocratic learned societies was the select but obscure Académie d'Agriculture, founded in 1761 as the Société Royale d'Agriculture. By the mid–twentieth century, these organizations had social prestige but almost no influence on the majority of French farmers.

The July Monarchy (1830–48) laid down a more popular layer of rural organization in the *comices*. These were local rural fairs intended to improve farm productivity at the grass roots. In principle, a *comice agricole* functioned in every arrondissement, at least in wealthier agricultural regions. Each year the *comice,* managed by a committee of leading citizens (not necessarily farmers themselves), awarded prizes for the best animals and crops and the most loyal tenant farmer and hired hand *(domestique)* and hosted a convivial lunch at which the more substantial farmers— owners and big tenants—rubbed shoulders with the local deputy and senator and listened to elegant speeches. In the 1930s, *comices* were still a lively social occasion in many rural communities. Indeed some *comices* were reviving in the 1930s after a period of slumber,[121] while others were marking their centennials.[122] Dorgères said the *comices* were "meant only to chloroform peasant anger"[123] and sent his people to jeer any deputies, senators, or ministers who might turn up.

A layer of much more dynamic farm organizations was laid down in the 1880s: the *syndicats agricoles* (SAs). A law of 21 May 1884, best known today as the statute that legalized labor unions in France, also authorized other economic groups to organize to defend their professional interests. Farmers used this law with alacrity to set up SAs in most departments of France. From the first, their distinguising feature was a commercial role: the first *syndicats* were the work of rural grandees who sought to protect themselves and their smaller neighbors from fraudulent fertilizer dealers by buying large quantities in common.

The SAs' expanding mercantile function was confirmed in 1908 when they won legal authorization to set up cooperatives to buy and sell in common for their members, over the protests of private feed and fertilizer stores. The "Chéron law" of 12 March 1920 confirmed and enlarged the SAs' commercial capacities. Even the most rudimentary SA bought wagonloads of fertilizer at wholesale prices for its members; the more enterprising ones operated warehouses and silos, administered insurance funds, established and oversaw the use of restricted labels *(appelations contrôlées)* for regional specialties, and bought and sold a wide range of products for their members.

Most *syndicats agricoles* were limited to one department. In several cases, regional groupings of SAs formed mighty economic empires. The Union des Syndicats Agricoles du Finistère et des Côtes-du-Nord was the biggest operation of this kind in the conservative west; it was familiarly known by the name of the town where its headquarters and main offices were located: Landerneau (Finistère).[124] The Union du Sud-Est at Lyon was another vast conglomerate of cooperatives, insurance funds, retirement funds, and sales and purchase organizations, covering seven departments of the Rhône Valley.

The head of such regional groupings of SAs could be a formidable local or even national personage. The head of Landerneau, the comte Hervé Budes de Guébriant, was a major figure in Brittany (and an active supporter of Dorgères at least through 1936); he was later in charge of putting the Vichy Corporation Nationale Paysanne into operation. Félix Garcin, head of the Union du Sud-Est and, simultaneously, a law professor at the Catholic Faculty of Lyon, lacked the inherited social power of the comte de Guébriant, but he was the undisputed master of every agricultural organization in the region around Lyons in the late Third Republic and under Vichy.

Confronted with the fluctuations of the world market and eager for state support, the producers of the principal commercial crops thought of forming specialized associations of producers similar to the industrial cartels so successful in the late nineteenth century. The first to organize were the winegrowers, forced by the overproduction of the years just after 1900 to work together or perish. They formed the Confédération Générale des Vignerons du Midi in 1907.

After World War I a new wave of specialized organizations arose. The most powerful was the Confédération Générale des Planteurs de Betteraves (CGB), which was formed in 1921 for sugar beet growers. Its power came from the wealth and influence of the big sugar beet farmers of the north of France, from their capacity to regulate production, and from their long history of successful lobbying for state support. The wheat growers' Association Générale des Producteurs de Blé (AGPB), formed in 1924, was also powerful because of the importance of wheat in the French rural economy, although the more dispersed, wheat producers were harder to discipline. The specialized associations for producers of meat, milk, cider fruit, and linen were weak, for their members were small, dispersed, and individualistic.

The main task of these specialized associations was to negotiate on behalf of their numerous members with the French state and with other economic powers. The CGB, as we have seen, negotiated the terms on which the state bought excess sugar beets and distilled industrial alcohol, a culmination of the long history of government support since the Napoleonic era. The CGB also negotiated in 1931 an accord between beet farmers and sugar refiners to put a stop to the wild fluctuations in the internal sugar market, exacerbated by the Depression.

With offices in Paris, staffed by trained professionals, the specialized associations lobbied the parliament and the press to promote public support for the government measures that they sought to support their particular crop. The secretaries-general of the strongest specialized associations—Jean Achard, Pierre Hallé, and Charles du Fretay (the three musketeers)—were highly skilled professionals who played important roles in the politics of agriculture between the wars and under Vichy. These specialized associations were more influential in the 1930s than today because there was no unified peak farmers' organization like today's FNSEA.

One step toward giving farmers corporate representation was to provide seats on the National Economic Council (Conseil National Économique, 1925). But these representatives were mostly notables, mere weekend farmers, and the council itself a mere forum for talk. More promising for peasant representation were the *chambres d'agriculture* (CAs), established in 1924. Although only consultative, the CAs were appreciated by farmers as a forum for the expression of their opinions in public and with the government. The members were elected by the votes of all farmers, including those women who ran farms in person (thus the CAs were the only official representative body in France for which women could vote before 1945).

The farmers voted in two colleges: one for individuals and the other for SAs and other farm organizations—a further sign of the spread of corporate representation in France between the wars. Farmers participated widely in these elections and showed esteem for the *chambres d'agriculture*. But the CAs had little impact unless the government chose to listen to them. André Tardieu did so in 1930, and Laval's Minister of Agriculture Pierre Cathala did so in 1935, and both won undying gratitude in the countryside; Pierre-Etienne Flandin refused to receive them in 1934–35, and thus won deep enmity there.

Now we must complicate this chronological account with the second grid: the political. The most significant formative period of French farmers' associational life began when the Third Republic was attempting slowly and painfully to establish its legitimacy in the 1870s and when farmers' associations became legal under the Associations Law of 1884.

In conservative regions of France, small farmers and rural workers still remained subject in the 1880s to the powerful influence of conservative notables and the church. The Republic wanted to recruit small farmers, along with other social strata new to politics (the *nouvelles couches sociales* of which Léon Gambetta spoke in the 1870s), in support of the new regime. So Republican leaders set up their own network of agricultural institutions. At the top was a national farmers' organization, the Société d'Encouragement à l'Agriculture, set up by Gambetta in 1880. It presided over a local network of pro-Republican credit, insurance, and cooperative associations for farmers. Since the Republicans controlled the apparatus of the state, they could fortify their farmers' organizations by obtaining the help of other public officials. These included the official agricultural services in each department: the *directeur des services agricoles* (law of 16 June 1876) and his assistant, the *professeur d'agriculture,* who dispensed technical advice and recommmended local leaders for government awards such as the Ordre du Mérite Agricole. They also had the power of the state behind their lending offices, so that abundant cheap credit was a powerful attraction for potential members. Most ministers of agriculture (an independent ministry since 1881) came from the world of the Société d'Encouragement and its network of Republican credit and insurance associations. This universe of Republican farm associations tended to think of their clientèle as citizens who happened to farm, farmers *(agriculteurs),* rather than as an organic culture and profession of *paysans.* Peasants from conservative parts of France felt estranged from them.

On the Catholic side another network of *syndicats agricoles* developed, based on paternalist and social Christian principles, powerful in the conservative regions of France. If not actively anti-Republican, they were indifferent to electoral politics and rested their power on the inherited authority of the great landowners, often noblemen or, in some cases, priests, who founded and ran then. Their doctrine rested on the social Catholicism of Albert de Mun and René de La Tour du Pin, who had founded one of the first farmers' cooperatives and who valued peasant life for its moral qualities. They thought of their world as a distinct organic corporation that responded to a different economic logic from that of the cities, and they referred to it increasingly as the "peasantry."

Thus two rival networks of local farmers' *syndicats, caisses, mutuelles,* and *cooperatives* were drawn up in mortal competition with each other. Each was known by the address of its central offices in Paris: la rue d'Athènes for the conservative Union Centrale des Syndicats Agricoles, and le boulevard Saint-Germain for the Republicans' Société d'Encouragement. Thereafter, "the history of agricultural organizations [in France] is nothing but one long rivalry between the noble landowner *[châtelain]* and the Radical-Socialist deputy."[125]

Both reached out competitively toward the small farmer but from different social bases. The pro-Republican and anticlerical boulevard Saint-Germain spread its network of credit unions and insurance funds and cooperatives outward from the market towns, relying heavily on sympathetic parliamentarians and public officials and on the attractions of cheap credit and official recognition. We have already met a splendid example in the person of Senator Chéron of Lisieux (Calvados). One hears many stories of local conservative *syndicats agricoles* unable to get loans from the quasi-official farmers' bank, the Crédit Agricole; of having cool relations with the minister, the *directeur des services agricoles,* and the *professeurs d'agriculture;* and of being left off the list for the Ordre du Mérite Agricole. Dorgères loved to ridicule this award as the leek *(poireau)* and its recipients as sycophantic incompetents. One understands, therefore, why the conservative SAs considered themselves "unpolitical" and professed to despise politics—politics meant the machinery used by their rivals.

Rue d'Athènes built its departmental or regional SAs upward from the hereditary social and cultural power of local landowners and priests. Sound political tactics, as well as social Catholic paternalism, encouraged them to spend more time than did boulevard Saint-Germain on training leaders and forming close social and ideological links with their clientele.

The rivalry of the two farmers' networks came to seem an annoyance, an embarrassment, and even an impediment to effective defense of farmer's own interests. The unification of the farmers' interests was a major rural aim between the wars. Each side (plus the emerging socialist and communist peasant organizations) blamed the others for the division and claimed to represent the entire rural society. Dorgères was no exception. For him, it was the Republic that divided the peasants, and his *comités de défense paysanne* were the most plausible representative of the entire rural universe. That claim was absurd, but it shows how powerful was the thirst for unity.

It was not clear in the 1930s who would emerge as the unifier of the French agrarian interest. But in retrospect, it was rue d'Athènes that deployed the most dynamism, organizational skill, and local roots. Without neglecting the technical and commercial needs of local farmers, they pursued more general political goals aggressively. Its SAs claimed to be instruments of "peasant emancipation" (the phrase is Jaques Le Roy Ladurie's) by enrolling the smaller farmers in the SAs; engaging them in SAs activities; and educating them in the doctrines of rural unity and corporatist, professional self-administration. At the same time, they reaffirmed the social hierarchy of the countryside They imparted a heightening sense among farmers of their own identity and power, under a natural inherited leadership. Their central organization, the Union Centrale des Syndicats Agricoles (UCSA), became the Union nationale (UNSA) when Jacques Le Roy Ladurie became its secretary-general in 1934 and reorganized its credit operations, which had been financially troubled by the Depression.

Le Roy Ladurie, a leader of driving energy and strong antirepublican and corporatist convictions, aspired to a major political role. The UNSA was to be the root on which the Peasant Corporation was built during the Vichy regime. And even though that link was a heavy liability at Liberation, the young Fourth Republic's attempt to build a new unified agricultural organization based on day laborers and consumers, as well as farmers, was stillborn. The Confédération Générale Agricole (CGA), brain-child of the socialist Minister of Agriculture François Tanguy-Prigent—who had helped roll Dorgères on the ground during a meeting on 26 January 1936 at Bégard (Côtes-du-Nord)[126]—could not overcome the old SAs' social solidity at the grass roots. It was veterans of the UNSA and of the Corporation Paysanne (including even a few Dorgérists) who realized definitive unity in the postwar FNSEA.[127]

We need now to overlay briefly a third and final grid: the social. Each one of these farmers' associations drew on particular elements of rural society and used particular forms of mobilization. The SAF consisting mostly of nobles of ancient title, remained limited to its exalted sphere. The *comices* became the realm of republican politicians and their friends. The SAs were run by big local landowners, not all of whom actually farmed. Up to World War I, all of this rich associational life was domi-nated by an oligarchy of rural notables. Even the republican notables were drawn from the upper levels of society; the conservative notables were if anything more likely to cultivate their own farms (though there were many absentee landlords among them, too, and very few muddy boots). The normal arrangement was leadership by the principal notable of the area, aristocratic or republican.

Each group had its particular social flavor. The *comices* were festive occasions bringing together prosperous republican farmers and local poli-ticians. The SAs—whether republican or conservative—had a more perma-nent structure: their base was cooperatives and mutual insurance and credit associations. Their heads were hard-working, rooted local notables, aristocratic or not. The specialized associations were run by professional managers, well-trained officials of impressive qualifications (the Achards, the Hallés, the du Fretays).

Two notable local agrarian leaders of the 1930s may serve as examples, one from the republican network and one from the Catholic-conservative network. From the latter side, Jacques Le Roy Ladurie (1902–88) is a natural choice because of his energy, verbal brilliance, and powerful social and political vision. He came from a substantial bourgeois family with ties to the nobility. His father, a professional army officer in the same class at Saint-Cyr as the future Marshal Pétain, was expelled from the army in 1902; he refused the command to ensure order during the crisis opened when the republican government of Emile Combes excluded members of Catholic religious orders from teaching. That political purge soured the family permanently on the Republic.

A sickly adolescent, advised by doctors to live in the country, the young Jacques settled on the family's country property of Villeray, at Les Moutiers-en-Cinglais (Calvados). There he discovered farming. After training at the Catholic *ecole d'agriculture* at Angers and serving as apprentice to conservative landowners for another two years, he entered the career of farming "as one enters into religion."[128] His health restored—one is reminded of Theodore Roosevelt—he deployed an abundant energy in multiple directions, including playing the harmonium in the local church for fifty-four years. The head of the Syndicat Agricole of the Calvados, the comte d'Oilliamson, recruited the young Le Roy Ladurie as his organization's secretary-general, and the young firebrand was soon at the head of a pyramid of interlocking posts, extending from mayor of his commune up to secretary-general of the UNSA at the rue d'Athènes. From these positions, he preached a gospel of peasant self-awareness, united organization, and self-administration independently of the allegedly hostile republican state.

An excellent example of a notable republican leader of agricultural associations is Joseph Faure (1875–1944): creator and animator of a whole network of agricultural organizations from the local to the national level and eventually senator (1921–38). Faure was born to a modest farm family in the Corrèze and never ceased being a farmer there. But he had a passion for organization, and he spent his life building and running farmers' associations. In 1905 he began by organizing a *syndicat* in his native region of Argentat (Corrèze). In 1918, he assembled most of the farmers' organizations of the Corrèze into a federation at the departmental level, the Fédération des Associations Agricoles Corréziennes. Casting his eye wider still, he assembled a regional Fédération des Associations Agricoles du Centre-Sud, which eventually covered fourteen departments. Its bulletin was called *Défense paysanne,* a militant title he invented before Dorgères gave it a different twist.

Meanwhile, in 1921, Faure had been elected senator from the Corrèze. He was instrumentral in helping found the *chambres d'agriculture,* and when the CAs formed a nationwide assembly of all its departmental presidents in 1927, he was elected president. He was the CAs' main spokesman and the inevitable president of republican committees or councils involving farm issues. For example, he headed the agriculture committee for the Paris World's Fair of 1937 and even international committees. He was a vice-president of the Confédération Nationale des Associations Agricoles (CNAA), a 1920 effort to unify all agricultural organizations, which only succeeded in adding another layer. By now, one wonders how often he managed to find a few moments for his farm in the Corrèze. His normal workplace had long ago ceased to be the field and had become the committee room or the public meeting.

Faure sat at the apex of a pyramid of farmers' organizations or, more accurately, of several interlocking pyramids. There was his pyramid of local sAs, federated at the departmental and regional level. Next came the pyramid of the *chambres d'agriculture,* from the departmental to national level, of which he was the top official as president of the Assemblée Permanente des Présidents des Chambres d'Agriculture (APPCA). One is amazed by the number of offices Joseph Faure managed to accumulate. One wonders how he found time for all of it, and at the powers of concentration and the personal ascendacy they demanded. But such pyramids of offices turn out to be a common pattern in farmers' organizations, both Republican and Catholic—as it is generally in French political practice, as in the frequent combination *(cumul)* of the positions of local mayor and deputy in parliament.

In the 1930s, this universe of agricultural associations had to persuade its members that its traditional leaders were able to cope effectively with the Depression, with the disappearance of rural life, and with the underrepresentation of farmers in the Third Republic. Their failure to do so shook their legitimacy. They failed even at what they claimed to do best, run a sound commercial organization *(syndicat boutique).* Many local cooperatives and credit associations went bankrupt. Even at the summit of the hierarchy of the *syndicats agricoles,* the UCSA was in financial difficulties; it was apparently by assembling rescue capital through his brother Gabriel, of the Banque Worms, that Jacques Le Roy Ladurie became secretary-general in 1934.

The economic crash of the 1930s coincided with a challenge from farmers who cultivated their own soil (the *cultivateurs-cultivants*) to take their own affairs in hand. The sAs were all dominated in the 1930s by rural notables, men who functioned simultaneously within rural society and within the larger world and established their social power on their capacity to link the two.[129] Faced with the crises of the 1930s, they risked losing their legitimacy on both levels, removed from agriculture and inefficacious in the wider world. The republican notables were just as vulnerable as the conservative ones to such charges. Indeed, they were more often non-farmers (like Chéron) or ex-farmers (like Joseph Faure) than were the conservatives.

Dorgères was a leader in the challenge to the traditional rural leadership in the 1930s, but he was by no means alone. As we shall see, the Abbé Mancel had already challenged it in Brittany in the 1920s, and the Communist party embarked on a serious bid in the 1930s to represent those small farmers for whom anyone well-to-do *(les gros)* was the enemy and who were willing to think of themselves as rural members of the working class, peasant-workers *(paysans travailleurs).* In conservative parts of France, the Catholic Farmers' Youth Organization (Jeunesse Agricole Chrétienne, JAC) became the most successful channel of young farmers' disillusion with their traditional leaders. The future was to belong to them, but not before Dorgérism and the Communist party had competed for the leadership of dissident farmers who no longer accepted the authority of the established agricultural associations.

To take Joseph Faure as an example once again, the senator faced a challenge from dissident peasant movements on both the Right and the Left in the Corrèze after 1933. On the Right was Fleurant Agricola's Parti Agraire and Paysan Français (PAPF), which had enjoyed a modest success in the legislative elections of 1932 and was at the peak of its activity, with a series of simultaneous rallies in every department of France in February 1933. On the Left was Renaud Jean's Confédération Générale des Paysans Travailleurs (CGPT). We see in Chapter 3 how Jean persuaded the Central Committee of the French Communist party to give a higher priority to work among the *paysans travailleurs* in February 1933. Both organizations began their activities in the Corrèze in late 1933, and in early 1934 were reported by the prefect to be in "take-off" *(plein essor)*.

Surprisingly, these two seemingly incompatible and rival organizations made common cause against Joseph Faure and the direction of the Fédération Départementale des Associations Agricoles Corrèziennes. They could work together because Renaud Jean was anticipating the Popular Front's overtures to the middle classes and because the PAPF always contained a radical element that rejected the conservative stance of the leaders and was to break away from the PAPF in February 1936. The CGPT and the PAPF cooperated, in fact, in several other departments in addition to the Corrèze, notably the Côtes-du-Nord.[130] The prefect of the Corrèze reported, therefore, in early 1934 that "their actions are combining." Communists and agrariens "are exploiting the real discontent that has been in evidence for several weeks."[131] By the end of 1934, Faure was in serious difficulty. The prefect of the Corrèze now reported that "Joseph Faure is no longer in command of his troops. He is overwhelmed by his constituents."[132]

At the annual congress of the Fédération Départementale of the Corrèze in February 1935, Joseph Faure was submitted to rough treatment quite outside his experience. The Agrarians and the Communists had packed the meeting, usually so docile. Instead of functioning as the usual well-oiled machine, ratifying all official motions automatically, the meeting slipped out of Faure's control. Speaker after speaker condemned the "lack of energy" and the "official character" of the traditional organizations. They demanded a march on the prefecture, noting that the authorities had not listened to farmers' complaints seriously in the Beauce until the peasants had occupied the prefecture at Chartres. The prefect reported after this stormy meeting that "the peasants [he identified them as solid proprietors and heads of cooperatives] are more agitated than they have ever been before." [133]

Eventually, Faure was able to salvage his position, at least for a time. But his recovery was due more to disagreements among his enemies than to his own skills. The Agrarians began to realize that the Communists were gaining more from their joint action than they were. Thus in October 1935, the Agrarians came back into Faure's camp. [134]

In general, rural notables like Joseph Faure, though shaken, did not lose their power in the 1930s Third Republic. There was less loss of legitimacy by the established farm leadership in France than there was at the same moment in Germany, where traditional farm leaders lost their place to Nazi farm leaders in places like Schleswig-Holstein even before Hitler came to power. [135] While the French Republic remained intact, so did its rural cadres. But their authority had faltered, which gave Dorgères the opening he exploited by offering his direct action formula to frustrated French peasants.

The three crises facing the French peasantry in the 1930s—economic, cultural, and political—were separate but interlocking. The economic crisis confronted the parliament with a challenge beyond its capacities and thus weakened the Third Republic's legitimacy in the countryside. The economic crisis simultaneously hastened the decline of the peasant way of life. Together, these interlocking crises made many French farmers ask whether the Third Republic was for them or against them. Many of them were ready to accept another kind of politics and another kind of leader.

two
· · ·

THE RISE OF DORGÉRISM

The Creation of Henry Dorgères

NOTHING IN HENRY DORGÈRES'S origins or youth seemed to prepare him to become the main rightwing peasant agitator of 1930s France. He was not raised on a farm. He was born Henri-Auguste D'Halluin in Wasquehal (Nord), near Lille, on 6 February 1897, the eldest son of a butcher who also fattened a few cattle for slaughter. The *D'* is not the noble particule *de,* as the Left press kept insisting in the face of Dorgères's energetic (and, for once, accurate) denials that he was the "vicomte d'Halluin." The *D'* was simply an ordinary kind of family name in the Nord. When Henri-Auguste's father died young, his mother and all the children struggled to keep the butcher shop going.

The boy was bright and determined in primary school. Like so many public figures of modest background in the Third Republic, he rode upward on the Republic's main mechanism of social ascent: the highly competitive system of examinations and scholarships that led talented and ambitious boys from the village primary school to the *lycée* and from there to teaching, a profession, or politics. Upon finishing his *certificat d'études* (primary school) in 1908, Henri D'Halluin won first prize for the Department of the Nord, which earned him a scholarship to the *lycée* of Tourcoing.[1] He had just passed the written part of the rigorous *baccaleuréat* and was about to take the oral when war broke out in August 1914. In 1923, after interruptions caused by the war, he finished a law degree *(bachelier en droit).*[2]

World War I caught the adolescent Henri-Auguste D'Halluin behind German lines in the occupied Nord. Thus he lived the war years very differently from most young Frenchmen of his age, under German occupation rather than in uniform. Dorgères always insisted that in his own way he had been a war hero. According to his own account, he was arrested in October 1914 for preparing false identity papers and spent forty days in prison. In February 1918, he was arrested again by the Germans while trying to cross the Dutch frontier, probably trying to join his family, which had been repatriated to the south; in 1945, he told an examining magistrate that he had been caught smuggling Allied intelligence into Holland.[3] Imprisoned in the fortress of Bruges, he managed to escape on 4 October 1918 as the Germans were preparing to retreat. Today we cannot authenticate these adventures, but Dorgères clearly felt it important to affirm a link with the great national epic that had occurred without him.

Dorgères was to put the peasant experience in World War I at the very center of his movement's appeal. His principal lieutenants had been decorated in action, and many of his followers belonged to the veterans' generation that had started farms in the 1920s only to be caught by the Depression with their initial debts not yet paid off. He claimed incessantly that the victory of 1918 had rested mainly on peasant qualities and peasant sacrifices. He often gathered his angry farmers around monuments to war dead, and he founded a veterans' association for peasants, the Union des Paysans Anciens Combattants.[4] And when another war loomed in the late 1930s, he opposed another disproportionate "blood tax" (impôt de sang) on farm boys.

Only when D'Halluin was a law student of twenty-two is there independent contemporary evidence of his political leanings. In March 1919 he published a series of four short notes in the main French royalist daily, L'Action française.[5] Commenting on the shortcomings of reconstruction in the postwar Nord, D'Halluin blamed the excessive centralization and paperwork of the French republican state and called for more reparations from "les boches." Although some of Dorgères's later themes—antistatism and anti-Germanism—were already present, the focus was industrial rather than agricultural. Writing for L'Action française seems, however, to have established a crucial contact with Bishop Charost of Lille. Charost appears to have found a job for the young D'Halluin with the principal local agricultural association, the Syndicats Agricoles du Nord, led by an aristocratic Catholic layman, count Octave d'Hespel. Soon Henri D'Halluin was writing for its newspaper, the Echo des syndicats agricoles.

In 1922, D'Halluin moved to Rennes (Ille-et-Vilaine) to work for the local Action Française newspaper there, Le Nouvelliste de Bretagne, from 1922 until 1927. We cannot be certain why he went to Rennes. His first employer there, Eugène Delahaye, director of *Le Nouvelliste* and a native of the Nord, testified at Dorgères's trial in 1945 that he had known the young D'Halluin in the Nord in 1918 and invited him to work for him in Rennes.[6] The principal scholars of Dorgères's beginnings[7] believe that it was Charost himself, by now archbishop of Rennes, who brought D'Halluin to Rennes to help him in his efforts to counter the progressive Christian Democratic movement that was spreading in Brittany.

Brittany was the region where the reconciliation of French Catholics to the Republic (the *ralliement*) was producing its most vigorous impact. The newspaper *Ouest-Eclair,* founded at Rennes in 1899 and edited by the Abbé Trochu, was at the center of a lively growth of the Christian Democratic organization and militancy that filled the space left vacant in rural Brittany by the weakness of a secular Left. In that predominantly agricultural setting, it was only natural that the Christian Democratic *abbés* of Brittany should place the peasantry at the center of their mission.

In 1920, the Abbé Mancel, who was already suspect to the Catholic hierarchy for having participated in Marc Sangnier's Le Sillon,[8] founded an independent network of Christian peasant organizations, the Syndicats Paysans de l'Ouest (SPO). The SPO, familiarly known as the *cultivateurs-cultivants,*[9] proposed to help small tenant farmers, sharecroppers, and farm laborers achieve economic, social, and spiritual independence, not only from their urban exploiters, the anticlerical bourgeois republican bankers and merchants, but from the great aristocratic and conservative landowners as well. From the point of view of traditional Breton rural authorities, the *cultivateurs-cultivants* were a fifth column, threatening from within a rural social hierarchy buttressed by the doctrine that all farmers, from the humblest day laborer to the greatest noble landlord, shared a common interest.

The *cultivateurs-cultivants,* by contrast, proclaimed that small farmers' interests conflicted with those of landlords, and they urged small farmers to take their fate into their own hands and seize the leadership of rural organizations from absentee landlords. The marquis Louis de Vogüé, then president of the main conservative national farmers' association, the Société des Agriculteurs de France, as well as of its offspring, the Union Centrale des Syndicats Agricoles (the rue d'Athènes), saw the stakes very clearly:

> The enemies of social peace and of the Fatherland have found unexpected allies in the very ranks of those whom they are fighting against. I can not imagine for what purpose attempts are being made around France, in Christ's name, to divide the agricultural family and to cast out as unworthy those who don't till the soil with their own hands.[10]

Archbishop Charost considered the Christian Democratic *abbés* to be the main threat to social stability in Brittany, the socialist and communist Left having only peripheral toeholds there: in the Brest navy yard and in some fishing ports. He fought their influence in the countryside. It may have been with the archbishop's encouragement that D'Halluin began writing editorials for a struggling new farmers' weekly, the *Progrès agricole de l'Ouest* (PAO), in March 1926, while continuing to write for *Le Nouvelliste*, and that he became its editor-in-chief *(directeur)* in April 1927.[11] The archbishop certainly had ties with the PAO, for it was printed by his own printer, Hyacinthe Riou-Rieuzé.

D'Halluin's beginnings as an Action Française journalist in Archbishop Charost's circle led his opponents to refer to him commonly as the "vicomte d'Halluin" and to portray him as an agent of the church, of the Action Française, and of the Breton nobility. As *directeur* of the PAO and later as head of his own peasant movement, however, Dorgères seems to have wanted to establish his independance from his early backers. Although the Abbé Mancel and "Grindorge," the agricultural correspondent of *Ouest-Eclair,* were among his favorite targets, Dorgères never mentioned Catholic doctrine and practice in his editorials and speeches. His paper and movement were totally secular. Indeed, Dorgères could sound outright anticlerical at times.[12] He never mentioned the restoration of a monarch. His movement was populist and nationalist, seemingly indifferent to religion and inherited social hierarchy. But Dorgères never renounced the attachment to village, family, and craft that he had imbibed as an adolescent with the Action Française, along with the conviction that the Third Republic was only the transitory regime of the moment, without authentic legitimacy.

Dorgères and the Agrarian Press

The *Progrès agricole de l'Ouest* had been founded in 1925 but had not done well. Henry Dorgères—as he now signed his editorials, after the name of a nearby village—proved to be an enterprising and dynamic *directeur.* He printed the market quotations and technical information customary in France's dozens of local farmers' weeklies, of course. He also offered concrete advice on taxes and other administrative problems and news of meetings and political issues that affected farmers. There was even a womens' page. More originally, the PAO offered individual help to subscribers with tax problems. Dorgères spiced each issue with a highly personal and argumentative editorial that gave vivid expression to small farmers' anxieties and animosities. The paper was printed on green paper, a color that he soon helped to transform into a symbol of peasant militancy.

By the middle 1930s, the PAO had a weekly press run of 27,000.[13] In 1933, Dorgères put the paper on an apparently sound financial basis by setting up a corporation, the Société de Presse Agricole, whose principal shareholder was the duc d'Harcourt, the conservative deputy of Bayeux (Calvados).[14] Although young, the duc d'Harcourt exercised a powerful hereditary influence over his dairy-farming region on the coast of Normandy, the Bessin. For example, he donated the prizes awarded each year for the best animals and for the most loyal servants; he raised prize-winning dairy cattle himself.[15] We have not been able to learn how Dorgères met the duc d'Harcourt or to determine what exact role he played in the PAO and in Dorgères's career.

The duc d'Harcourt's financial participation in the company that published the PAO led the Ministry of the Interior to conclude, erroneously, that Dorgères was his "spokesman" and a "royalist agent,"[16] and the Left press to label him Action Française or Camelot du Roi. The duc's own political views were Catholic, monarchist, and paternalist, as expressed in the *Indicateur de Bayeux,* which he owned outright. By 1937 that paper was supporting Colonel de La Rocque and his Parti Social Français rather than Dorgères. The PAO, in contrast, pursued its own line, which differed in significant ways from the duc's. The PAO was hostile to religious activism in politics and indifferent to the monarchist cause. Dorgères tried to play down the duc d'Harcourt's influence on his paper when the police interrogated him in 1935, and he seems to have been accurate on that point.[17] The duc d'Harcourt, for his part, omits any mention of Dorgères in his memoirs.[18]

The second major shareholder of the corporation that published the PAO was Riou-Rieuzé, the paper's printer, who was also the printer for the Archdiocese of Rennes. There is no evidence that he exercised any editorial influence, either, over what was, for all practical purposes, Dorgères's own newspaper. Several great Breton landlords were also (mistakenly) believed to be shareholders: the marquis de Kérouartz; another conservative Breton deputy, Etienne Le Poullen; and count Roger de La Bourdonnaye, the president of the Chambre d'Agriculture of the Ille-et-Vilaine.[19]

The *Progrès agricole de l'Ouest* was probably modestly profitable.[20] During the worst of the Depression, when some agricultural weeklies had to cut back on their publication schedules,[21] the PAO kept up its weekly rhythm. About 25% of each twenty-four-page, tabloid-sized issue, on the average, consisted of advertising, about normal for a farmers' weekly of that time. There were full-page ads occasionally for Renault and Ford tractors, half-page ads frequently for major fertilizer producers like Saint-Gobain, and smaller ads for important agricultural items such as Als-Thom electric motors. Huiles Lesieur often had the largest ad, reflecting the long-term backing Dorgères received from its owner, Jacques Lemaigre-Dubreuil.

There is no direct evidence of support from other major advertisers or of advertisers' influence on Dorgères's editorial positions, though it is noticeable that in his attacks on powerful economic interests he singled out the state phosphate company rather than the private fertilizer companies that advertised in the PAO. Of course, he received no ads from big flour-milling companies and international grain traders, the "international finance capitalists" whom he denounced regularly as the peasants' enemies. Unsurprisingly, his advertisers were those who sold to the peasants, not those who bought from them.

Gradually Dorgères expanded his newspaper operations until he was head of a modest press empire. In April 1933 he published the first number of a monthly called *La voix du paysan,* which he edited jointly with Joseph Cadic, a former deputy of the Morbihan who had lost his seat in the elections of 1932. Cadic was mainly interested in winning back his seat; his electoral aims drew him closer to the Parti Agraire in 1934, and he thus disappeared from Dorgères's immediate circle (though he remained a distant ally after again winning a seat in 1936). Left alone with this monthly, Dorgères changed its name in May 1937 to the more emphatic *Le cri du paysan.*

In early 1936, Dorgères bought a Loire Valley weekly called *Le paysan du Centre-Ouest* (PCO), which had been published since 1932 at Saumur and Tours by the Parti Agraire and edited by J.-B. Jahan. Jahan was now elderly (he died in 1937) and the Parti Agraire in disarray. Dorgères may have been assisted in this purchase by his printer, Riou-Rieuzé, who printed this additional weekly in Rennes after the number of 7 June 1936. The PCO claimed a circulation of 24,000,[22] mostly in the Loire Valley, and had a comfortable spread of advertising, covering about 30% of its four to six pages. The paper's editorial expenses could not have been very burdensome, moreover, since many of its articles came from the PAO.

Also in 1936—possibly with help from Jacques Le Roy Ladurie,[23] a Norman gentleman farmer then emerging as one of France's leading conservative agrarian leaders—Dorgères founded another weekly in Paris called *Le cri du sol.* By this time Dorgères had national ambitions. In 1935, he had rented offices in Paris, at 10, boulevard du Montparnasse. The new weekly—on full-sized white paper—was intended for peasant militants throughout France. It had more illustrations and cartoons and less technical advice and news of local events than the PAO and the PCO. It was mainly devoted to Dorgères's editorials and articles on national agrarian issues. This was the one paper that Dorgères chose to continue to publish after 1940, during the Nazi occupation, when there was not enough newsprint to go around.

In March 1936 Dorgères started a monthly paper, *Haut les fourches,* for the Jeunesses Paysannes or Chemises Vertes. In May 1938, finally, he launched a regional monthly, *La Provence paysanne,* aimed at a rural audience in the Midi. By 1939, therefore, Dorgères was running three weeklies and three monthlies from his offices at 10, boulevard du Montparnasse, serviced by a common advertising agency, the Office Fédéral de la Publicité Agricole. In addition, he had strong editorial influence on two small agrarian weeklies in the southwest, *L'Action paysanne* (Toulouse) and *La Défense paysanne* (Aurillac), though they became cooler by 1937 and were absorbed by a rival. After the war, Dorgères claimed a total circulation of 300,000 for all his prewar papers combined.[24] Although Dorgères almost certainly inflated this figure, as was his habit, it is likely that this little press empire supported his modest life-style in Rennes in the 1930s, at least some of the costs of his Paris offices after 1935, and even some of the expenses of his movement.

Dorgères, the Peasant Tribune

Dorgères lived frugally in the 1930s. His personal needs were relatively simple. He lived from about 1927 until 1941 in a small house in Rennes, for a long time at 13, rue Saint-Malo, then in the rue Edith Cavell (which was perhaps why he thought of telling one judge the unlikely tale that he helped Nurse Cavell during the German occupation in World War I). In 1937, the Public Prosecutor *(procureur-général)* in Paris, scrutinizing for possible prosecution Dorgères's role as one of the main organizers of the strike of market gardeners *(maraîchers)*—which closed the main Paris fruit and vegetable market (Les Halles) three times in the fall of 1936—and who would have been delighted to uncover some private pecadillo that the state could use against Dorgères, concluded that "Henry Dorgères has not been the object of any special notice concerning his private life."[25] His concierge in Paris, questioned by the police in 1945, reported that Dorgères paid his rent regularly and did not have a "grand life style."[26]

The image Dorgères chose to portray in his books and speeches, of nights spent on the hard bench of a third-class railway carriage as he traveled from meeting to meeting, seems reasonably accurate. He devoted himself totally to his newspapers and to a prodigious schedule of public speaking, sometimes several times a week in widely scattered country towns. Dorgères claimed that he averaged 250 speeches a year before

World War II,[27] a figure that is certainly far above reality. Painstaking counts of the speeches reported in Dorgères' own *Progrès agricole de l'Ouest* suggest that the real figure was nearer one-third of his claim: 82 in 1929, 65 in 1930, only 8 in 1931, 44 in 1932, 77 in 1934, and a peak of 119 in 1935.[28] At times, the rhythm could indeed be very strenuous. We learn in the PAO of 26 meetings in thirteen days in January 1930.[29] Over three days in September 1935, Dorgères addressed an important rally in the Paris suburbs at the beginning of the market gardeners' strike on Saturday, 26 September; then he was in Caen (Calvados) on Sunday to address a major rally (the press reported that he was "visibly ill"). The next day, Monday, he was back in the Paris region for the market gardeners' strike.

In addition to a heavy schedule of speechmaking, Dorgères wrote five or six articles a week and saw into the press three weeklies and three monthly publications. It was a life of hard work and few frills. Efforts by some hostile witnesses to portray him as needing money to pay "debts from gambling and women"[30] have no basis. Luxurious living belonged to conventional political mudslinging of the period: Dorgères also liked to so accuse trade union leaders such as Léon Jouhaux.

The young editor learned how to sway a peasant audience and won his first public notoriety by campaigning against social security. France's system of obligatory *assurances sociales,* initiated by the "Loucheur law" of 5 April 1928, provided for assistance in cases of illness, incapacity, or maternity; funded by joint monthly contributions by workers and employers, it was extended under somewhat different rules to farm workers in 1930.[31] The delay was caused by the legislators' discovery that farm workers were not simply factory workers in the open air. Whereas social security could be applied without serious strain to big farms with salaried employees, the far more numerous family farmers with one or two employees, some part time, who might well be family members or neighbors, found it unthinkable.[32] Many of them were innocent of paperwork and bookkeeping, and few handled much cash. It was not only the payments that enraged them; they also had to fill out forms and enmesh themselves in a bureaucracy. Social security inserted the state between the farmer and his own son or cousin or neighbor, who had for years done occasional paid labor at planting or harvest time.

The farmers' rage over social security offered fertile ground for a demagogue. Even some urban workers, who doubted that they would ever get anything back, opposed social security payments.[33] This scattered urban opposition was minor, however, compared to the tidal wave of rejection that social security aroused in the French countryside. Dorgères was able to gather 12,000 people at Vannes (Morbihan) on 28 December 1928 for his first great protest meeting against it.

The campaign against social security was more successful in the west than in any other region of France.[34] The prefect of the Finistère reported in March 1935 that social security had never been accepted by rural populations there.[35] In effect, in large areas of western France, the social security system simply did not function for farm workers for many years—not until during or after World War II in some cases. The west was, after all, one of the areas of France where salaried farm workers were rarest and most likely to be family members. Dorgères took a leading role in the west's refusal of it.[36] According to one police estimate, Henry Dorgères and Fleurant Agricola, founder of the Parti Agraire et Paysan Français (PAPF), between them gave 200 speeches against social security in 1930 alone.[37]

At the beginning, without an organization of his own, Dorgères usually appeared as a speaker for the Taxpayers' League (Ligue des Contribuables), a militant antitax movement that was to take on anti-Republican coloration in the middle 1930s under Jacques Lemaigre-Dubreuil. Soon Dorgères formed his own organization. On 2 January 1929, he gathered twenty to thirty farmers in his newspaper offices at 13, rue de la Monnaie in Rennes to create a Comité de Défense contre les Assurances Sociales. This was the local branch of a similar committee already set up in the Eure-et-Loir by Henri Doublier and Rémy Sédillot.[38] Never willing to take orders from anyone else, Dorgères soon appropriated the name Comités de Défense as his own creation and played down the original founders.[39]

The high point of the campaign in the west against social security came on 1 February 1930, just before the farmers were supposed to register their employees with a local insurance fund *(caisse)*. Dorgères and Agricola organized a huge rally in Morin's car repair shop in Rennes. (Morin was in trouble with the tax collectors, too, and provided a link among the Ligue des Contribuables, the peasants, and the truck drivers, another group hostile to state regulation). Between 5000 and 6000 *cultivateurs* and *ouvriers agricoles* came from six western *départements,* according to the prefect. They were first warmed up by ten speakers and then chanted a litany of responses as Dorgères asked them questions: "Do you want the Social Security law? NO! Do you want the law as modified? NO! You won't pay? NO! You will tear up the inscription forms? YES!"[40]

The social security system was also the occasion for Dorgères's apprenticeship in direct action. He first drew national attention by mounting a mass demonstration on 18 June 1933 that blocked the sale of Valentin Salvaudon's farm at Bray (Somme). Salvaudon had refused on principle to make social security payments for his employees. The administration seized his farm and put his equipment up for auction to recover the amount he owed. Dorgères's obstruction of the sale brought him twenty-eight days in prison and notoriety as "the prisoner of Péronne." It also gave Dorgères an undying enmity for Radical Interior Minister Camille Chautemps, whom he blamed personally for his jail sentence, a sentiment that influenced his career several times later. (We look more closely at Dorgères' actions against the judicial sale of farms in Chapter 3).

Dorgères and his followers could be truculently aggressive. A rather tawdry example from the early days was the Cadoret affair. François Cadoret was a Radical deputy from Quimperlé (Finistère), the purest type of the species of parliamentarian whom Dorgères liked to threaten to throw into a manure pile. On 29 January 1933, Dorgères and some associates, returning flushed from a rally followed by a pause in a bar along the way, found themselves in Riec-sur-Belon (Finistère) before Deputy Cadoret's house. The deputy was not home. Nevertheless Dorgères and his friends tried to enter and had an altercation with Mme. Cadoret. Dorgères claimed he was slapped, and two windowpanes were broken. He attempted to pass the matter off in the PAO with bravado: now, he wrote, at least they listen to us.[41] But he had made a lasting negative impression on members of parliament. Edouard Daladier, head of Cadoret's party and prime minister, denounced in the Senate on 30 May 1933 "disorderly gatherings, threats, violations of the homes of representatives of the people" and vowed to "put a stop to that sort of thing."[42]

As the Great Depression escalated from mere hardship to catastrophe, and especially as wheat prices began to collapse in late 1932, Dorgères widened his horizons. He extended his attention beyond social security to the general economic, social, and political situation of peasants in France. This meant gradually freeing himself from the Ligue des Contribuables. Although he remained a frequent speaker at league events through 1933, he devoted more and more of his time to his own organization, no longer Comités de Défense contre les Assurances Sociales, but now, more broadly, Comités de Défense Paysanne.

By the turn of 1932–33, his central theme had become the collapse of wheat prices and the necessity to overthrow a Republic that did nothing to save its farmers from ruin. In meeting after meeting, Dorgères gradually established local CDPs across the Ille-et-Vilaine and, eventually, throughout much of northern and western France. This network of CDPs in many communes of western and northern France was to become by the middle 1930s Dorgères's principal organizational base.

When Dorgères opened an office in Paris for his newspaper chain in May 1935, he also created a summit organization for his CDPs: the Comité Central de Défense Paysanne. He was only its *secrétaire-général;* Jean Bohuon, a small farmer from the Ille-et-Vilaine, was president. Dorgères typically rewarded his ablest lieutenants with the presidency of his summit organizations, retaining effective control for himself from an apparently subordinate post such as secretary-general or delegate for propaganda. Soon after, in the fall of 1935, he set up a parallel organization, the Ligue des Paysans de France. In May 1936, he changed the name of his *comités* to Syndicats Agricoles de Défense Paysanne.

These incessant organizational adjustments at the top seem less a sign of vitality, however, than a tacit admission of their ephemeral nature. The real strength of Dorgères's movement lay with those local branches lucky enough to have a dynamic leader. At that level, Dorgères' organizations could well be powerful when there was a burst of passion to fuel them, at least until the passion passed. Even at their most vigorous, however, they lacked the glue of daily economic activity that gave the *syndicats agricoles* (SAs) their impressive continuity and durability.

Nevertheless, Dorgères's movement could claim to represent a considerable force in rural France, at least in the west and north, in 1935. He never offered very precise membership figures, which in any case must have been volatile. At the beginning of 1935, the CDPs may have had about 35,000 members.[43] In the fall of 1935, a time of high excitement following Dorgères's trial and conviction for impeding tax collection, he claimed his membership had quadrupled.[44] Dorgères's strength lay not with a solid organization with stable membership, however, but with his ability to mobilize huge rural audiences around particular grievances. Some of his crowds in the most dynamic years, such as the rally held in Rouen on 25 August 1935 to protest Dorgères' sentence for promoting the refusal of income tax payments, must have approached 20,000 people.[45] That power to stir and motivate the rural masses was something the traditional leaders of rural France could no longer ignore.

Dorgères against the Republic

As the decline of farm prices became an avalanche and as Dorgères became aware of his way with a crowd, he began to nurture thoughts of using the peasants' mass discontent for some kind of seizure of power. If only the *classe paysanne* could pull together its inchoate forces, Dorgères told his mesmerized crowds, it would be powerful enough to take the place it deserved in the economy, society, and government of France. Given sufficient peasant pressure, the Third Republic—run (as Dorgères saw it) by lawyers, businessmen, and schoolteachers; forced by its working class to provide cheap bread at the expense of those who grew the wheat; and too enfeebled by parliamentary palaver to resist Anglo-American free trade and German expansionism—would have to give way. In its place would appear a new regime, and the peasants would have to be ready to ensure that it was an authoritarian, corporatist, prolific, paternalist, and autarkic one, whose backbone would be the family farm.

We know his private thinking quite well in this period from some letters, dated between November 1932 and March 1934, seized by the police when the ministers of finance and the interior began to consider Dorgères a danger to the state.[46] Among others, Dorgères wrote to Maurice Foissey and Georges Lambert, farmers in the Somme who had been with him at Salvaudon's sale, that he wanted to "organize violent demonstrations all over." He believed that the peasants' movement and the taxpayers' movement could together create a movement—ready to "step outside legality"—strong enough to demand "full powers to change the bases of the constitution of our country" and found a new regime based on the craft and the family.[47]

Dorgères (unlike his more sophisticated associate, Jacques Le Roy Ladurie) was not in touch with the organizers of the great antiparliamentary demonstration of 6 February 1934. That exclusion only whetted his appetite for some kind of peasant action, however. On 14 March, he wrote another associate that it was time "we decided to take power quickly." If the *contribuables,* the war veterans, and the peasants agreed on a common political program based on "the family, the craft, and the region," Dorgères asserted, "in very little time we could manage to combine our efforts and take power."[48]

Although his young action squad, the Chemises Vertes, would later sing, "With bare arms and pure hands, we will go clean up Paris,"[49] Dorgères does not seem to have ever seriously planned a physical assault on the French state. In any event, the lesson of 6 February was that the Republic could not be overthrown frontally. By 1935, at least in public (we don't know what he was saying or writing to friends by then), Dorgères admitted that the Republic could be transformed neither electorally nor by force. But "the illegal seizure of power seems to me possible"[50] if the peasants make life so miserable for Republican governments that they abandon power voluntarily. "No need to spill blood for that. It is pacifically, by the force of their numbers and their convictions, that the peasants must succeed in taking power."[51] By a strategy that was avowedly illegal yet cautious, Dorgères managed to lay claim to the activist terrain without offending the fundamental orderliness of French peasant society in the west and north.

It is worth noting that Dorgères refused to reject the label of fascist in the spring of 1934.[52] More reserved by the end of 1935, he took his lasting position on the matter: "I am neither fascist nor anti-fascist; I am for order, justice, property."[53] Since fascism has become corrupted as an epithet both vague and actionable, I propose to leave to Chapter 5 a careful examination of Dorgères's relationship to it, where I have the space and time to consider carefully how that highly charged term is best understood.

Committed publicly to a policy of selective illegality designed to unseat the Republic, Dorgères had to select tactics that would undermine the state without causing bloodshed. He had been advocating a tax strike since the end of 1932. In 1934, determined not to be left behind while the urban-based *ligues* were profiting from the anti-Republican momentum of the February riots, Dorgères enlarged his arsenal. In November– December 1934 he alluded often to a secret "action plan," to be revealed in due course, by which the peasantry, with its immense power, "will rise up and chase out the politicians and take power."[54] The "action plan" turned out to be the mass withdrawal of peasants' savings from public and private savings banks, a step he was convinced would bring down the state. (He later asserted that it was the young Inspecteur des Finances Henri Dumoulin de Labarthète—in 1940–42 Marshal Pétain's *chef de cabinet* at Vichy—who drew his attention in 1934 to the French state's vulnerability to a mass withdrawal of savings.[55])

Dorgères tried to carry out his fiscal assault on the state in 1935. At a mass rally in the Cirque de Rouen on 22 February, he revealed his "secret plan": refusal of taxes or payment in kind and withdrawal of savings from state savings institutions.[56] Accounts differ about exactly what, in the heat of the moment, Dorgères urged his hearers to do. A hostile newspaper reported the words "we should take our guns and let them have it" *(tirer dans le tas)*.[57] That report provoked Henri Guernut, deputy of the Aisne and president of the League of the Rights of Man (Ligue des Droits de l'Homme), to interpellate the government on its failure to repress the peasants' violence. The government then prosecuted Dorgères under a 28 February 1933 statute against advocating the nonpayment of taxes. In July 1935, the Tribunal Correctionnel de Rouen found him, along with several of his associates (two of whom, the rural mayors Pierre Suplice and Jean Chalony, we encounter more closely in Chapter 3), guilty of "collective refusal to pay taxes."[58]

Legal troubles always spurred Dorgères on. Associated by this time with the Parti Agraire, the Union Nationale des Syndicats Agricoles, and other agrarian organizations in a Peasant Front, Dorgères spent the summer and early fall of 1935 building up suspense around a strike of all peasants' purchases and taxes (he now prudently called it a "moratorium"), which he threatened to set off in October. (We look more closely in Chapter 4 at the Peasant Front and the involvement of French rural notables in Dorgères's tax strike.)

Dorgères also reacted to prosecution by taking his first dip into electoral politics. In May 1935, he ran in a by-election at Blois for the seat in the Chamber of Deputies vacated by the election to the Senate of his old enemy, the Radical Deputy Camille Chautemps. Profiting from the disarray of the local notable agricultural leaders because of the Depression, and from the division of the Left between cautious reformers and socialists, Dorgères came in first on the first round. For the second round, however, the Left reunited (as was indeed always foreseeable) to keep him from winning Chautemps's former seat. It is curious that Dorgères should have run at all, after spending years denouncing all parliamentary politics as a sink of iniquity. Did he run for Chautemps's seat in order to spite his old enemy? To strengthen his political position? Or simply to gain parliamentary immunity from the prosecution then in progress for advocating a tax strike?[59] We do not know. In any event, even though he was never to serve in the Third Republic's Chamber of Deputies,[60] Dorgères had become a national figure.

Militant political organizations were expected in the 1930s to have a youth organization and some kind of uniform. Dorgères took this step in the summer of 1935 with the establishment of the Peasant Youth (Jeunesses Paysannes), popularly known as the Greenshirts (Chemises Vertes). For some time, he had noted that his meetings needed "protection squads" for the intimidation of the inescapable hecklers. He also liked to promise his audiences that he had "mobile teams" ready to come to their aid if their farms were seized and sold for taxes or social security arrears.[61] Given his position by the summer of 1935 as the central figure of rightwing rural agitation in France, Dorgères must have been embarrassed to have to call on other movements to guard his meetings. On 25 July 1935, it was the action squads of the Croix de Feu, the *dispos,* who guarded an important meeting at Bény-Bocage (Calvados), during which Jacques Le Roy Ladurie and other rural notables rallied rural opinion against the state's prosecution of Dorgères.[62]

The Greenshirt idea seems to have crystallized on 10 June 1935, when Dorgères made his one visit to Alsace to speak at a meeting organized at Ingersheim, in the outskirts of Colmar (Haut-Rhin), by Joseph Bilger's Bauernbund. This radical Right peasants' movement, with some 6000 members—middling producers of milk and wine in the Haut-Rhin[63]—already had a shock troop dressed in green shirts to guard its meetings. Dorgères always admitted that he got the green shirt idea from Bilger, even after rivalry cooled their relationship.[64]

Already a CDP delegation had marched with green neckties at the Joan of Arc Festival in Rouen in May 1935.[65] On 25 August 1935, Dorgères fielded his own guards with green brassards at a giant meeting in Revel, near Toulouse.[66] Four days later, as he harangued a huge crowd in Rouen on the day of his sentencing, he, Bilger, and Félix Dessoliers (one of his most militant propagandists), stood together on the platform in green shirts.[67] Dorgères was in a green shirt again at Beaupréau (Maine-et-Loire) in September.[68] Green-shirted youths policed meetings for the first time at Rosporden (Finistère) and Formerie (Oise) in the first week of October 1935, and Dorgères announced that henceforth members of the Jeunesses Paysannes must wear their green shirts to all official functions.[69]

The Greenshirts grew rapidly. Their first annual conference on 11 December 1935 at Bannalec (Finistère) assembled 8,000–10,000 participants, who heard the movement's most famous notable supporters such as Jacques Le Roy Ladurie.[70] Modeste Legouez, only twenty-six years old, who farmed twenty-five leased hectares in the Eure, was the Jeunesses Paysannes' first president; he was to gain notoriety the following year by using anti-Semitic themes to come within 700 seats of beating Pierre Mendès France at Louviers (Eure) in the parliamentary elections of May 1936.[71]

The Greenshirts were meant to do more than merely guard meetings. The movement tried to give farm boys pride in their *métier;* it was also intended that they would do battle with the Left in a strike of farm labor or even with the police in an action against the sale of farms for arrears in taxes or social security payments. The movement stirred their spirits with tales of heroic deeds carried out by their fellows, such as the action of the Dessoliers brothers and the Comité de Défense Paysanne of Oran in throwing sacks of imported Canadian wheat into the harbor at Mostaganem in October 1935.[72] The Greenshirts permitted Dorgères to claim parity with other militant movements in 1930s' Europe, with their youth squads, uniforms, badges, mottoes,[73] anthems, and salutes. Dorgères had long ceased to refer to the mobilization of peasant forces for taking power, but he familiarized the rural youths of northern and western France with this more intense, new style of belonging, typical of mass movements in the era of fascism.[74]

In 1935 Dorgères reached what was probably his highest point of influence. His relationships were closest then, through the Peasant Front and its Comité d'Action Paysanne, with the notables who ran the agricultural organizations of France.[75] He also came nearest in 1935 to commanding some firm power base, either as a deputy or as the head of an important nationwide farmers' protest movement. It was also the moment when the French state most feared him, as we shall see.

Dorgères was now getting national media attention. He was the subject of a cover article in the illustrated weekly *Vu* on 20 March 1935, he wrote regularly in the Paris dailies *Le Matin* and *Le Jour*,[76] and he was the subject of several favorable works.[77] *L'Illustration,* France's most widely read glossy pictorial weekly, devoted several pages to Dorgères's giant rally at Revel (Haute-Garonne) on 18 August 1935.[78] On 5 April 1935 he was invited to speak in the Théâtre des Ambassadeurs lecture series—a prestigious platform. He admitted to nervousness: "I affront two perils," he told his audience of 500, the examining magistrate (the equivalent of the grand jury in the Anglo-American legal system) at Rouen—who was deciding whether the government's case against him for advocating a tax strike should go to trial—"and this audience." As he mounted the stage to speak on "The Peasant Will Save France," his partisans in the room set up a chant against Chautemps: "Down with Camille!"[79] In those spring and summer months of 1935, Dorgères was as close as he ever came to being a major figure in French national politics.

For the Ambassadeurs's speech, as well as for the Blois by-election, Dorgères needed to show that he could address the fears and demands of audiences other than those of peasants. On that occasion he muted his style and broadened his content: he told his Paris audience (uncharacteristically) that there was no urban-rural conflict.[80] But the transition to national, cross-class "catchall" politics was not one that he made comfortably. Afterward he seemed more at ease in returning to the more limited role of peasant militant, free to fan antiurban and anticommerce prejudices. This failure to transcend an exclusively peasant interest is what distinguished Dorgères most clearly from the successful fascist leaders of his period.

The electoral victory of the Popular Front in May 1936 and the strike wave that followed it in June and July offered Dorgères a significant new opportunity. The strikes of farm workers in the summer of 1936 and again in the summer of 1937 in the regions of extensive agriculture around Paris and in the northern plains were the most widespread rural labor conflict ever known in France, and they created anxiety among farmers far beyond the centers of strike activity. Dorgères discovered a new identity as the Popular Front took power: France's best defense against rural communism. He organized volunteers against farm workers' strikes during both summers, 1936 and 1937. He boasted of creating a Green Belt *(ceinture verte),* a barrier of suburban farmers and market gardeners to contain the Red Belt of the Communist industrial suburbs around Paris. As we see in Chapter 3, Dorgères never really became the indispensable barrier to communism that he claimed to be. Although he organized his Greenshirts to fight strikes on farms and in factories that treated farm products, they had very little scope in which to play their role. The French state and the big landlords restored farmers' control over their employees without much more than symbolic help from Dorgères.

Dorgères's other response to the Popular Front was to increase his movement's efforts to recruit agricultural workers. His movement had always claimed that it spoke for a unified and harmonious peasant interest, ranging from hired hands to great landlords. Now it had to prove that the *comités de défense paysanne,* and not the Popular Front, spoke for the hired hands. Changing their name from comités to syndicats agricoles de défense paysanne (SADP) on 28 May 1936, he urged the local branches to set up special workers' sections,[81] and he advocated mixed arbitration commissions to resolve labor conflicts. So did most other conservative agrarian organizations during the Popular Front's rise, with limited results.

Dorgères's following among farm workers cannot be known with certainty, but it was probably limited to a few family retainers. Dorgères liked to claim that most of the Chemises Vertes were farm workers,[82] which might be technically true if one remembers that most of them (all of them in the case examined in detail in Chapter 3) were sons of owners or renters who were working on their fathers' farms. Only a very few agricultural workers appeared as officers of SADPs or on the lists of small contributors, a franc or two, published in almost every issue of the PAO.[83]

Dorgères opened one more frontier in the fall of 1936 when he himself became the organizer of strikes, this time strikes of agricultural producers. The market gardeners of the suburbs of Paris, upset by declining prices and labor problems, attempted three times to prevent the arrival of fresh fruit and vegetables at Paris's great wholesale market, Les Halles: 28–29 September, 19–20 October, and 16–18 December 1936, the last time with some support from provincial market gardeners. Although Dorgères was not solely responsible for these strikes, he attempted to assume their leadership, and he was arrested twice in the midst of demonstrators who were attempting to close down the market.[84]

In retrospect, we know that by the mid-1930s Dorgères' movement had gone about as far as it would go and that some of its vital energy ebbed in 1936 with the improvement of agricultural prices. But the French state and the French agrarian notables did not know that. Dorgères loomed large in the French press and in political circles in 1935–36 as a threat—or as a promise.

three
. . .

FIVE SCENARIOS OF
PEASANT ACTION

IF WE TRY TO understand Dorgères's movement by laying out a table of organization and listing a program, point by point, we will miss the mark. Institutions and ideology, those staples of most studies of contemporary political life, are not the best keys to a movement whose structures were loose and whose appeals were not primarily to the intellect. Dorgérism was most itself in the heat of the moment and in the distinctiveness of each village that was swept up in it for a season.

Thus in this chapter we observe Dorgérism in action. The drama and emotion of these encounters bring us closer to understanding how it functioned at the village level. These narratives have several common features. In each the peasants have material grievances that, they are convinced, neither the Third Republic's democratic politics, with its new urban majority,[1] nor the traditional rural leaders can resolve. Dorgères's kind of direct collective action also offers a sort of emotional satisfaction that the Republic and the traditional agricultural organizations deny. In each confrontation, hitherto obscure small farmers emerge into leadership roles. As the protestors' peers, supplanting their customary paternalist notable leaders, they are capable of arousing a powerful village solidarity against an outside world deemed uncomprehending and hostile and of shaking the entrenched rural oligarchies of the late Third Republic.

Each confrontation also contains a rich repertory of symbolic actions: peasants try to dramatize their plight and demonstrate control over their own destinies; rival rural leaders and the state's agents try to display their prestige, authority, and legitimacy. Behind it all stands a vague but powerful vision of an agrarian utopia in which independent small farmers are sufficiently numerous and united to overcome their weakness in the marketplace and their inferiority in the social hierarchy. Taken together these stories help show how Dorgères managed to recruit—at least for a time—a sizable fraction of some peasant communities of northern and western France. They also reveal something of the texture of French rural life in its final generation with a numerous peasantry as it awakened to its potential importance in the national life, its distinctiveness from urban civilization, its shrinking share of the benefits of French citizenship, and its impending disappearance.

Giving the Peasants a Voice: The Market-day Rally

The market-day rally was Dorgères's most important propaganda medium. He reached many more people in this way—at least for an hour or two—than by his string of newspapers, and he roused them to peaks of excitement far beyond anything the printed page could stimulate. Dorgérism was first and foremost a visceral phenomenon. Dorgères initially seized on most of his followers by the immediate experience of his oratory in an excited crowd.

The traditional weekly market day offered Dorgères a ready-made and responsive audience. On that day, the farm families of an extended area came together to buy and sell, see the *notaire* on business, gossip, eat and drink, and look for a little excitement.[2] In addition to the weekly market day, annual fairs and saints' days drew even greater crowds from an entire region in a mood of receptive expectancy. Although Dorgères was capable of assembling up to 20,000 people on ordinary days for moments of special drama (such as in Rouen on 25 August 1935, when he was awaiting his sentence for advocating a tax strike), he and his most compelling orators—Bohuon, Suplice, Coirre—timed most of their propaganda meetings to coincide with the weekly market. Lesser speakers had a more modest opportunity after mass on Sundays in pious towns, where most of the women went to church while the men waited in the café.

Dorgères came on the scene at what was probably the apogee of the middle-sized market town in France. Rural fairs and markets had long been a base of peasant sociability, but they had become concentrated geographically in the early twentieth century.[3] Improved transportation had weakened the village markets and transferred much of the excitement to the regional centers, the chief towns of a canton or an arrondissement. The decade of the 1930s was a unique moment in the evolution of market day: it came after the bus and a few cars had concentrated rural business in the larger towns but before the universal recreational automobile, the dominance of television, and the last spurt of rural exodus had thinned rural sociability.[4] Thousands of people could assemble once a week in the chief town of a district, and they wanted to. Once there, they intended to do more than just transact their business and go back home. Market day was a full day's outing. It was the only occasion for many isolated families to enjoy amusement, excitement, and a crowd. It was the main setting for rural recreation. Dorgères's market-day rallies offered entertainment and spectacle along with the message he wanted to transmit.

Market day was a setting for social and political conflict, as well as the more benign kinds of sociability. On even the most ordinary market day, sharp conflicts arose between urban buyers and rural sellers, frequently to the latter's disadvantage. Whereas the many unorganized small sellers had perishable products on their hands, the buyer, in contrast, was often a single, well-financed agent for large firms, who could wait. Market day often rubbed peasants' noses in their economic and social inferiority.

On certain special days, the difference between a good year and a bad one was played out in one charged moment in the market square. Then the social tension could come close to snapping. In the Beauce and Touraine/Anjou one such day was the *louée*, on the holiday of Saint-Jean (24 June), when labor contracts were negotiated for the coming year. Conflicts between widely dispersed employers and employees reached their most concentrated point. Communist organizers learned to "work" the *louée* in the 1930s. In June 1936 *louées* in the main Beauce towns—Chartres, Auneau, and Chateaudun—were marked by demonstrations, fights, and demands for better working conditions. The employers responded by boycotting the hiring process.[5] In June 1937, the Confédération Générale du Travail (CGT) planned to organize meetings during the *louée* at Chartres, but angry farmers warned that they would do what their colleagues had done (they heard) at Sully-sur-Loir and chase them out of the market square with pitchforks.[6]

Another tense moment in many parts of France was the Saint-Michel, 29 September, when land leases *(fermages)* traditionally expired and had to be renegotiated. The Depression subjected land leasing to almost unbearable stress. Leasers faced bankruptcy and expulsion because the crash of their sale prices left them unable to pay rents agreed to in prosperous times. Proprietors had been happy enough when they were permitted to revise rents upward with inflation in 1927, but they were reluctant to revise them downward with depression in the 1930s. The government took emergency measures to cut land rents twice (April 1933 and July 1935) to stave off waves of bankruptcies,[7] but the Third Republic was not able to settle longer-term issues such as the tenant's rights of renewal and whether a departing tenant should be indemnified for improvements to the farm during his tenancy *(droits du fermier sortant)*. Vichy began to regulate these matters, and tenants received broad statutory rights at Liberation.[8] But in the 1930s *fermage* problems set rural tenants and owners at each other's throats.

All these conflicts made market days and fairs a rural demagogue's best regular opportunity to mobilize the usually dispersed members of the crowd for some political purpose. If one wanted to persuade a large number of people to vote for a resolution *(ordre du jour)* that might be delivered to the subprefect or prefect at the head of an imposing procession (and perhaps even passed on to the government in Paris), that was the time to do it. However, in a mood of exacerbated tension and excited emotions, often heightened by the press of a crowd and by drink, violence was possible.

Public speeches and debates before live crowds were still important in the 1930s. The drama of verbal confrontation made them a major rural amusement, as well as a medium of information. The market-day public was as quick as Neapolitans at the opera to jeer a poor speaker or to walk out on him. They were equally quick to savor and cheer a clever or passionate one. The public storyteller, such as one still sees in the market of, say, Marrakech, had long gone from literate France, but public political debate was still flourishing.

These debates followed a well-established ritual. If a meeting was open to the public, it must have a bureau: a president and one or two *assesseurs,* local worthies who sat on the platform and took responsibility for the maintenance of public order and decorum. The bureau was elected by the crowd. The bureau, handpicked by the meeting's organizer, was usually ratified as a matter of routine, but the organizer of a public meeting could lose control of it at this point in the proceedings. In hostile territory, his enemies might plan in advance to have an unsympathetic bureau elected. This trick was turned on Dorgères once or twice, and he occasionally worked it on the Left in conservative western country towns, where the crowd was on his side. For example, a group of Dorgérist activists headed by Pierre Suplice took over a meeting that Renaud Jean was rash enough to organize on 26 July 1936 at Yvetôt (Seine-Maritime), a railroad center at the edge of the agrarian Pays de Caux, and gave Jean a severe beating.[9]

The rules required a public meeting to allow time for a "contradiction." In Dorgères's meetings, the "contradiction" was usually delivered by the local schoolteacher (as often as not, in the west of France, the only Socialist or Communist in town) or perhaps by a local CGT official, if there was a railroad center or a factory nearby. In Dorgères's own newspaper accounts of his speeches, he (or the orators that he trained and encouraged) always triumphed over these contradictors, ensuring their rapid and ignominious defeat. The contradictor was a symbolic presence and not merely the spokesman for a different point of view. He was the physical embodiment of the enemy, the representative of the dominant cultural and economic power of the urban consumer, politician, or intellectual, whose humiliation a peasant audience found to be a satisfying reversal. Such reversals gave a carnival tone to a successful market-day rally. Occasionally the contradictor was roughed up a bit in the process, and on rarer occasions there was a real brawl. Normally, however, the violence of a Dorgérist meeting was more verbal and ritual than physical.

Dorgères gave careful attention to the aesthetic setting of his rallies. They often took place in a field, sometimes because a mayor had denied permission to use the municipal meeting hall or covered market. Whether outdoors or in, the stage was set to demonstrate pride in the agricultural profession, readiness to act, and control of the situation. Dorgères often spoke from a farm cart drawn up to serve as a speaker's platform. It was decorated with wheat sheaves or some other symbol of agrarian bounty. Rows of pitchforks were frequently part of the decor, the symbol of the violence Dorgères's peasants threatened to use, if necessary, to get their way. The presence of young men in green brassards or (by the fall of 1935) green shirts, served to demonstrate the peasants' supremacy over their space. Impressions of menace, virile vigor, and control were very important to a successful Dorgérist meeting.

Now we come to the speakers themselves. A curious but revealing Dorgérist institution was the orators' school.[10] Dorgères took particular pains to find and cultivate peasant orators—young men of authentic farm backgrounds with a gift for salty phrases and enough courage to stand up to a hostile crowd—and teach them to enjoy the rough and tumble of a market-day rally. He brought them to Paris for a few weeks, but mostly he turned them loose in minor meetings and encouraged them by praising their progress in his newspaper.[11]

Thus, partly by trial and error and partly by training, Dorgères discovered and promoted some champion peasant orators. He recruited two of his best from the *cultivateurs-cultivants* of the Abbé Mancel in Brittany: Jean Bohuon, who farmed eighteen hectares in the Ille-et-Vilaine and whom Dorgères praised for "passionate intensity and high spirits,"[12] and François Coirre, an old colonial army sergeant who also cultivated a small farm in the Ille-et-Vilaine. Others were rural mayors who had won their spurs in village politics, like Abel Néel, "a colossus"[13] with tax troubles, mayor of Le Fournet (Calvados) and veteran of many protest meetings on behalf of the *bouilleurs de cru* of the Pays d'Auge. And there was Pierre Suplice, a young farmer well connected with the landowners of the Pays de Caux and mayor of Bourg-Dun (Seine-Maritime) since the age of

thirty. He had come to the prefect's notice when he organized rural protests against the appointment of the Communist schoolteacher Darius Le
Corre in October 1934 and brought the work of the local agricultural
statistics committee (Commission Cantonale de la Statistique Agricole) to
a halt to protest the wheat price collapse of 1933.[14] A few, like Robert
Fiche, were barely out of school. Dorgères's speakers were genuine farmers (unlike himself), men with whom peasant audiences could identify.

A gifted peasant orator could speak a long time if he was good (I say
"he" because public oratory remained an exclusively masculine role in
rural France at this time). At one rally in 1937 Bohuon spoke for two
hours, at another for an hour and a half. The speaker had to maintain a
high pitch of excitement during every minute of this time, for he faced a
volatile audience. The public would desert him the instant he bored them.
The speaker needed to use pithy language and tread the edge of vulgarity.
He needed to display conviction and energy and make sense of the apparently senseless situation in which a peasant might work hard and still fail.
Above all, he must help the peasants express the anger and resentment
they felt but could barely articulate, hold out some hope that something
could be done, and cover their enemies with gratifying ridicule.

The Dorgériste orator usually touched on a wide variety of themes—
economic, political, and moral. The economic crisis always had a place.
The collapse of farm prices was often blamed on some particular person,
such as the deputies who had approved commercial treaties or the big
grain importer Louis Louis-Dreyfus (le roi deux-Louis). There was almost
always some reference to the corruption and inefficacy of politicians.
Dorgères's orators were moralists, quick to contrast the peasants' austere
virtues with the decadent amusements of their rich urban enemies.[15] The
peasants were reminded that they were the victims of the Republic and
of the middle and working classes, and then they were raised from despair
by some story of the heroic actions of some peasant militant. Jews were
often singled out as enemies, more often in an individual capacity as
merchants or politicians than as the agents of some vast racial conspiracy.

Humor was an essential weapon. The Dorgériste orators found pithy
phrases, often drawn from the barnyard, to personify their enemies and
make them laughable. One friendly journalist wrote of Dorgères's style:
"Ah! Dame, you can't expect academic perfection in his harangues, but
they flow thick and fast and he gets off some good ones."[16] Making fun
of politicians, merchants, and intellectals was Dorgères's way of helping
the peasants refuse to be cowed by these people's power over broad
reaches of public space: schools, electoral politics, the urban life-style, and
most of the written word.

To close the meeting, the crowd usually voted a resolution, or *ordre du jour*. The text had, of course, been prepared in advance by the meeting's organizers. This was a moment to confirm the speaker's mastery of his crowd, not to open spontaneous debate. Once voted by acclamation, this text was delivered formally to the authorities, which often meant marching in procession through the enemy's turf in town. Sometimes the assembled crowd went en masse to the prefecture or subprefecture, carrying the petition. Sometimes they went to the war memorial, to show that the peasants had not forgotten that they had borne the brunt of World War I. They sometimes deposited wheat sheaves there, as their own particular sacred symbol, instead of the urban citizen's wreath.

While the market-day rallies generated excitement and temporary mobilization, Dorgères's newspapers provided a more permanent connecting tissue. Each issue brought dramatized accounts of peasant orators' success to the larger peasant world. They read a bit like the sports pages today, except that the contests of will or physical force always ended in the peasants' favor. Indeed, Dorgères was not unhappy if the debate or the ensuing procession produced a fistfight: it brought him publicity, and sometimes new allies, and created the impression that the peasants were capable of mastering their own domain and overcoming their weakness and division.[17]

The rituals surrounding the market-day rally concerned prowess and turf. The speaker and his audience communed less over a program than over an incantation of peasants' virtue and victimhood and control over their own realm. Once united, the peasants could demonstrate their superiority over the Left, its captive state, and its missionaries in the schoolroom. The debate was a form of combat—a "verbal joust." As in a boxing match, the audience received pleasure in watching one speaker skillfully outdo another, especially if the victorious speaker was "one of their own" and the loser was a condescending schoolteacher or official. It gave them vicarious pride and prestige. At the heart of the matter were the peasants' self-respect, sense of moral worth, and control over their own fates. The initial issue of *La Voix du paysan,* the paper Dorgères founded with Joseph Cadic in 1933, proclaimed across its front page: "We are nothing, we want to be someone!"[18] Echoing the Abbé Sieyès, speaking for the Third Estate in 1789, and emulating Marx, speaking for the working class, Dorgères wanted to free the peasants from their chains of self-doubt, division, and ignorance and make the "peasant class" conscious of its merit and power and historic mission.

The transformation of the word "peasant" in the early twentieth century from a term of ridicule to a proud title was a major part of Dorgères's program, although that transformation was not his work alone. As late as World War I, "peasant" had had a pejorative meaning. Traditionally, the *paysan* was the brutish and exploited creature in the famous sketch by La Bruyère, known to every French schoolchild.[19] Nineteenth-century realist novelists gave the term an additional connotation of individualistic greed. Balzac's peasants cut up estates into mean parcels; Zola's grasping peasants pushed aside their aged parents and fought for control of the family acres. The first signs of change were also literary. Agrarian novelists of the turn of the century, such as René Bazin,[20] revived the romanticists' belief in the simplicity and nobility of peasant life, flavoring it with the new fin de siècle dread of national decadence.

The term *paysan* entered the French political lexicon in a favorable sense at the end of World War I. The term's positive usage in public affairs was fortified by the discovery of peasants' military virtues—fertility and stoicism—in a war in which farm boys made up a disproportionate number of front-line soldiers. In any event, it was in 1918 that a number of rural deputies set up a Groupe de Défense Paysanne in the Chamber of Deputies—one of the first, if not the first, positive use of the term *paysan* in French politics.

As soon as small farmers began to call themselves peasants with pride, the time had come for both Left and Right to try to appropriate the term for their own uses. The trade union movement before 1914 focused its rural efforts on day-laborers, whom they considered twin brothers of urban workers—rural workers *(travailleurs de la terre)*. The Left did not entirely neglect the peasantry before 1914, however. The Parti Ouvrier Français defended small peasants against their creditors and landlords as early as 1892, and the great French Socialist leader Jean Jaurès denounced the exploitation of peasants by landlords, creditors, monopolists, and employers in a celebrated three-day address in the Chamber of Deputies in June–July 1897. In his usage, however, peasants were simply rural citizens, deserving the same protection as other citizens from the bosses, not members of a special rural culture that deserved preservation. When the Communist party began in 1929 to try to recruit small landowners and renters, as well as rural wage laborers, and to expand its rural base beyond the customary *travailleurs de la terre,* it coined the term "peasant-workers" *(paysans-travailleurs)*. The Confédération Générale des Paysans-Travailleurs (CGPT) of that year was formed to recruit small farmers who personally worked a small plot they owned or rented. The Left used "peasant" as an economic criterion—it set small against large—with an added echo of militancy borrowed from the revolutionary peasant soviets of 1917.

Conservatives also used the term "peasant" for partisan purposes, but in a very different sense. They used it to affirm the unity of rural society against Communist and Socialist efforts to divide rural laborers and small tenants from big landowers. For conservatives, the term stood not for an economic category but for an organic society, a bulwark of social harmony, as in their favorite image of the hired hand and the landowner sharing the harvest table. Conservatives, too, relished the word's militant tone, as in the Masse de Combat des Paysans, an aggressive peasant movement in the Somme in the late 1920s.[21] By the 1930s, even large farmers, who had formerly preferred to be called "farmer" (*cultivateur* or the even more distinguished *agriculteur*) began to use the term *paysan* positively to identify a way of life that they shared with all cultivators of the soil and that they wanted to preserve and to lead. In 1937, the Norman gentleman-farmer and secretary-general of the UNSA, Jacques Le Roy Ladurie, changed the name of the UNSA's journal to *Syndicats paysans*.

This process had begun earlier in Germany: *Bauern* had become a positive term before World War I, used by both Right and Left in ways parallel to the French agrarians' new usage of *paysan* in the 1920s and 1930s. In the English-speaking world, however, the equivalant term—"peasant"— never acquired a positive connotation and so never became a useful political label. In the United States, where the agricultural interest was a powerful one, the functional term "farmer" was normal, whereas the term "peasant," with its broader social connotation of a traditional way of life, was used only pejoratively, and rather rarely at that.

Dorgères liked to claim credit for this positive reworking of the word "peasant." He portrayed his movement as the force that had transformed the peasants from pariahs into the foundation stone of a healthily "balanced" society. Before, Dorgères said, paysans had been the subjects of "hatred" and "contempt," "beggars" whom the rest of the population had to "subsidize."[22] The *paysan* had been despised and silent; Dorgères made him a *classe paysanne*, with as much claim to attention as the working class, and gave him pride and a voice.

In fact, this profound shift of values had begun before Dorgères became active and was the work of many organizations and individuals. Peasants' self-esteem was also a central theme of the fast-growing Young Christian Farmers (Jeunesse Agricole Chrétienne, JAC) in the 1930s.[23] Jacques Le Roy Ladurie, who discovered the cause of "peasant emancipation" after he began to cultivate his family's estate in the Calvados in the middle 1920s, decided to promote the local *syndicat agricole* by personifying peasant symbols, in the way that Michelin marketed tires by their famous trademark, the rotund rubber personage known as Bibendum.[24] As secretary of the Syndicat Agricole du Calvados, he changed the title of its monthly newsletter from the colorless *Bulletin* to *Mait' Jacques,* personified by a crusty Norman farmer who proclaimed in *patois* on the masthead of each issue, "I have my rights and I stand up for them" (J'ai mon droit et mé my tiens).

Le Roy Ladurie maintained that he had not named the *syndicat*'s newspaper after himself, still less after the hypothetical leader of the medieval *jacquerie*, but after one of his family's tenant farmers. Even so, his personal imprint was strong in the newspaper. It was his energy and passion and gift for words that built *Mait' Jacques* into a weekly farmer's newspaper with a wide readership in Normandy and with close links to Dorgérism from 1933 to 1937. Le Roy Ladurie also called the *syndicat*'s offices in Caen "the peasant's house" *(la maison du paysan),* and he affixed the *Mait' Jacques* logo to all of the fertilizer and other farm necessities bought in bulk for members and to the agricultural products sold on the members' behalf. Some older notable landlords ridiculed this adoption of a once-despised term, but Le Roy Ladurie had the backing of his *syndicat*'s president, the revered comte Pierre d'Oilliamson. By the middle 1930s, it had become almost chic for a large farmer with a keen sense of rural identity and interests to call himself a *paysan.*

Dorgères didn't rescue the word "peasant" all alone, but in a characteristic propaganda victory he came to personify that transformation. Fifty years later, an old Dorgérist militant, veteran of many a market-day rally and dust-up, retained one main memory of those days. Before Dorgères, the peasants had been an "interior colony."[25] With Dorgères, the peasants had found their voice.

Pushing Back the State: The Battle of
Bray-Sur-Somme, 18 June 1933

Conflicts between peasants and the state reached their flash point when some official violated a peasant's home. Farmers resented the visit of the social security inspector.[26] The resentment darkened to rage in the *bouilleurs de cru* country, when the tax man came to check on an illicit distillery, sometimes when only a wife was at home. The most fateful form of state invasion of domicile was the arrival of the judicial clerk *(huissier),* who came, perhaps accompanied by a gendarme, to seize an indebted farmer's equipment and furniture and put them up for auction *(vente sur saisie).* Sales for debt, arrears in rent or tenant's shares, back taxes, or social security payments during the Great Depression could whip a whole commune into a fever of agitation. Finding some way to block a judicial sale was a sure way to rural celebrity. Obstructing it came to be the tactical centerpiece of both the Dorgérists and the Communist party in the French countryside during the Great Depression.[27]

Dorgères's *comités de Défense Paysanne* (CDPs) and Renaud Jean's Confédération Générale des Paysans Travailleurs (CGPT) both staged mass actions against judicial sales. Usually such manifestations had only one political color, green or red, according to the area's leanings. Occasionally, however, Communists and Dorgérists competed for credit for the same action against a judicial sale.[28] It can be difficult, when one reads some rural weekly newspaper's account of a mass obstruction of a *vente sur saisie,* to know whether its organizers came from the Left or the Right. In general, however, Dorgères specialized in protests against state seizures of property. Cases in which the delinquent owed money to his landlord were tricky for him, for he feared accusations of supporting "lazy tenants" against their landlords. He was willing, he said, to defend a hard-working *fermier* who needed a chance to recover.[29] Renaud Jean, in contrast, left social security cases alone. He preferred to block sales for debts owed to landlords by sharecroppers or renters. There was also some geographical specialization. Jean worked mostly in the southwest, plus a few islands of *paysan-travailleur* strength elsewhere, such as the western half of the Côtes-du-Nord. Dorgères was most active in conservative regions of northern and western France.

Protests against judicial sales were an elemental expression of rural anger and could take place spontaneously. Dorgères did not invent them. The Left actually preceded him, Renaud Jean beginning in August 1932.[30] Jean may even have actually carried out more actions of this type than Dorgères, but Dorgères probably gained more national attention with his skillful use of this tactic. Indeed, he gained his first nationwide notoriety by organizing an action of this type: a mass demonstration to obstruct the judicial sale of Valentin Salvaudon's farm equipment at Bray-sur-Somme on 18 June 1933, for failure to make his monthly social security payments for his hired hands.

Valentin Salvaudon was well chosen to play the role of victim of the state. He was a decorated war veteran, the father of six children, and worked his farm with his own hands. These simple verities made Salvaudon the perfect image of the timeless, suffering peasant as victim of the state. Dorgères assured the readers of the PAO that Salvaudon had bought his farm at Bray-sur-Somme in order to till French soil near a place he had defended heroically during World War I. In fact, the area had been a British sector in that war, and the military cemetery across the road from Salvaudon's house, to which Dorgères made frequent allusion, was British.

Many other facts about Salvaudan were slightly different from Dorgères's image of the stoical peasant, pillar of the nation but victim of the state. Salvaudon was certainly not a small peasant. He owned 240 hectares (over 500 acres) of rich Somme farmland, and he employed eighteen full-time hired hands and twenty seasonal workers.[31] Among the property that the *huissier* put up for sale on 18 June were a small truck and an automobile. *L'Humanité* called Salvaudon a "kulak" and deplored the support that his workers gave him (some of Salvaudon's employees didn't want to make social security payments either). The Communist newspaper later urged its peasant readers not to be misled by demagogues into lending their support to a "fascisto-agrarian" protest, as many small farmers had done at Bray-sur-Somme.[32] According to the prefect (who was not a neutral observer either), Salvaudon was "of *limousin* origin but of *gascon* temperament, hot-headed and verbose."[33]

Salvaudon had already started building a political career out of intransigent opposition to social security. He was already well known locally as a speaker in farmers' meetings. He had won an upset election on an anti–social security platform as *conseiller d'arrondissement* for Bray-sur-Somme in October 1931 (one step up from the lowest rung on the electoral ladder, the *conseil municipal,* at the commune level). He had won a respectable 2568 votes in the first round of the legislative elections of 1932. He was to run (unsuccessfully) in the cantonal elections of October 1934 for the Conseil Général of the department of the Somme.[34]

Salvaudon decided to refuse to make any social security payments for his hired hands and to face the consequences. He goaded the state to react. When the sale was scheduled for 11 June 1933, he asked for a week's delay because of his children's first communion. The prefect suspected that he used the time instead to summon a mass demonstration of neighbors and sympathizers to obstruct the sale. Salvaudon did indeed appeal to the Action Française, to the Ligue des Contribuables (an antitax pressure group), and to Dorgères to assemble a crowd at his farm on 18 June. Expecting disorder, the prefect advanced the time of the sale from the hour that had been announced (2 P.M.) to 9 A.M. and closed the road leading to Salvaudon's farm to automobiles.

It should not surprise us much that the local officials' account of the mass demonstration in the courtyard at Salvaudon's farm on 18 June 1933 differed substantially in tone and in details from accounts by Salvaudon's friends. The day was a confusing one, with lots of action designed for symbolic effect, difficult to describe clearly. Each side, moreover, had pressing reasons to spread its own version.

The local gendarmerie and the prefect wanted their superiors to believe that they had never lost control of the situation. They insisted that Dorgères, Salvaudon, and their friends had acted first, pelting the gendarmes with bricks, pots, and pieces of wood from the windows of the house, making the horses rear and thereby forcing the gendarmes to react. If the *gardes mobiles* unsheathed their swords, they did not charge the crowd in that position, according to the gendarmes' report, echoed by the prefect. Instead, they moved the crowd back slowly and carefully.

Dorgères and Salvaudon were to give a very different account of the gendarmes' actions in the *Progrès agricole de l'Ouest* (PAO) and from the podium during dozens of market-day rallies across western France for the next year and a half. Dorgères's account pits heroic peasants against vindictive gendarmes. The latter, Dorgères said, charged without reason, with bared sabers. Action Française and most of the conservative press supported Dorgères's version and blamed Prime Minister Edouard Daladier for what they saw as the Republic's overreaction.

Both sides treated the Salvaudon sale as theater. Each side staged things in a way calculated to appeal to its own audience. The state brought in employees of a social security office in Amiens to keep the bidding going and frustrate Dorgères's effort to prevent anyone from bidding at all. The state was also eager to place the blame for disorder on the demonstrators and to portray its use of force as the minimum necessary to ensure that the state would not be revealed as powerless or humiliated in this contest of wills. The public officials in the Somme were determined not to permit a rabble of demonstrators to challenge the authority of the French state. The prefect reported to his superiors that "the eforts to foment disorder have failed and the sanctity of the law has been upheld."[35]

Dorgères's version of the script was intended to provoke the gendarmes to overreact, to intimidate all bidders, and to demonstrate to the small farmers of France that they could disobey the state with impunity if they followed their intrepid leader, Dorgères. Dorgères's tone is one that we have come to expect from the PAO: the outnumbered peasants mock and taunt the brutish police; they outwit and humilate them by clever exploits appropriate to the physically weaker party, in Robin Hood fashion.[36]

The prefect claimed at least a tactical victory: the sale took place. After the first efforts by Salvaudon's allies to intimidate all bidders had failed and the employees of the social security office in Amiens had raised the bidding, some friends of Salvaudon quickly bought enough farm material to reach the required sum. The whole affair thus ended quickly at the end of the morning. The gendarmes arrested eight people who had led the demonstration or committed phyical violence (including one woman who struck a gendarme with her umbrella) and brought them to trial in the district criminal court in the arrondissement capital, at Péronne.

Since the records of the trial at Péronne of Dorgères, Salvaudon, and their associates have apparently vanished,[37] we must rely on press reports.

On 22 June 1933, the Tribunal Correctionnel of Péronne sentenced Dorgères to three months of prison, plus a fine of 100 francs, and four other demonstrators to lesser terms.[38] Dorgères actually spent twenty-eight days in a cell at Péronne before being freed in the 14 July amnesty. However uncomfortable those days were for him, they had enormous publicity value. At this point, Dorgères became well known in France and something of a hero to many small farmers. The Republic began to watch the Dorgérists closely as a threat to public order.

Dorgères used the Bray fracas and his prison sentence at Péronne over the following eighteen months or so to inspire audiences. Salvaudon accompanied him on many speaking engagements in western France and as far away as Aurillac, Tours, the Pas-de-Calais, and Paris.

The Bray scrap had two important consequences for Dorgères. It won him national celebrity, and it won him the public support of some leading rural notables. The most eminent of these new friends was Adolphe Pointier, a big wheat and sugar beet farmer in the Somme who was already the president of the departmental agricultural federation and was to be elected the following year national president of the wheat growers' federation (AGPB). In 1941–44, Pointier even served as top executive—*syndic national*—of the Vichy regime's Peasant Corporation. Pointer was present in person at Salvaudon's sale and Dorgères's manifestation at Bray-sur-Somme. Pointier also testified in Dorgères's favor at a later trial in Rouen for advocating nonpayment of taxes, and he organized a rally in support of Dorgères at Amiens in September 1935 when the court in Rouen was about to issue its sentence.[39]

From much further away, Dorgères received a telegram of support from Jacques Le Roy Ladurie, the emerging young agrarian leader who had already dominated the farmers' organizations in the Calvados and was to become the secretary-general of the main conservative national farmers' organization, the UNSA (ancestor of today's FNSEA), in 1934. Le Roy Ladurie had already been appearing with Dorgères on platforms since June 1929[40]; now he took up the defense of the "prisoner of Péronne" in his editorials and speeches. After June 1933, therefore, Dorgères enjoyed public support from two of the most influential conservative agrarian leaders in France. He had become a national figure.

Dorgères's defense of the family farm from the encroachments of the state was a theme that served him well in the short run, for the French state—its paperwork, its tax collectors, its schoolteachers, and its inspectors—aroused strong antipathy among small farmers, especially in the north and west. But Dorgères's anti-state rebellion served him badly in the long run, for agriculture is "an affair of State,"[41] and nowhere more than in France. After bringing him notoriety and an audience in 1935, during the worst days of the price decline, Dorgères's integral antistatism finally separated him from the agrarian notables.

We see in Chapter 4 how, after joining him in protest in 1934–35, the leaders of most of the *syndicats agricoles* and their national federation (the UNSA), and the officials of the specialized associations began by 1937 to prefer to work within the French state, even a Republican state, in an effort to construct locally, from the ground up, institutions of corporatist self-administration. "Better to build than to demolish," wrote Jacques Le Roy Ladurie in an editorial of May 1939.[42] Without ever ceasing to be an "astonishing conspirator,"[43] never avoiding a good fight, Le Roy Ladurie came to believe that it was possible to build the new corporatist self-administration of agriculture within the existing constitution—perhaps while awaiting the arrival of a better one. Thus he constructed his own autarkic wheat-trading arrangements in the Calvados in 1933, which he called "the wheat corporation," a first stone on which "will rise the new society."[44] He praised the quota and price agreements of 1931 between sugar beet growers and sugar refiners as another step toward corporatist construction.

So while Dorgères wanted to destroy the whole plan to apply the new family support payments *(allocations familiales)* to agriculture unless the state paid all the costs, the agrarian notables preferred to seize the opportunity to set up their own offices to manage such benefits *(caisses des allocation familiales)* as a building block of the new corporatist regime. They had come to see Dorgères as a threat to the practical realization of corporatist joint admininstration through teamwork between the state and the organized rural notables (the system that would be called *cogestion* after World War II).

As for Dorgères's more modest peasant followers, they were not quite sure what they wanted the state to do. They wanted its help but not its interference. Most of them wanted state aid in some form or other, particularly the larger, better organized ones. But most wanted to avoid state interference in any market decisions that might be profitable. The large producers' pressure groups (e.g., AGPB) wanted self-regulation under state sanction. The smaller, unorganized farmers wanted at least protection against imports and fraud. The Communist party hardly mentioned its rejection of the existing bourgeois state and its ultimate goal of collective farms during this Popular Front period, but it advanced the most precise program of state aid: "crisis benefits" *(allocations de crise)* for the poorest small peasants.

The Dorgérists' attitudes toward the state shared the ambivalences of the poorly organized but conservative small owners and renters for whom they spoke. They never ceased to demand that the state stop imports and control what they saw as the widespread fraud of the milling and whole-sale businesses. But they were admanant about keeping the state out of their farmyards. In the end, these ambiguities won them neither mass support nor alliances with the notables.

Pushing Back the Reds

Strikes of Farm Laborers

Dorgères liked to claim that he and his Greenshirts were France's best protection against the Marxists. He liked to call his market-gardening sup-porters in the outer suburbs around Paris a "green belt" that encircled the "red belt" of the Communist-dominated industrial suburbs.[45] There was no communism, he boasted, where his *comités de défense paysanne* were strong.[46]

For most agrarian conservatives, defending the peasantry was synony-mous with fighting the Left. In their eyes, the Left promoted everything that was going wrong with French society: rural exodus, full-throttle in-dustrial growth, declining religion, cheap bread, agricultural modernization that arrayed farm workers against ever more concentrated agribusinesses, and someday the ultimate nightmare: collectivized farms *(kolkhoz)* where once there had been family farms. These old themes took on new urgency in May–June 1936 when the Popular Front won parliamentary elections and France's first Socialist prime minister, Léon Blum, took office.

Dorgères was in step with this rhythm. During the parliamentary elec-tions of April–May 1936, his priority began to shift from agricultural prices to the communist menace. By summer 1936 the "red peril" drowned out everything else in the pages of the *Progrès agricole de l'Ouest,* the *Paysan du Centre-ouest,* and the *Cri du sol.* It became even easier to maintain this focus after agricultural prices improved a bit in the winter of 1935–36 and when social conflicts boiled over in the countryside in the summer of 1936. When agricultural workers struck the great wheat and sugar beet farms of the Ile-de-France and the plains of the north, in the summers of 1936 and 1937, Dorgères helped to organize "harvest volunteers" to break the strikes. His "green belt" was mobilized in the fall of 1936, when he succeeded, for a time, in organizing the market gardeners *(maraîchers)* around Paris. Dorgères's response to the social ten-sions of the Popular Front was to offer to fearful conservatives his mili-tant family farmers and their sons, mobilized in green-shirted action squads, as France's most effective bulwark against the advancing Marxist tide.

Dorgères's best opportunity to pose as France's savior from communism presented itself in the summers of 1936 and 1937 when France's principal labor union, the Confédération Générale du Travail (CGT), mounted the most massive strikes of agricultural labor in French history.

Agricultural wage laborers are hard to organize everywhere, for a number of reasons. Farm employees, "hired hands," usually work alone or in small groups rather than in large factories (except for brief gatherings for certain seasonal tasks in common, such as grape picking, haying, harvest, or thinning and weeding the sugar beets). They often live on the premises under the immediate influence of the employer and his family. Most of them are drawn from the most uneducated stratum of society. Another obstacle is the yearning of many farm workers to buy or rent an acre or two of their own. This age-old longing to possess land has made even the poorest among them resistant to Marxist collectivism. However desperate and bitter toward their employers and city merchants, even the poorest landless laborers, those who would seem most available to Marxist agitation, are often more attracted by the eternal rural dream of a few acres of their own than by the socialist project of nationalized collective farms.

French farm workers were even less organized than those of other major European countries in the 1930s. This low unionization rate reflected the small average size of French farms, as well as the relatively lower levels of organization of French labor in general than in Britain and Germany. Also, many of the wage laborers on the biggest farms of the plains in northern France were foreign immigrants—usually Poles or Belgians—which made them doubly hard to unionize. Foreign field hands were both vulnerable to their employers' pressures and excluded by language and culture from the usual channels of union recruitment.

As for the next rural stratum from the bottom—marginal sharecroppers, renters of a few acres, and day laborers with small plots of their own (farmers with one foot on the ladder of social ascent)—nowhere in Europe did they want anything to do with Marxist land collectivizers *(partageurs)*. Anticollectivism was even stronger among small but independent family farmers. Marxist organizers, for their part, spent little time trying to recruit small farmers, who were not only too dispersed to organize efficiently but also destined to disappear as they were undersold by big agribusinesses—the rural version of "proletarianization." Since Marxists expected to collectivize all land sooner or later—small farms, as well as big ones, along with all other factors of production—they rarely tried to enlist the struggling small and middle farmers.[47]

Marxist organizers faced a special problem in France, which was half peasant. How could one build a mass party and win elections without attracting peasants' votes? The Parti Ouvrier Français began as early as 1892 to take up the grievances of small landowners and renters, despite the opposition of purists at the summit of the Communist International, like Friedrich Engels. Before 1914, Jean Jaurès understood (as did his Bavarian colleague Georg von Vollmar) that electoral socialism must deploy a plausible peasant strategy in regions where half the working population was still rural. Before World War I, the CGT enjoyed some local successes among woodcutters in the center, sharecroppers (métayers) in the Landes, and wage laborers in the Paris basin.[48] At the end of World War I, however, when many Socialist and Communist strategists believed that urban revolution was imminent, small farmers seemed even less useful for the cause than before. French trade unionists allowed their rural branches to stagnate or even decline in the 1920s, even in those areas where they had established some outposts before 1914.

The French Left turned back toward the peasants once again in the early 1930s. When fascism—once limited to Italy—began to spread across Europe and when Fleurant Agricola's Parti Agraire and Dorgères began to prosper in France, the Left began to worry that small farmers in France were turning fascist. Instead of deeming them a retrograde social stratum that was doomed to disappear, the Communist party now considered them honorary members of the working class as *paysans-travailleurs,* potential supporters who must not be abandoned to the fascists because of doctrinal narrowness.

Renaud Jean, Communist militant of the Lot-et-Garonne and party specialist on peasant issues—he had founded the Confédération Général des Paysans Travailleurs (CGPT) in 1929—helped turn the Communist party toward encouragement of the *paysans-travailleurs* in 1933 to counter the success of the rightwing "agrarians" among small family farmers. He wanted to build socialism in cooperation with farmers rather than in indifference or even hostility toward them as obstacles to collectivization, doomed by industrial progress. He thus espoused Bukharin's proposed model of development in the Soviet Union and served as a pioneer in establishing the Popular Front, that shift of strategy in which the immediate goal of keeping the entire middle class out of fascist hands took precedence over the long-term goal of socialist revolution. He quietly abandoned the distinction between "kulaks," who employed hired hands, and worthy peasants who worked alone, for this sectarian rigor would have excluded many small family farmers in France—those with a hired hand *(domestique)* or two, in many cases the family's sons.

Renaud Jean presented a vigorous report on the peasant issue to the Central Committee of the French Communist party on 10 February 1933. The party, he complained, had almost "completely neglected" the "peasant problem" since the last party congress. While the "sterile action" of the party had produced "mediocre results," the Parti Agraire was growing, and even the Socialist party (SFIO) had increased its rural influence. At that very moment, in fact, during the second week of February 1933, the PAPF was holding giant rallies all across rural France, obliging the notables of the agricultural associations to join them for fear of losing their own troops. The CGPT, Jean continued, left to itself, had not been able to prevent its newspaper, *La Voix paysanne,* from "declining considerably" in sales.

Renaud Jean proposed that the party give higher priority to the peasants, on the basis of a "program of demands well conceived and studied and capable of drawing the mass of poor and middling peasants into the CGPT unions."[49] The program included militant actions to block sales for debt or taxes (as Dorgères would begin to do four months later), propaganda in favor of protection, and such touchy issues as the revision of land-rent contracts downward during the crisis (all supported by Dorgères), as well as a "crisis benefit" *(allocation de crise)* payable to the poorest farmers (Dorgères, with his myth of the unity of the *classe paysanne,* proposed to help them all with higher prices).

Thus after 1933 the French Communist party built an active program around the immediate grievances of the small peasantry. Renaud Jean's CGPT enjoyed some successes in his native Lot-et-Garonne and in a few other departments with a Republican tradition among peasants: the Corrèze,[50] for example, and the western half of the Côtes d'Armor, then known as the Côtes-du-Nord. He is thus the ancestor of the party's postwar support of declining small peasants, through the Mouvement d'Orientation et de Défense des Exploitants Familiaux (MODEF). Jean, and the postwar French Communist party after him, recognized that while hired hands mostly disappear with the modernization of agriculture, family farmers, struggling to survive by adopting "small producers' capitalism," remain a potential recruiting ground in traditionally Left-leaning rural regions of southern and southwestern France.

The Socialists also began to devote special efforts to peasants in the 1930s, but less ambitiously than the Communist party and without much success. The SFIO founded a Confédération Nationale Paysanne (CNP) in 1933 at Limoges, led by Henri Calvayrac of the Haute-Garonne. In the southwest and the Côtes-du-Nord, the CNP had some modest success in the years before the Popular Front, but its influence was to be significant only after the Liberation.[51]

Simultaneously with the Communist party's rediscovery of the *paysans-travailleurs,* the CGT revived its work among its more traditional rural clientele, hired hands on big farms. Organizing farm labor was the province of the unions rather than of the party. The architect of the giant mobilization of agricultural wage laborers after 1933 was the CGT's principal farm organizer, André Parsal. Parsal targeted the work force of the great wheat and sugar beet farms of the Ile-de-France and the northern plains and the industrial vineyards of the Midi. His strategy in the north was to use the fingers of suburban development that thrust deep into the farmland of the Ile-de-France as bases for organization and propaganda. These suburbs at the edge of the open fields—towns like Mitry-Mory and Roissy-en-France, which lie today under the concrete of the Charles De Gaulle airport—often had Communist mayors in the 1930s. They provided meeting rooms and militants to help recruit the hired hands of the nearby great farms of the Seine-et-Marne and the Seine-et-Oise.

Agitation built up among farm workers in the Paris basin in the early 1930s. The first reaction of the big planters to falling prices was to cut wages. Farm workers in the Seine-Maritime were paid 10%–12% less by 1935 than they had earned in 1932 (already little enough).[52] The prefect described wage reductions in the Beauce as "massive."[53] In the Paris basin, the cuts approached 30%.[54] Union activity, dormant there since 1914, began again in 1933, and strikes broke out that summer at Tremblay-les-Gonesse (now Seine-Saint-Denis) and Mitry-Mory (Seine-et-Marne).[55] The stage was set, during the Popular Front summers of 1936 and 1937, for the most massive strikes of agricultural laborers ever known in France.

These great agricultural strikes occurred at the intersection of two apogees in French agricultural labor history: the moment when a peak of revolutionary militancy coincided with the historic maximum of salaried farmhands. The big wheat and sugar beet farms of the Paris basin and the north were at their most labor-intensive. Although they were modern enterprises in many ways, specialized in producing high yields through the use of selected seeds and large quantities of fertilizer, they were not yet mechanized. They required the concentrated effort of large numbers of field hands and their families at crucial moments: weeding, hoeing, and thinning sugar beets (sarclage, binage, and démariage); digging up the beets (arrachage); and harvesting the wheat.

It was the 1936–37 strike wave, in fact, that persuaded the big cultivators of wheat and sugar beets in the Paris basin and the northern plains to begin to replace their fractious workers by machines and the labor-intensive weeding and thinning with chemical herbicides.[56] Today, when the historian visits these big farms in the Aisne or the Brie, where in June 1936 the strikers occupied the buildings, one sees empty courtyards. Where sixty years ago dozens of hired hands and their wives and children bustled about, the visitor today sees only a tractor and a combine harvester parked in the farm's hangars. The courtyards are silent.

Massive strikes of farm labor, often combined with the occupation of the farms by the strikers, had the impact of a bombshell in the summer of 1936. The Popular Front's farm strike wave has never received the serious historical study it deserves. It has been overshadowed by the simultaneous strikes of industrial workers and commercial employees. We do not know exactly how many farms and workers were involved over the two summers because the Ministry of Labor chose to stop collecting strike statistics in 1935.[57] Several thousand farms and tens of thousands of hired hands must have been affected, but the exact number would require combining figures from many different *archives départementales.* These conflicts deserve more attention, for they were even more bitter than industrial or commercial strikes. They had none of the conviviality of the latter, none of the festive dancing of shopgirls in the aisles of the Bon Marché department store.

As in all strikes, salary settlements increased production costs at a difficult time for owners. But special features of agricultural strikes made them even grimmer than the industrial and commercial ones. The strikers had to decide whether or not they would care for the animals. In especially bitter cases they did not, and the unmilked cows and unfed horses added pain and anger to the confrontation. A second irritant stemmed from the perishable nature of the farmers' products. The strikers understood perfectly how to withhold their labor at a strategic moment, when the wheat was ripe or the sugar beet seedlings needed separation *(démariage),* and when the delay of a few days could cost the farmer his crop. A final embittering factor was that while occupying a factory enraged the owner and wounded his sense of ownership and mastery, occupying a farm meant, in many cases, occupying the boss's residence, as well as the seat of his business. The sense of invasion and injury thus went even deeper among the owners of occupied farms than among owners of factories.

French farmers were convinced that outside agitators were exclusively to blame for the strikes, a conspiracy theory abetted by the large proportion of foreigners among the strikers.[58] The planters laughed and applauded when Dorgères denounced André Parsal and his fellow organizers as "strike-growers" *(gréviculteurs)*—those who could produce nothing but division and conflict while the *agriculteurs* produced the bread and wine of life. And in cases in which the French state did not protect their interests fast enough or firmly enough, some of them were willing to go beyond speechmaking and take direct action against the strikers.

One of the bitterest cases involved gunfire on an estate in the Seine-et-Marne on 3 July 1937. The proprietor of a farm at Moissy-Cramayel fired on a group of CGT militants who arrived on bicycles in an attempt to persuade his men to stop hoeing his sugar beets. Words led to an exchange of stones, and then the proprietor fired several times with his shotgun (four shells were found by the police). Seven CGT representatives were wounded. The birdshot was removed easily from six of them, only those pellets in the eye sockets posing difficulties, but a seventh, with about fifty bits of lead in him, had to be hospitalized in Melun. The proprietor was jailed briefly and eventually sentenced to six months' suspended sentence.[59]

Strikes on the farm touched a sensitive nerve on the Left as well. Hungry cities summoned up recollections of provincial separatism (*fédéralisme*) during the French Revolution, when the rural districts refused to feed the cities. The Left's heroic memories included the dispatch by the Committee of Public Safety of Revolutionary Armies, groups of urban volunteers who forced the reluctant peasants to disgorge the food needed by the revolution.[60] The Popular Front was not unsympathetic to the plight of farm workers, however. Agriculture Minister Georges Monnet began gathering information about working conditions on 2 July 1936, with the intention of improving them.[61] But the Popular Front had no intention of allowing the food supply to cities to be interrupted.

On 7 July 1936, Interior Minister Roger Salengro promised an agitated Senate (and its many rural landlords) that the government considered occupations of farms to be illegal and would repress them. The Popular Front government dealt promptly and severely with farm strikes. Anyone reading the accounts of the strikes during the summers of 1936 and 1937 is struck by the rapidity with which the police arrived on the scene to protect "the right to work"—much more speedily than in industry. This is the greatest difference between France in 1936–37 and Italy in 1920: the state, even Léon Blum's state, intervened at once to stop the agricultural strikes, whereas the big farmers in Giolitti's Italy in 1920–21 believed that they needed to hire vigilantes—Mussolini's *fasci di combattimento*—to protect them from militant organized labor.[62]

Even so, many big French farmers accused Léon Blum's Republic of not protecting them adequately. The word went around among conservative agrarians that in the Aisne (where Agriculture Minister Georges Monnet's own farm was located) the police kept volunteers from carrying out farm work to avoid provoking the strikers.[63] These bitter, highly personalized conflicts created an opening for the Dorgérists to come to the rescue of enraged farm owners, as the Fascists had done in the Po Valley in 1921 and as the *Freikorps* had done in East Prussia in 1920.

Typically, a *comité de défense paysanne* recruited a bus-load of young men from an area of conservative family farmers to harvest the wheat left untouched by the strikers. Dorgérist propaganda never referred to these young men as "strikebreakers." They were "harvest volunteers" sent to "save the harvest" (the "people's wheat," rather than the more commercial sugar beets). The goal was not merely the practical one of getting in the wheat before it rotted, although the farmer's entire annual income might well depend on those few days of concentrated effort. These actions were also laden with symbolism. They were designed to recall the sacredness of the land and of the harvested wheat sheaf and the high values of peasants' "mutual aid," that warm cooperation among all levels of society in the chief rituals of the agricultural year, which made rural society, in agrarian opinion, morally superior to urban individualism, with its class conflict.

The photographers pictured the volunteers cutting the wheat by hand; no tractors are visible, although the harvest volunteers probably normally used a harvester-binder at this date. At the end of their day's labor, the volunteers went to the local war memorial to place a symbolic sheath there, combining the ideals of patriotism, social order, mutual aid, and the sacredness of farm work in a single gesture. The press, especially on the Left, always called these volunteers "Dorgéristes," whether Dorgères had anything to do with them or not. Whatever else he accomplished, Dorgères surely won the propaganda battle of the harvest volunteers.

When I began this project, I expected to find that the Greenshirts were widely involved in fighting strikers on behalf of the big owners in the Paris basin and the northern plains during 1936 and 1937. In fact, I found only a limited number of cases in which an official Dorgérist *comité de défense paysanne* had organized "harvest volunteers." Those whom we can clearly identify as Dorgérist came mostly from areas of middling family farms in the Seine-Maritime and the Pas-de-Calais, rather than from the regions of great farms in the Paris basin and northern plains. The largest group, 180 members, was recruited by Pierre Suplice in the Seine-Inférieure in July–August 1936 and sent to the Somme,[64] where Dorgères's powerful ally Adolphe Pointier had issued an appeal for volunteers in the name of the comité d'action paysanne.[65] Suplice also sent two teams of volunteers to the Pas-de-Calais in August 1936.[66]

By 1937, the Pas-de-Calais had become the most active center of Greenshirt "harvest volunteers," under the impetus of Pierre Leclercq, departmental leader of the CDP and later national president of the sugar beet lobby. Seven young people desribed as Chemises Vertes went from Aire-sur-la-Lys (Pas-de-Calais) to the Calais area to replace striking workers on 7–9 June 1937,[67] and Leclercq prepared to send 300 volunteers to the *Cambrésis* (Nord) at about the same time to help with the hoeing of sugar beets.[68] The last "harvest volunteers" we know about were active in the Pas-de-Calais in June 1939.[69]

Many of the harvest volunteers, however, had nothing to do with Dorgères. Some were recruited by Colonel de La Rocque's Parti Social Français (PSF), which began a major effort to enlist farmers in 1937.[70] The PSF offered to defend struck farms in the Paris basin,[71] and in the Aisne they were at the center of a clash between harvest volunteers and the government (as we see in the following discussion). There are shadowy traces of the recruitment of Parisians by the Comité National des Volontaires pour l'Agriculture at 23, avenue de Messine in 1936[72] and at 104, rue de l'Université in 1938, with no apparent relation to Dorgères and to which he alluded very rarely.[73] The whole operation was carried out with such discretion that it is impossible today to identify its organizers.[74]

The big farmers of the Paris basin did quite well by themselves without much help from Dorgères or any other outside force.[75] Caught unprepared by the wave of strikes that began in May 1936, they negotiated at first. The main agricultural association of the Paris basin, the Fédération des Organisations Agricoles de la Seine-et-Oise et de la Seine-et-Marne, agreed under government pressure to sign a regional collective contract with the reunited farmworkers' union, the Fédération Nationale des Travailleurs Agricoles (FNTA), on 23 July 1936. Its negotiator, Aimé Monmirel, a great sugar beet planter of the Seine-et-Oise and president of the Confédération Génerale des Planteurs de Betteraves, was disovowed by many planters for recognizing the union and sacrificing the bosses' initiative to government mediators. A new and more intransigent Union (later Association) Centrale des Employeurs Agricoles (ACEA) was formed in July 1936 under the presidency of Paul Caffin, a big vegetable and fruit grower at Poissy (Seine-et-Oise) and early proponent of the Peasant Front.[76]

By the spring of 1937, when the 1936 collective agreement expired, both sides had hardened their positions. The union had a new list of demands. The ACEA refused to accept it as legitimate, refused all contact with the union, proposed to index any salary increases to the wheat price, and prepared to sacrifice part of the sugar beet crop if necessary (expecting to hold the state responsible for the loss). The planters fired union activists and seized the opportunity to stop feeding and lodging their workers.

When strikes began again at weeding and thinning time (May 1937), the ACEA set up a command post with telephone contacts and prepared to find substitute labor. The planters used the urban unemployed from Meaux, their own sons and neighbors,[77] Belgians, and volunteers sent by various organizations in other parts of northern France. Although the union called all the volunteers "Dorgérists," only one of some half dozen contingents was actually sent by a CDP: ninety volunteers from the Cambrésis (Nord), on 22–23 June, with Dorgères himself present on the twenty-third.[78]

The powerful French agricultural associations were quite capable of defending themselves against strikers in 1937. They did not become dependent, like Italian or German big farmers in 1920, on auxiliary movements to protect them. The ACEA entered into frontal conflict with the Popular Front government in the Aisne during strikes of beetroot workers at the end of July 1937. Determined to break the farm workers' union and acting according to daily strategic advice from Paul Caffin, the big planters of the Aisne (including one sugar-refining company) brought in harvest volunteers. The prefect had orders from Agriculture Minister Georges Monnet (who had a farm in the Aisne) to keep the harvest volunteers and the strikers from coming to blows. On 29 July, the *gardes mobiles* kept 200 volunteers organized by the PSF from crossing a police line.[79] The ACEA and the PSF[80] drummed up a major propaganda campaign around this incident, alleging that since the French state under the Popular Front had sided with the strikers, it was thereby promoting violence. Consequently the farmers had the right to take the maintenance of order into their own hands. Their story, along with its justification of agrarian vigilantism, made the rounds of the conservative agrarian press, including Dorgères's PAO.[81]

Dorgères played a relatively small role in the Aisne antistrike action, however. Only eighty-five volunteers seem to have been Greenshirts, and the prefect reported that several of them had to be locked up for drunkenness after their ceremony at the Monument aux Morts, on the day they left, 5 August. A larger number were PSF members, and most of the harvest volunteers seem to have been recruited locally by the farmers themselves. Dorgères was already cool to the big planters, finding them ignorant of their social duties and too ready to come to a purely economic agreement with the Communists[82]; and the big planters seem to have had little interest in anything about Dorgères but his oratory.[83]

For a time harvest volunteers were on the front pages.[84] Some of those who came from Paris and got themselves photographed in the Paris press were the urban unemployed, and others were intellectuals and political activists. Many of them found the field labor heavy going. The Left press tended to call all of them Greenshirts even when Dorgères had nothing to do with them. The harvest volunteers had only momentary significance, however, in the absence of a more general collapse of Republican legitimacy, as in Italy or Germany. But antistrike action led to something closer to local power for a Dorgériste organization in the Seine-Maritime, and we now look more closely at that case.

Organizing against Farm Workers' Strikes
Bourg-Dun (Seine-Inférieure), 1936–37

The Dorgérists worked most effectively against agricultural strikes in areas where a strong personality was present to take things in hand. Strikes aroused particularly bitter personal feelings on middling family farms. This made some areas in the west of France that were threatened by strikes ripe for Dorgères's *comités de défense paysanne*. One such case involved the Caux, a region of the Seine-Inférieure (as the Seine-Maritime was called then), where one of Dorgères's most effective lieutenants, Pierre Suplice, was the mayor of Bourg-Dun (Seine-Inférieure).

The Caux is a chalk plateau that extends along the coastal highlands facing the English Channel northeastward from Dieppe: a windy upland celebrated for the independence of its productive farms and its closed society.[85] It was then a region of largely self-sufficient, middling family farms, practicing polyculture and dividing their time among wheat, flax, milk, and meat.

As strikes threatened in the summer of 1936 and developed in the summer of 1937, Mayor Suplice came close to establishing his CDP as the effective arbiter of farmer–hired hand relations in his part of the Caux. This was a far more solid achievement than the mere dispatch of a few harvest volunteers for a day or two. The CDP became the pole around which the threatened proprietors of the Caux organized themselves in a permanent fashion to prevent strikes; they drew hired hands into their organizations and set up mixed committees of arbitration. This could be seen as the embryo of a local corporatist administration, with farmers' self-administration taking the place of the state. The prefect watched this situation closely, for the CDP was beginning to encroach on the state's guardianship of order and monopoly of force. For a short time, the *Comité* exercised de facto local authority over labor-management relations on many of the farms of the Caux. But it operated within Republican legality, in the absence of any national movement that significantly challenged the Republican order.

Pierre Suplice was a much-decorated war veteran who was elected mayor of his rural commune, Bourg-Dun, in 1925, at the age of thirty.[86] He cultivated a large farm with nine employees (more than average for the region) that belonged to his aunt; hardly a marginal peasant, he was married to the daughter of another mayor. The Subprefect of Dieppe described Suplice in July 1934 as "young, ardent . . . basically a good person but with an intransigent character and easily moved to suspicion"; he had the reputation of getting along very badly with the local authorities (a reprehensible quality, in a prefect's view). At the end of 1934, as a member of the regional farm statistic commission *(commission cantonale de la statistique agricole),* he provoked a "major incident" by persuading his colleagues to break off all contact with public authorities, which led to the revocation of the chairman of the commission.

If Suplice got along badly with public officials, he was hardly more accommodating with the traditional agricultural associations. He belonged—like so many Dorgérists—to that generation "which did not know the prosperous era, and had serious difficulties in running their farms. . . . The agrarian movement, which has crystallized so much discontent among young farmers, was bound to attract him."[87] By November 1934, five months after he had become president of the Comité de Défense Paysanne for the whole department of the Seine-Inférieure and a militant Dorgérist, Suplice was described by the subprefect as "a hot-head whose activities must be watched quite closely."[88]

The farmers of the Seine-Inférieure were until 1935 solidly in the grip of an agricultural oligarchy. The rural "boss" of the area was Senator Gaston Veyssière, who had accumulated all the major agrarian posts in his department according to the common practice of rural notables of the Third Republic. He was not only the unmovable senator (Union Ré-publicaine, i.e., conservative) of the Seine-Inférieure; he was also president of the Syndicat Agricole de la Seine-Inférieure, which comprised about half of the cultivators of the department (a smaller Fédération, formed in 1934 on corporatist principles, had grown to about 200 branches by the outbreak of the war).[89] In addition, Senator Veyssière was president of the Chambre d'Agriculture of the Seine-Inférieure. The other senator of this department, André Lavoinne, was also active in farm organizations. A descendant of the family that had developed the Norman breed of cattle and established the Normandy Herd Book, he was president of the national meat producers' association (Association des Producteurs de Viande).

As the 1930s began, the first cause of tension in the Caux and even more in the Bray, a dairy region of rich grassy valleys a little further inland, was the antagonism of small farmers toward the big companies that bought their milk on the companies' terms: Gervais, Maggi, and Fermiers Réunis. Fleurant Agricola's Parti Agraire et Paysan Français (PAPF) was the first agrarian activist movement to try to exploit those tensions in the Caux and the Bray. The PAPF ran an Agrarian candidate in a by-election in the Bray in 1929 and tried more generally in the legislative elections of 1932, without much success. The PAPF candidate in 1929 got only 2000 votes, and in 1932 the PAPF seems to have been unable to field a candidate at all.[90] In the early 1930s, the notables of the Seine-Inférieure still had the agricultural structures of the department well in hand in spite of the severe crisis of confidence the Depression produced in their authority.

Then Dorgères became active in the Seine-Inférieur in 1934. "With him," reported the subprefect of Dieppe, "the tone has changed. He is a leader who knows how to move people."[91] Dorgères invested major time and energy in the department of the Seine-Inférieure, speaking there seven times in 1934. By January 1935, the Subprefect of Dieppe reported that "we found ourselves confronted by a new organization, methodically led, laid out along the same lines as the *Syndicat agricole.*"[92] The department's main city, Rouen, was the site on 22 February 1935 of one of the greatest rallies of Dorgères's career, the one in which he urged a tax strike, using language that brought him his second prison sentence.

Pierre Suplice was Dorgères's main agent in the Seine-Inférieure. When a departmental *comité de défense paysanne* was set up at a rally in the Rouen circus pavillion on 22 June 1934, Suplice was elected president. He then set out to organize the department, aided by a paid CDP official, Emile Lefebvre, Dorgères's "secretary" and journalist at the PAO. Suplice's first issue was an "impetuous campaign" in November 1934, supported by "several hundred farmers," to prevent the nomination of Darius Le Corre, a Communist, as a schoolteacher in Bacqueville (Seine-Inférieure).[93]

Building on the emotions aroused by the Le Corre case, Suplice spent much of the following year actively building the CDP in the Seine-Inférieure by establishing local sections, especially in the Caux and in the adjacent Bray, immediately to the east. There were thirteen CDP rallies in the Seine-Inférieure in the six months from July 1934 to January 1935,[94] and there were another half dozen rallies during the next month, working up the great audience of 20,000 that heard Dorgères in Rouen on 22 February 1935. Suplice was prosecuted for participating in that meeting, in which Dorgères urged a tax strike; he was clearly a major confederate at that point.

Between public meetings, CDP activists worked markets and fairs, making contact with individuals and small groups. The department sent over 600 delegates to the Peasant Front rally in Paris on 28 November 1934— one of the biggest delegations of any department of France. The subprefect of Dieppe estimated in January 1935 that there were "several thousand people who have heard [Dorgères], the great majority of whom have remained sympathisers" in the Seine-Inférieure.[95]

The agricultural notables of the Seine-Inférieure, as elsewhere in western France, had to decide in 1935 whether they were going to fight the Dorgérists, share power with them, or try to moderate them. They had fought the Parti Agraire of Fleurant Agricola, but this had required only a few public expressions of disdain. Dorgères was a more serious matter. It was also three years later, and rural anger and despair were far greater. Meat and milk prices, in particular, collapsed in 1935, after having been the main remaining resource of many family farms after grain prices had collapsed in 1933. The year 1935 marked the high-water mark of Dorgérist success in associating the CDPs with the traditional elites of rural western and northern France, and the Seine-Inférieure was a notable example of this process of alliance with rural notables. The subprefect of Dieppe reported on 22 January that the parliamentarians, "unrelated, even indifferent" to the old PAPF and "suspicious" toward Dorgères at first, "now walk with the Peasant Front."[96] The well-entrenched conservative deputy of the Bray, Charles Thureau-Dangin, who had regarded the PAPF with a "suspicious eye," declared publicly his "entire approval" of the CDP program during a rally of 500 farmers at Neuchâtel-en-Bray on 29 December 1934.[97]

The next rural notables to associate with Dorgères were the leaders of the powerful Syndicat des Agriculteurs de la Seine-Inférieure (SASI), presided over by Senator Veyssière. The SASI devoted its regular annual meeting in Rouen on 17 September 1935 to the speech of Pierre Hallé, secretary-general of the national wheat growers' association (AGPB) and militant antirepublican. Hallé explained the comité d'action paysanne (CAP)[98] and its petition campaign then circulating throughout France. In the Seine-Inférieure, 15,000 had already signed the CAP's petition and its associated "action order." The climate was feverish. The "big associations," said Hallé, don't want the desparate small peasants to throw themselves into "the extreme movements" (did he mean communism?). The CAP, "that is, all the big associations, weary of presenting resolutions and petitions to which no one pays any attention, has turned towards the mass movements" (i.e., the CDP). The petition, affirmed Senator Veyssière, his tone becoming as militant and threatening to public authorities as the senator ever permitted himself, "is only a beginning." The CAP hoped that the government would understand the situation and work with the agricultural associations, but if not, "they will call upon all the mass movements."[99]

Senator Veyssière thus shared a platform with Pierre Suplice, who spoke briefly at the end. The strategic decision of the elites of the Seine-Inférieur in 1935 to work with the Dorgérists could not have been more clearly expressed. Dorgères was their battering ram. If the government did not find a way to bring farm prices back up, the traditional leaders of the farm populations of the Seine-Inférieure, normally cautious men, indicated that they would help Dorgères arouse a vast peasant protest movement in their department.

Next came the other agricultural organization, the Fédération, whose secretary-general, René Lerebours, shared the platform with Suplice; with one of the Dessoliers brothers (among Dorgères's most fiery lieutenants); and with Max Govare, departmental president of the PAPF, at a Peasant Front rally in Dieppe on 28 September 1935.[100] Lerebours was also simultaneously a vice-president of the CDP of the Seine-Inférieure for the Fécamp region. This was a much more heated meeting than the SASI annual assembly. Dessoliers, in particular, attacked the government violently. Suplice, while denying that he was advocating the nonpayment of taxes by those capable of paying (Dorgères had been convicted for using careless language about a tax strike in Rouen a few months earlier), urged those whose financial situation was desparate not to pay taxes: "we are not against the payment of taxes," but if a peasant can't pay, he can send the tax forms to the secretary of the Peasant Front.

Even the Syndicat des Producteurs de Lait du Pays de Bray, which had boasted in March 1935 that its members did not "break windows" like Dorgères,[101] also drew closer to the CDP in early 1936. Its president, Antoine des Courtils, was present at a CDP meeting at Gournay-en-Bray on 12 February 1936.[102]

Despite all this activity and the support of the agrarian elite in 1935, the Comité de Défense Paysanne in the Seine-Inférieure described itself in early February 1936 (in PAO) as "without resources" and obliged to ask for dues of 5 francs per member to continue local propaganda activities. Beginning in February 1936, Sulpice started a new round of rallies, centering on the iniquities of the futures market (Bourse de Commerce) and of cut-rate stores (both dominated by Jews, he said) and the necessity for peasants to organize their own corporatist self-government. One has the sense that all of Suplice's efforts to give Dorgérism momentum in the Seine-Inférieure had left few permanent results until the strike wave in the summer of 1936 gave it the occasion to assume a para-governmental role.

In the six months beginning in June 1936 there were 479 strikes in the cities of Dieppe, Le Havre, and Rouen, but no farms in the Seine-Inférieure were struck that first summer of the Popular Front.[103] The Caux teetered on the brink of a farm workers' strike, however, and of course the cultivators of the Seine-Inférieure looked on with horror at agricultural strikes in nearby regions of big farms in the Vexin and the western Paris basin. Already in July–August 1936, the *comité de défense pay-*

sanne sent volunteers to counter the strikes in the Somme and the Pas-de-Calais, as we already saw. As for their own farms, they began to "react against the visit of anyone foreign to farm work," fearing efforts by the CGT to mobilize the farm workers.[104]

And well they might. A departmental labor union for farm workers (Union Départementale des Syndicats des Travailleurs de la Terre), affiliated with the CGT, was formed in the Seine-Inférieure on 13 August 1936. The efforts were directed by Coudray, the CGT leader in Rouen; by Féron, from the fishing port of Fécamp; and by Gaonac'h, the schoolteacher (a Communist militant), in the village of Bois-Robert in the Canton of Fontaine-le-Dun[105]—three good examples of the kinds of Left strongholds from which the CGT could mount forays into farm country. Their recruitment activities provoked the landowners into firing troublemakers among their employees and preparing to defend themselves.[106] In fact, the CGT seems to have preached calm in the Seine-Inférieure during that summer. They weren't ready for a strike there yet, which explains why the first agricultural strikes broke out in that department only in the summer of 1937.

In the meantime, the farmers of the Seine-inférieure put themselves in the hands of Pierre Suplice and his CDP to defend their farms against strikes and occupations. In May 1937, Suplice was even made secretary of the departmental *syndicat agricole,* whose head, Senator Veyssière, had only recently become willing to cooperate with such rash newcomers.

So the farmers of the Seine-Inférieure were ready to be tough when agricultural strikes reached the Caux in the summer of 1937. Agricultural strike activity there had the shocking impact of pure novelty. There had never before been a Marxist farm workers' organization in that region. Even the *paysans-travailleurs* were unknown, though the average size of farms in the canton of Dieppe was an upper-middling forty hectares.[107] As for agricultural laborers, they were quite numerous but scattered among the many middle-sized farms. The subprefect of Dieppe reported as late as November 1933 that there was "no revolutionary syndical propaganda here" and doubted that if there were any it would have any effect.[108]

When the first farm workers' strike in the Seine-Inférieure broke out on 27 May 1937 in Ourville-en-Caux, both sides had learned how to manage a strike since the first wild days of June 1936 in other departments. The strikers cared for the animals and milked the cows. They were quite calm. As for the employers, they had formed a new farm owners' association (Chambre Patronale des Agriculteurs) by fusing the traditional Syndicat des Agriculteurs de la Seine-Inférieure, presided over by Senator Veyssière, and the Dorgérist CDP, headed by Pierre Suplice.[109] Suplice thus became the principal negotiator for the employers, assisted by Jean Lepicard, mayor of the affected commune.[110]

The fusion of the notables' *syndicat agricole* and the Dorgérists' *comité de défense paysanne* was a landmark: it carried to an ultimate conclusion the cooperation of the traditional agrarian elites with the Dorgérist activists begun in 1935, and it made the CDP the agent of the entire agricultural establishment. In effect, the CDP was in power at the grassroots in the Seine-Inférieure in the summer of 1937.

This first agrarian strike wave lasted a week and affected a maximum of 70 farms and about 300 hired hands at its height on 3 June 1937. A few days later, agitation reached the farm workers of the canton of Fontaine-le-Dun, and Suplice sat down with the CGT delegates—led by the teacher Gaonac'h—for a first meeting on 8 June. They could reach no accord. On the morning of 16 June strikes broke out on the farms in the valleys of the Saane and the Dun. At its peak, this second strike wave involved 200 farms and 650 workers.[111] Although the strikers occupied no farmyards, the owners were very bitter at this unprecedented affront to their authority.

The local brigades of gendarmerie were reinforced at once and began patrols on the night of 17 June. Suplice alerted his followers in the CDP that same day to prepare to intervene on the farm owners' side. The following day, according to a phone call from the subprefect of Dieppe to the prefecture, Suplice had twenty "strong-arm men of the Peasant Front" at his farm ready to act in case they were needed to protect the "right to work" of those who wished to work.[112] Suplice had let it be known that forty more would come if needed from the neighboring communes of Saint-Saens and Bellencombre. These CDP volunteers were as visible as Suplice could make them (though they do not seem to have worn green shirts or any other distinctive mark). He no doubt meant them to serve as a deterrent to discourage possible occupations of farms.

While he was assembling his forces, Suplice was also meeting with the local union leaders. He and the landowners were willing to bargain with their workers individually, even willing to raise salaries, but they remained totally unwilling to accept the authority of the CGT to act as the lawful representatives of the department's farm workers. Union recognition was what the local union leaders most wanted to gain from these strikes, but it was the one labor demand the landowners were least ready to accept.

Meanwhile, the CGT leaders sent out groups of strikers on bicycles to try to draw more workers away from their work. At four in the afternoon on 21 June, a group of 200 cyclists led by the Communist schoolteacher Gaonac'h passed directly in front of Suplice's house in Bourg-Dun "without making the slightest gesture," reported the subprefect by phone, but their very passage was a powerful provocation. On 23 June the CGT leaders tried in vain to draw Suplice's own workers into the strike. We do not know what it was that kept Suplice's workers from going on strike that day: whether it was fear of their redoubtable employer, acceptable working conditions on Suplice's farm, or even personal affection for him. In any event, whether by force or by persuasion, Suplice kept his own workers from striking.

Meanwhile, some employers were less hard-nosed than Suplice. Three of the thirty-five cultivators present at a strategy session on 18 June were in favor of settlement. On 20 June the region of Luneray settled with the strikers. Suplice, under pressure for a settlement, reached an agreement on terms on 28 June. Though the employers agreed to wages and hours that were acceptable to the strikers, they declined to sign a contract.[113] Thus they ended the strike without recognizing the legitimacy of the CGT to represent "their" workers.

After the strikes ended, French landowners hoped that a more radical form of corporatism would save them from a future of steady confrontation with the CGT. Many of them (including Jacques Le Roy Ladurie in the Calvados) began to organize workers' branches within their farm organizations in order to deprive the CGT of clients and eliminate it from their area. Pierre Suplice transformed his *comité de défense paysanne* into a more corporatist *syndicat de défense paysanne* (SDP), including a workers' section, as well as an employers' section. This corporatist *syndicat* was intended to demonstrate the priority of common agrarian interests, uniting farmers and their hired hands over any class divisions that might separate them. The SDP was corporatism in action in a purely distilled form. Suplice had never wanted to let the CDP appear as simply the strong arm of the employers. He declined to intervene against one strike in the Vexin, on the grounds that it was justified.[114] As for Dorgères, he had already changed the name of his central organization from Comité Central to Syndicat Agricole de Défense Paysanne in May 1936.

Despite these efforts, however, the Dorgériste movement melted away in the Seine-Inférieure after the excitement of the strikes of 1937 and the fear of one in 1938 were over. Apathy was the besetting problem of the CDPs: they oscillated in a rhythm of boom and bust between intense excitement and collapse. They lacked the prosaic but permanent activities of the *syndicats agricoles,* with their cooperatives for storage, insurance, and group purchases and, increasingly, with programs of moral and agrarian instruction such as correspondence courses and lectures. The *syndicats* were even trying by 1936 to keep up with Dorgères in the realm of propaganda and not leave the moral, cultural, and political turf entirely to him.

By 1938, the CDP had become so weak in the Seine-Inférieur that it was attached to the Normandy regional office under Modeste Legouez and the secretary was dismissed. Legouez organized in 1938 and 1939 some fiery meetings against the proposed family benefits payments program and against war, described as attempts to "reorganize" and "recreate" the movement. When the regime changed after the defeat of France in 1940 and the Vichy government set up the Peasant Corporation, the major roles went to the Lepicard brothers, of the Fédération,[115] and Suplice was only *syndic* of his commune.

It is true that Suplice was elected to the Peasant Corporation's departmental assembly in the election of December 1943. But the Dorgérist movement had clearly spent its energies on the antistrike excitement of 1937–38 (and had perhaps made some enemies among the big farmers who wanted to settle). That was typical of Dorgérism's long-term weakness: boom or bust (like the early labor movement). Thus the CDP was briefly "in power" in a few communes of the Seine-Inférieure in the summer of 1937; but in the absence of any national power to which local power could be permanently linked by patronage and other rewards, local power soon returned to the hands of the local notables and the more prosaic commercial operations of the *syndicats agricoles*.

Breaking Industrial Strikes Isigny (Calvados), August–December 1936

Another opportune setting for Dorgères's anticommunist peasant action was the industrial strikes that affected farmers' interests: at sugar refineries and milk treatment plants, for example. Work stoppages at food-processing plants put farmers under even more intense stress than that of other kinds of suppliers to industry. The furnishers of agricultural raw materials have a perishable product on their hands. If strikers close a milk treatment plant, the cows cannot be turned off. Within twenty-four hours, the milk spoils—and more keeps coming. Even sugar beets spoil in a few days if a sugar refinery goes out on strike. Processing farm products is highly seasonal work, moreover. Their poorly paid employees know exactly how to apply maximum pressure: go on strike at peak time.

There were many such cases during the 1930s, and they could lead to violent conflict between the striking workers and the farmers who supplied raw materials to the factory. Sugar beet planters fought striking North African workers at the sugar refinery at Toury (Eure-et-Loir) on 15 October 1936. The farmers got rather the worst of it: half a dozen suffered injuries, and two were hospitalized. The Toury incident involved the Parti Agraire and not Dorgères, although the PAO contributed to the intense propaganda the event generated on both the Right and the Left.[116] Flax growers broke up a strike in a hemp-stripping factory in Tréguier (Côtes-d'Armor) in February 1937, again independently of Dorgères.[117] It was the *comité de défense paysanne,* however, that mobilized farmers in the Nord against striking factory workers, who had invaded markets in June 1936 and forced the farm women to lower their butter prices.[118]

Strikes at milk-processing plants offered particularly fertile terrain for Dorgères in the 1930s. The case we examine in some detail is the butter and cream plant operated by the Dupont firm at Isigny (Calvados), which was struck by its workers twice in late 1936: 31 August—2 September and 8–10 December. These strikes offered an opportunity for action to the Greenshirts of the Calvados and to their leader, Germain Boullot, who was subsequently promoted to national chief of the Chemises Vertes.

Isigny was much more politically polarized in 1936 than most of Catholic and conservative Calvados. Isigny had an important bloc of Communist votes, and the Communist candidate for parliament, Louis Colette, came in second after the incumbent duc d'Harcourt in the parliamentary elections of April 1936. Isigny had the second-highest Communist vote in the whole arrondissement of Bayeux in this election.[119] Conservatives in this arrondissement were correspondingly tempted by the New Right. In addition to the city of Bayeux itself, Isigny also contained the only other autonomous local branch of Colonel de La Rocque's Parti Social Français in the Calvados. The rural areas around Isigny were even more deeply anti-Communist. Isigny's political polarization created a climate in which many citizens were prepared to accept direct action, such as that offered by the Greenshirts.

Not only were political tensions high around Isigny in the summer of 1936, but also this milk-producing area faced sharp economic tensions. Dairy farming engendered particularly acute feelings of powerlessness in the 1930s. The producers of milk, most of them small farmers, invested in animals and equipment and then depended on selling their product to one large purchaser, either a milk distributor or a processor of butter and cheese. The farmers felt vulnerable and weak when dealing individually with giant corporations like Nestlé or a large local firm like Dupont d'Isigny. Buyers were able to set purchase prices unilaterally and did so arrogantly, a power that seemed particularly abusive during price declines, as in the late 1920s and early 1930s. If the farmer who wanted to sell his milk did not like the price set by the purchasing company, there was not much he could do to improve it. During conflicts between the farmers and the big firms, the latter always had a powerful weapon: they could simply decline to pick up the milk of some farmer whom they wished to coerce.[120]

The milk market was also plagued by problems of quality control. Some small dairy farmers were tempted to adulterate their product. In the absence of any self-policing by the small milk producers, the state was beginning to edge toward government inspection—which threatened the house searches and other statist horrors that the distillers of the nearby cider country were already experiencing. Quality control was a particularly sensitive issue in the Bessin region of coastal Normandy. The milk of the Bessin was mostly used to produce a butter famous throughout France: Isigny butter. Increasingly after 1900, commercial firms were using the term fraudulently, mixing milk from the Bessin with cheaper milk from other places and producing an inferior product. This damaged the milk producers of the Bessin in two ways: they lost sales to other areas, and the high reputation of their product was undermined.

Dairy farmers in many regions of France began learning in the late 1920s and 1930s to take their destinies into their own hands. They formed producer cooperatives and syndicates to meet both their needs by their own efforts: to ensure quality without state intervention and to deal on an equal footing with big buyers. The farmers' responses to the milk crisis easily took on a political color in the 1930s. The farmers blamed the Republic for permitting too many imports during the Depression. They wanted to keep the state out of their farmyards, but they wanted the state to protect them from competition. Their organizations could take on a distinctly antistate, corporatist, and even antirepublican tone.

For example, a milk-gathering cooperative was the power base of Joseph Bilger, the inventor of the Greenshirt symbol and the animator of the militantly rightwing *Bauernbund* in Alsace, who cooperated with the Nazi occupiers of Alsace after 1940. Another example was the Gervais plant at Gournay-en-Bray, this time in a stronghold of Dorgérism, where the local *comité de défense paysanne* assembled 1200 peasants to force the solution to a strike in June 1936.[121] A further area where Dorgères encouraged milk producers to defend their interests was the Guérande peninsula in the Loire-Atlantique. But the milk producers of Isigny-sur-mer (Calvados) were probably Dorgères's most enthusiastic supporters.

Isigny was the setting of a particularly militant cooperative of milk producers who were just beginning to "take back in hand their own market and defend the quality of their product."[122] Henry Babeur, a leading corporatist apostle, formed a milk producers' cooperative at Isigny in 1930 and a union of butter and cream producers (Syndicat des Producteurs de Beurre et Crème d'Isigny) in 1931. Babeur wanted the dairy farmers to be able to stand up to the buyers, but he did not want confrontation. He wanted to organize the entire commercial chain by which butter was made and marketed, from the small milk producers through the processors to the commercial distributors. He called this kind of corporatist organization an "interprofession": the farmers, processors and distributors would work out their own market structure, through negotation among organized professions, without the intervention of the Republican state or labor unions or any other "outsiders."[123]

One of Babeur's young associates, Germain Boullot, a twenty-seven-year-old livestock raiser at Deux-Jumeaux, near Isigny, was much more interested in direct action than in organization. By the summer of 1936, Boullot was already well known in the Calvados as an impulsive hothead. He was secretary of the Syndicat Agricole of Longueville-Deux Jumeaux, of which Babeur was president. On 11 September 1935, this syndicat took up a collection at its regular meeting and gathered 80 francs to support Dorgères, who was at that time under indictment at Rouen for having advocated a tax strike in a big rally the previous February.

Like many Dorgérists, Boullot was in trouble with the tax collectors himself. He was much bolder and more confrontational about his tax problem, however, than most of the others. On 9 March 1936, he wrote to the prefect of the Calvados, asking for relief from the tax on agricultural profits. Boullot's letter took a remarkably belligerent tone. He warned the prefect that he could not be bought off with some compromise: "I am not the sort of person that can be appeased by satisfying their particular interest." If the prefect let legal action proceed against him and his friends, Boullot threatened, "I can't answer for what might happen." Boullot's letter then suggested that "to rip up the tax-collector's office" would be "an attitude . . . worthy of a man."[124]

The prefect believed that Babeur—who was mayor of Longueville, as well as president of the *syndicat agricole* of which Boullot was secretary and creator of the milk producers' organizations just discussed—did not support Boullot's petition for tax relief. We know nothing about Babeur's reaction to (or even possible participation in) the raid of about "150 individuals, mostly notables of the region of Isigny-sur-Mer," who descended on Neuilly-la-Forêt on the evening of 26 July 1936, where they thought a pro–Popular Front meeting was going to be held. That meeting had been canceled, but Boullot harangued the night riders about corporatism anyway for about twenty minutes before the crowd headed home.[125] The local gendarme identified the night riders as members of the "dissolved group of the 'Croix de Feu,'" but Boullot, at any rate, was the head of the Greenshirts of the Department of the Calvados, and so we presume that this was a Greenshirt raid. It is not surprising that Dorgères appointed a young farmer of Boullot's combative ardor to command his action squad in the Calvados or that in 1937 Boullot would become the national chief of the Greenshirts.

Boullot and his Greenshirts were in no mood for passivity when they learned on Monday, 31 August 1936, that the Dupont butter factory in Isigny had been closed that morning by a strike. Labor troubles had been brewing at the plant since the summer. In midsummer the employees had succeeded in forcing out the plant manager because he was "of foreign origin."[126] At the end of August, the management stopped making its evening pickup of milk, blaming the added expense caused by the Popular Front's social laws, which required the plant (so management claimed) to let twelve workers go. Some of the fired workers were delegates of the local CGT union. So, on that Monday, the union went on strike and the workers occupied the plant. The shutdown of the plant meant that no milk was being picked up at all by Dupont, a catastrophe for many small farmers of the region.

After Subprefect Roger Pinel of Bayeux had failed to persuade the strikers to let a few workers pick up the milk that the farmers had put out that morning, now spoiling, Germain Boullot summoned his Greenshirts in the afternoon. Evaluations of the Greenshirts vary. The Left press speaks of 200–250 "adolescents."[127] The conservative press speaks of 400 peasants "with their heads on right" (la tête solide), mostly small farmers.[128] In any event, they wanted to pick up the milk themselves, taking the workers' place, and transport it to another Dupont plant at Trévières before it could spoil. Threatening to liberate the plant by force unless the government did so first, they occupied the Town Hall of Isigny. In a scuffle, the balustrade in front of the hall was pushed over and one police officer was slightly wounded.

Witnesses differ about whether the subprefect was at one point a prisoner of the Greenshirts. Dorgères said so; Pinel hastened to assure his superiors he was always free in his movements.[129] For the rest of the day, at any rate, the violence was only verbal. Late in the afternoon Dupont agreed to negotiate. At 9 P.M., the workers ended their occupation of the plant, and work resumed at the milk plant the following morning.

Soon after the Dupont strike had been broken, the victors held a huge rally in a meadow across the road from Babeur's milk producers' cooperative, just outside Isigny, on 27 September 1936. This meeting associated the Greenshirts closely with the most eminent representatives of agriculture and commerce of the whole region. The meeting, billed as a "Peasant Front rally," was officially sponsored by the departmental union des syndicats agricoles. Jacques Le Roy Ladurie presided. Henry Dorgères was the principal speaker. The Jeunesses Paysannes had been ordered to attend in their green shirts, to provide the security force, or risk expulsion from the movement.[130] Germain Boullot had a place of honor: he read the resolution to be voted on at the close of the meeting. Between 1200 and 2000 farmers were present—a good turnout, although the organizers had hoped for 5000, according to the subprefect of Bayeux.[131] Important representatives of the chamber of commerce and of local commercial interests were also present,[132] no less interested than the farmers in defeating strikes.

The climax of the occasion was an oration by Dorgères. Le Roy Ladurie introduced him as "the peasant apostle."[133] Speaking from a farm cart decorated with wheat sheaves under a canvas tarp, Dorgères (who was suffering from a cold or flu and who was making a strenuous round-trip from Paris and back within twenty-four hours for this meeting) was not in his best form. Nevertheless, he made a vigorous attack on the Popular Front: the devaluation, which, coming after the price of wheat had been set, amounted to robbing the peasants; the Wheat Office, which instead of advancing peasants' interests simply created 196 new public sector jobs and whose director received 8333 francs a month; "Monnet the Innocent," the new minister of agriculture, who had managed to go bankrupt twice in prosperous years on good land in the Aisne; and the rumor that government inspectors were going to search private homes to enforce a coming embargo on the private possession of gold (a curious rumor, possibly an echo of Roosevelt's measures in 1933 to take the United States off the gold standard and forbid the private possession of gold).

Dorgères was followed by Modeste Legouez, the national head of the Greenshirts. Legouez, who, as we have seen, had just come within 700 votes of defeating Pierre Mendès France in the parliamentary elections of April–May 1936 with a campaign marked by anti-Semitism, followed a denunciation of communism and Marxism with a diatribe against Louis Louis-Dreyfus, "the richest man in France," who battened on wheat imports while French wheat growers were starving; against the state fertilizer company; against social security; against civil servants; and against "teachers sold to Moscow."

Closing the meeting, Jacques Le Roy Ladurie added his own denunciation of the Popular Front. France, he warned, had three capitals: it took orders from Moscow and Madrid in addition to Paris; he summoned the farmers of the Bessin to unite instead behind their natural leaders: Babeur, Boullot, and Brohier.[134] These three men, all active farmers, as well as heads of farmers' organizations, personified the three kinds of institution on which Le Roy Ladurie hoped the peasants of France would build a corporatist France at the grass roots, as a potential alternative to the currupt Republic.

Félix Brohier, who raised prize horses, was president of the Fédération des Syndicats Agricoles de la Région d'Isigny. He stood for the *syndi-cat*, the local unit of a national network of organizations by which peas-ants would manage their own affairs. Henri Babeur, president of the local milk and cream producers' cooperative and theorist of the "interprofes-sion," stood for the specialized marketing groups that would be the building blocks of corporatism. Germain Boullot, finally, the leader of the Greenshirts of the Calvados, stood for direct action: the use of force by the peasants' own militia when necessary to defend peasants' interests.

A second strike closed the Dupont plant in Isigny from Tuesday, 8 December, to Thursday morning, 10 December, because five workers had been fired. By this time, Dupont had signed a department-wide collective contract (26 October 1936), which set up more formal grievance-settling procedures. But even though the prefect of the Calvados and the subpre-fect of Bayeux came to mediate, the Greenshirts still became involved. The prefect and subprefect received at the Town Hall of Isigny not only delegates of Dupont and of the CGT but also Henri Babeur, on behalf of the the the milk producers' cooperative, and Germain Boullot, president of the Jeuneses Paysannes of the Calvados.[135]

Negotiations began around 3 A.M. Around 4 A.M., some 100 Green-shirts slipped into the plant and occupied it, intending to take the place of the striking workers, pick up the milk, and treat it themselves. At 8 A.M., it was agreed that pickup and treatment would resume during the negotiation, and the Greenshirts left the plant.[136] The prefect concluded that the strike did not conform to proper procedure (there had been no advance notice, or *préavis*), and the firings were legal. In the interest of public order, however, Dupont agreed not to fire the five workers, though he declared that he had the right to do so. Two of the dismissed workers had been hired as temporary replacements of regular workers during the new paid vacations, which the Popular Front had just insti-tuted; the other three had violated work rules. All the workers returned to their jobs at the Dupont plant on Thursday morning, 10 December.[137]

By the following summer, it was generally accepted that Boullot and his Greenshirts would smash any strike in the Calvados that farmers felt damaged their interests. Commenting on the smooth accomplishment of the harvest in August 1937, the police commissioner of Caen observed that any communist or labor-union propaganda among the harvest work-ers "would be quickly wiped out by the action that Dorgères's Green-shirts, of which Boullot is the commander for the Calvados, would not fail to carry out."[138]

Indeed, a large proportion of Calvados farmers were sympathetic to the Greenshirts and Dorgérist direct action during the Popular Front years. With two different centers of peasants' anger—the milk-producing Bessin and the cider-producing Pays d'Auge—deeply committed to him, and with local notables of the stature of Jacques Le Roy Ladurie enthusiastically backing him, Dorgères had very favorable terrain in the Calvados in 1935–36. He made at least a dozen speeches there between 1931 and 1936. By March 1935, the police chief of Caen concluded that Dorgères "enjoys real popularity" in agricultural circles.[139]

More important, Dorgérism penetrated established agrarian organizations more deeply in the Calvados than in any other department in France. Consider the *chambre d'agriculture,* for example. It was very rare for its elections to be contested. In the arrondissement of Vire, in the poor inland *bocage* region of the department, however, a slate of "admirers of Dorgères, Croix de Feu, or sympathisers" won narrowly, by about 2500 votes to 2300 votes in the *chambre d'agriculture* election of 9 February 1936, defeating a more conventional slate of rural mayors and *conseillers municipaux.*[140]

Dorgères's lieutenant Abel Néel, the fiery defender of the *bouilleurs de cru* and "the principal lieutenant of Dorgères in the Calvados," according to the police commissioner of Caen,[141] sat in the Chambre d'Agriculture for the arrondissement of Pont l'Evêque; and André du Boullay, who had handed Dorgères a check for 5000 francs (and got into trouble for it) when Dorgères was under prosecution for a tax strike, sat in the Chambre d'Agriculture for the arrondissement of Lisieux. In the Chamber of Deputies, a peasant candidate supported by Dorgères, Jules Radulphe, was elected to the seat at Vire in a by-election in the fall of 1936. According to the subprefect, the force behind this surprising election of a farmer to the Chamber of Deputies was the *syndicats agricoles* of the region, "in which one finds many admirers of Dorgères, many activists."[142]

The French state, however, left very little room for Dorgérism to function. Boullot was ready for strong-arm work, and the local farmers were ready to call on him if the state did not perform its functions. But the state did. Such local vigilantism could contribute to the establishment of agrarian fascism in other settings, such as the Po Valley of Italy in 1920–21, where the Liberal state had ceased to function and where a strong national Fascist party gathered all such local sparks into one great flame. But in the Calvados, where the French Republic still operated, they had little serious lasting effect.

Furthermore, many local farm notables cooled on Dorgères in 1937. Jacques Le Roy Ladurie, a major supporter earlier, failed to invite Dorgères to the great Peasant Congress he organized in Caen in 1937, as we see in Chapter 4. Dorgères was on his own in the Calvados after 1937.[143] The French state and the conservative rural notables together were too powerful to need the help of rural fascism.

Organizing the Market:
Le Pétrolage des Petits Pois, Finistère, June 1938

The village of Pleuven, south of Quimper, in the Sud-Finistère, was almost unanimously Greenshirt in 1936–38. The Comité de Défense Paysanne of Pleuven can be better known than most other local Dorgérist organizations because the municipal archives of Pleuven contain a small treasure. In the attic of the *mairie,* there is the account book of the local *comité,* containing the list of all the young men of the village who paid 15 francs in 1938 for a green shirt. There are also several sheaves of green ticket stubs bearing the names of seventy-three persons in the canton of Fouesnant, including thirteen from Pleuven, who paid their dues to the CDP.

The Comité de Défense Paysanne of Pleuven was a weak organization. Its members did not need a powerful organization because they could rely on the traditional solidarity of their rural community. Pleuven was a commune of relatively homogeneous family farmers, without extremes of wealth or poverty. They were either owners or renters *(fermiers),* the latter sometimes better off than the former. As farmers, they had already been organized in 1929 into a *syndicat agricole* affiliated with the Office Central at Landerneau,[144] the economic arm of the all-powerful Union des Syndicats Agricoles du Finistère et des Côtes-du-Nord, run by the comte Hervé Budes de Guébriant.

The case of Pleuven illustrates very well the importance of a local leader, preferably the mayor, in the successful implantation of Dorgères's *comités de défense paysanne.* The mayors of rural communes were an essential link in the Dorgérist network. Without a mayor's acquiescence, it was hard even to find a suitable meeting space. The organizers of Dorgérist meetings liked to have the mayor on the podium. If a mayor became a militant (and most of the leading militants were also mayors: Suplice, Bohuon, and Néel), his entire commune and even the region around it could be enrolled actively in Dorgérism.

The mayor of Pleuven, Jean Chalony, never became as conspicuous on the national scene as some other Dorgérist mayors such as Bohuon or Suplice. But his success as a local organizer may serve as an instructive example. He was simultaneously president of the Syndicat Agricole of Pleuven, and he had been mayor since 1927, when he was only thirty years old. He united most of his neighbors in a CDP in 1935, and he carried many of them with him into direct action in 1938. Chalony was a middling proprietor (about forty hectares); he employed two farm laborers *(domestiques)*, who lived on the premises,[145] slightly above average for the commune of Pleuven.

Chalony was propelled into political activism by a tax problem, like a lot of Dorgérists. When a revision of the land tax rolls *(cadastre)* imposed large tax increases on his village in 1933, at a time when farm incomes were down, Mayor Chalony asked for postponement. Instead, the tax collector threatened Chalony and three other farmers in Pleuven with the sale of their property for nonpayment of taxes. Chalony consulted Dorgères (every farmer in France in trouble with the tax collector had heard of Dorgères after the Salvaudon incident of 18 June 1933). Dorgères wrote to him on 22 November 1933, offering to organize a demonstration if the *fisc* seized his property.[146] Dorgères said he would raise "all of *Cornouaillè*" to defend Chalony and praised him as a tough guy and a leader.[147] That was the strongest accolade Dorgères knew how to bestow.

Mayor Chalony's problems with the tax collector seem to have been smoothed over somehow, for there is no evidence of a sale (there was a lot of bluffing in these matters). The mayor was now ready, however, to take a more active role in Dorgères's movement. Chalony was one of the speakers alongside Dorgères at a mass rally in Rouen on 22 February 1935. He appeared in Breton costume, although, to the surprise of some, he spoke perfect French.[148] This appearance got Chalony into trouble when Dorgères was quoted by a local newspaper as advocating from the rostrum a peasants' tax strike. The French state was very sensitive about antitax movements in 1935. It prosecuted Dorgères and everyone who had been on the platform with him in Rouen, including Mayor Chalony.[149]

Chalony was acquitted of the charge of "conspiracy to organize a collective refusal to pay taxes" by the Tribunal correctionnel of Rouen on 29 August 1935,[150] and thus got off without any real cost except the time and trouble of a trial. Despite these tangles with the state (or perhaps even because of them), Jean Chalony remained a popular mayor. He served from 1927 through 1944, being reelected over scattered opposition in 1935. Even after the German occupation, when many rural mayors became unpopular because they had had to administer hated German requisitions—as Chalony had to do for the German *kommandantur* at Fouesnant—he continued as assistant mayor and as *conseiller municipal,* and he served on the electrification board for four communes. He is remembered as a popular mayor, with a touch of the Don Quixote, who tried to help those who needed it.[151]

The dues-paying members of the Pleuven CDP can be identified on the *liste nominale* of the census of 1931. They were leading citizens of the commune: substantial farmers (both renters and owners), mostly with a hired hand or two living on the farm. It was their sons, whose names also appear on the *liste nominale,* who bought green shirts in 1938.[152]

Once hardened under fire by his prosecution alongside Dorgères, Jean Chalony was ready to use the CDP and the Greenshirts to help himself and his neighbors when their most important cash crop, peas, faced a very poor market in 1938. The commune of Pleuven, along with neighboring communes in the canton of Fouesnant, had recently invested heavily in the intensive cultivation of peas for the cannery in Fouesnant. These were small mixed farmers, rather new to cash crops. Their exposure to the perils of the cash market was thus relatively recent. They were small producers, with no organization to help them, for while the *syndicats agricoles* affiliated with the great Office Central at Landerneau were very well served with group purchases, insurance, credit, and other material necessities, they were not conceived for influencing a market. The buyers for the large cannery in Fouesnant had the advantages of size, unity, and organization.

Brittany had become a major center for vegetables since 1900, and certain communes had become highly specialized in particular products. Plougastel, for example, was the strawberry capital. It had become the principal supplier for both the French and the British markets in the late nineteenth century, after the strawberry beds of the Paris suburbs had been destroyed in the Franco-Prussian war. The strawberry producers of Plougastel were highly organized in a vertical production-marketing pyramid under the dynamic Mathurin Thomas, who amassed all the positions from mayor of the commune and president of the *syndicat* of strawberry producers up to the board of the Office Central at Landerneau. It may have been Plougastel's highly efficient cartel that permitted the strawberry growers to navigate successfully the crises of the 1930s. In any event, the strawberry growers of Plougastel do not appear to have resorted to direct action, nor did Thomas's little empire seem to leave any room for Dorgérist recruitment or tactics. At least, that is a likely explanation of why the strawberries of Plougastel make no appearance in Dorgérist chronicles. Dorgérism offered, instead, "weapons of the weak." [153]

Dorgérism became an important weapon, in contrast, for the vegetable growers of northern Brittany. Farmers along a narrow coastal strip on the north shore of the Finistère (Saint-Pol-de-Léon and Roscoff) and the

Côtes-du-Nord (Paimpol and Saint-Malo) turned at the end of the nine-teenth century to the specialized production of vegetables—potatoes, arti-chokes, onions, and cauliflower. They developed trade circuits with the British market. Itinerant onion sellers ("Johnnies") went from Saint-Pol and Roscoff to England each winter. In the 1930s, the situation became very difficult for the potato growers of northern Brittany, when an infesta-tion of potato beetles *(doryphores)* gave the British a good excuse to close their market. The growers turned in desparation to Dorgères.

On 27 June 1937, Robert Bougeard, secretary of the Comité de Dé-fense Paysanne of the Finistère, at the head of 200–300 excited farmers and aided by Jean Bohuon (who was summoned by telephone from the Ille-et-Vilaine), threw sacks of potatos from the train at Saint-Malo to protest low prices. Bougeard received twelve days in prison, for violence against a police officer, and praise in the PAO.[154] Northern Brittany was the main conduit whereby the example of direct action by farmers was transmitted from the Dorgérists to the peasant activists of the Fourth Republic, like Alexis Gourvennec, who led growers of potatoes and arti-chokes of Saint-Pol and Roscoff to block roads and invade the subprefec-ture of Morlaix in June 1961.[155]

Peas were another highly localized crop in Brittany, concentrated in Plougastel and the canton of Fouesnant (including the commune of Pleu-ven) in the Sud-Finistère south of Quimper. The production of peas for canneries could be quite lucrative, but it was also risky. The size of the crop could vary considerably from year to year. Either extreme could mean trouble: an overabundant crop lowered the price, whereas a small crop reduced everyone's income even if the price was good. The pods ripened all together in early June, moreover, and it was imperative to get the highly perishable crop picked and sold within a few days. The risk of overripening or spoilage gave the buyers for the big canneries (such as the one at Fouesnant) powerful leverage in the annual price negotiation. The pea growers, lacking any mechanism for withholding all or part of their product or regulating its flow, had no means of applying pressure in the negotiation of each year's contracts. They faced the buyers, moreover, with no organization to speak for them. Thus they staked everything on a one-sided negotiation, under pressure of time, which could decide whether their year of effort would produce a livable income or penury.

The pea harvest generated a powerful solidarity by its own rhythms. When the pods were ripe, the entire population of the village was sum-moned, sometimes by drum. Everyone took part in the picking—women; retired farm laborers in their *[penty]*, or retirement cottage; schoolchildren (school was of course suspended; it always took second place to agricul-tural work in farm country). Just as the pea harvest involved everyone, so did the fate of the crop. It was thus relatively easy to create a powerful peasant solidarity—even if only briefly—around it.

Until 1930 or so, the producers of peas in Brittany endured the fluctuations of the market as they endured the vagaries of the weather. Their resignation lessened as they observed the producers of other crops managing to control their markets more successfully. Their patience came to an end with the Depression.

In the early summer of 1934 the prefect of the Finistère warned his government that the agricultural situation was very bad. In early June, he reported that because of an abundant pea crop, the price paid by the canneries was dropping from the 80 francs per 100 kilograms (a quintal, about 220 pounds) previously paid and would probably stabilize around half that, 40 francs per 100 kilos.[156] In early July, he reported that the peasant population had had to "make one more knot in the old wool stocking" and that commerce was suffering from the decline in peasants' purchases. Some peasants asked the prefect, "Don't you think the Revolution is coming soon?"[157]

The following year, the prefect felt obliged to become involved in helping to negotiate the price paid by the canneries for peas. On 27 March 1935, he presided over a joint arbitration committee of farmers and canners (a *commission paritaire*) to head off an effort to inflame this issue for political purposes. He thought it was too early to set a price, but he recommended that the pea producers unite (something that was far from being realized as he wrote).[158]

Matters had not improved two years later. Peas sold poorly again in 1937. The following winter, the weather was unfavorable, and the spring was dry. Expecting another bad year, the growers were tense. By January 1938, Dorgères's chief lieutenant in the Finistère, Joseph Divanac'h, was working with the pea growers there.[159] He was famous in western France for the judicial sale of his furniture and cattle on 1 February 1936, which had been aborted by a mammoth crowd (in the presence of both Dorgères and de Guébriant, the latter trying to calm things down). The newly fashionable device of a *commission paritaire* was incapable of negotiating an agreed-on price between canners and growers in advance of the harvest. Some eye-witnesses suspected that Divanac'h wanted the negotiations to fail and deliberately asked for too much on behalf of the growers.

In the interim, the Popular Front had generated bitter feelings among many peasants. While salaried workers seemed to be receiving more and more social benefits, peasants felt that they bore only the costs and received none of the benefits of the forty-hour week and other social laws. Dorgères's newspapers had beaten this drum every week since the summer of 1936, and his vision had more influence in the Sud-Finistère than did the Popular Front's view. Witnesses to the "battle of the peas" remembered that the growers' bitterness against the canneries (and the cannery workers) contributed to the failure of setting prices in the spring of 1938, for the growers believed that the pay increases and additional benefits received by the workers forced the canners to offer the growers less. Dorgères's perception of city-country relations as a zero-sum game seemed very real in the canton of Fouesnant in 1936–38.

When pea-picking time arrived in June 1938, the Dorgérists of the Sud-Finistère decided to try to assert greater influence on the market by a producers' strike. At a meeting on 6 June in Quimperlé, Joseph Divanac'h carried a motion to impose a strike on pea deliveries. Divanac'h signed a tract warning that "patrols will carry out severe penalties against those who refuse to go along." [160] Dorgères himself, it must be noted, did not appear in person in the Sud-Finistère during this strike. But the action was entirely in keeping with Dorgères's rejection of an unregulated market, his belief in peasants' self-help, and his dream of an agrarian utopia where the growers could set their own prices. And his principal lieutenants there, Divanac'h and Jean Chalony, carried it out.

Producers' strikes were a controversial new idea among militant farmers' movements between the wars—the sort of thing a radical new movement might undertake but from which an established *syndicat agricole* would shrink. [161] It was not easy to enforce a producers' strike among scattered individualist pea growers, moreover. Wool stocking makers in the English Midlands early in the industrial revolution had faced the same problem of how to enforce discipline among scattered artisans and had discovered Luddism: machine breaking. The pea growers found something roughly similar to enforce discipline in their strike. Wherever growers had ignored the strike and placed their bags of harvested peas on the road to be picked up, Greenshirts squirted a few drops of gas (automotive fuel) into each sack, which was then spoiled by the odor. [162] This action went down in local legend as "gassing the peas" *(le pétrolage des petits pois)*.

Crop destruction was an uncomfortable action for farmers. But the pea growers' reluctance to destroy crops was outweighed by their resolve not to remain passive any longer. To overcome the reluctance to damage a neighbor's harvest, the Greenshirts employed for each action came from a different canton. Those who acted in Pleuven were bused in from Pont l'Abbé and assembled in the Pleuven meeting room, where a local farm worker, Nader, showed them to the right targets. Pleuven's Greenshirts and Mayor Chalony went to Ergué-Armel. [163]

The *pétrolage des petits pois* aroused considerable opposition. The victims among the growers, as well as the canners, were angry. Charges were pressed. Twenty-five Greenshirts or their helpers were arrested and fined for actions in four locations, including Divanac'h himself and four men from Pleuven. The largest action was at the cannery of Le Heneff at Pouldreuzic, where ninety-one sacks (4.5 tons) were spoiled and fifteen men arrested.[164] Twenty-five years later, one of the leaders—Auguste Le Calvez of Plobannelec—was still known to his neighbors as *le pétroleur*.[165]

Joseph Divanac'h tried to defend this controversial action in an open letter to the press.[166] It was necessary to use strong measures *(méthodes qui frappent)*, he claimed, to draw public attention to the pea growers' plight. Moreover, the intended goal had been reached: the price had been raised from 100 francs per quintal (below cost) to about 130. The victims were "lacking in discipline"; they disobeyed the strike order, and it was necessary to make examples to teach the importance of "professional discipline." As a good corporatist, Divanac'h wanted to organize the producers in order to seize a major role in the structured market of the future. He bridled at the accusation that his Greenshirts had wanted to destroy the harvest. Their aims were much higher: to "defend the peasants' bread and that of their workers" and to stop the desertion of the countryside by achieving better living conditions for both farmers and farm workers. Divanac'h was most irritated by comparisons between the CGT's occupation of the factories in 1936 and the Greenshirts' *pétrolage des petits pois*. There are two sorts of revolutionaries, he observed: those who destroy and those who restore. If stronger measures are needed, he concluded, "we will take them."

The powerful Office Central at Landerneau came to Divanac'h's defense. In his monthly newsletter, F.-M. Jacq, the secretary-general of the Union des Syndicats Agricoles du Finistère et des Cotes du Nord and himself a shipper of vegetables from Saint-Pol, defended such actions in the exceptional circumstances of the moment, though they might not be permissible "once order has been reestablished, order in our institutions."[167] One hears in Jacq's language an echo of the Action Française's tendancy to call the Republic the "established disorder." The incident shows how far into the agricultural elite of Brittany acceptance of direct action had penetrated, led by a group that openly favored replacing the French Republic with an authoritarian, corporatist state.

It was not only in Brittany that market gardeners *(maraîchers)* were attracted to Dorgères's tactics. He also recruited many of the *maraîchers* around Paris and around the mouth of the Rhône in and after 1936. In the Midi, market gardeners were Dorgères's main recruits. He enjoyed a "certain success" in the "area of speculative agriculture" around Cavaillon (source of the famous melons), where the growers were "the most vulnerable to unforeseeable fluctuations in the economic situation." The local Fédération de Défense et d'Action Paysanne tried to stop the supply of new potatoes to the markets in Arles, Cavaillon, and Orange in May 1937 and to keep factory workers with new leisure time, since the Popular Front's forty-hour week, from competing with professional market gardeners.[168]

We see once again that Dorgères's most impassioned followers were not the most traditional, self-sufficient small farmers—this point is worth repeating. They were small producers who had come to depend on a cash crop but were insufficiently organized to deal effectively with the canners and distributors who bought their product. The *comités de défense paysanne* offered them a structure and a technique—direct action—for giving them some weight in the market.

The most spectacular, though brief, example of Dorgérist direct action among market gardeners was the series of strike that closed the great wholesale fruit and vegetable market of Paris, Les Halles, three times in the fall of 1936: 28–29 September, 19–20 October, and 16–18 December. Dorgérist direct action thereby reached into Paris and to the very citadel of the French agricultural market system. One can doubt that Dorgères was the uncontested leader of the *maraîchers*. But he claimed to be, and he took pains to get himself arrested among the demonstrators at les Halles twice to prove it. In the early hours of 20 October 1936, accompanied by his friend Suplice, he sat down in the police station, refusing to leave until his arrested comrades had been released, and was finally detained overnight himself. These closures of Les Halles were only momentary and they were never complete, as the southern suburbs of Paris around Arpajon refused to join in.[169] Nevertheless Dorgères came close to touching a major economic artery of the nation at this moment, and he aroused passionate denunciations in *L'Humanité* as a "starver of cities" *(affameur)* like the counterrevolutionaries of 1793.

We return, in conclusion, to the Greenshirt mobilization in Pleuven. An observer is struck by its personal quality and its brevity. A vigorous, respected, and committed mayor could carry a majority of a village with him, but not for very long. The enemy of Dorgérism was less active opposition than indifference. After their burst of activity, in the absence of some prosaic but continuing task, the Greenshirts of Pleuven demobilized. After the excitement of the *pétrolage des petits pois*, the notebooks of the CDP in the *mairie* at Pleuven contain only one final entry, months later: the remaining funds are turned over to a liquidator. The movement is dead. The green shirts are hung up in the armoires of the Sud-Finistère.

four
. . .

DORGÈRES, THE AGRARIAN ELITE, AND THE STATE, 1934–44

WHEN DORGÈRES BEGAN gathering the biggest political assemblages ever seen in rural France and threatening public order, the state had to decide how to react. Should the police, prefects, and magistrates of the Third French Republic ignore Dorgères and thus deny him the publicity he sought? Should they wink at his excesses because he was keeping communism out of the countryside? Or must the state uphold due process and the rule of law against Dorgères's claim to lawlessness in a higher cause?

The conservative notables of the French countryside, too, had to decide what to do about Dorgères. Should they ignore him, oppose him, try to coopt his mass following to fortify their own shaken hegemony, welcome his anti-Republican violence from a safe distance, or simply throw in their lot with him? Some of all these responses occurred among them in the 1930s. The extent of notable cooperation with Dorgères tells us how deeply his movement penetrated the French rural world by the mid-1930s and how successful he was in detaching parts of their clientele from the Third Republic. We widen our canvas in this chapter, for Dorgérism is not fully comprehensible alone, without attention to the variegated mosaic that was French rural society in the 1930s and to the allies, rivals, and accomplices Dorgères found within it. But first we need to know just how strong Dorgères's movement had become by the middle 1930s.

Dorgérism, 1934–40: Who, Where, and How Many?

We cannot design a map of Dorgérism in one single dimension. Neither region, socioeconomic situation, type of crop, political opportunity, nor even the accident of local leadership, by itself, can explain Dorgérism's pattern of success and failure. All of these dimensions enlighten us, but only partially, for the Dorgérist map was emotional as well as social, political, and economic.

Dorgères liked to claim that he received the same eager response from one end of France to the other.[1] In truth, his movement had narrow geographical limits: it was strong only in the north and west. Fortunately we do not have to rely on Dorgères's own claims about regional coverage. The establishment of the Peasant Corporation by the Vichy government in 1941–43 provides the best picture of Dorgérism's geographical distribution as of the end of the Third Republic. The picture is convincing because the men in charge of setting up the Peasant Corporation (Corporation Paysanne), comte Hervé Budes de Guébriant, the head of the powerful agricultural federation of the Finistère and the Côtes du Nord (Landerneau), and his principal associate, Rémy Goussault, took pains to identify all the local agrarian organizations that had an appropriately "corporatist" spirit in order to graft the corporation's departmental branches onto these living roots. They excluded only those farmers' organizations closely tied to the Third Republic's Left. Although de Guébriant and Goussault favored traditional notables, they were willing to include Dorgérists who had authentic local support. Indeed both had appeared on platforms with Dorgères. Thus their census[2] gives us a snapshot of conservative agrarian organizations at the close of the 1930s.

The first step in setting up the Corporation Paysanne was to choose a regional chairman *(délégué régional)* for each department[3] to establish the corporation's structures within his territory. This official usually became the head *(syndic)* of the corporation for that department. Four departments wound up with Dorgérist *syndics.* Modeste Legouez, former national chairman of the Greenshirts, was regional chairman (and, subsequently, *syndic)* of the Eure.[4] The Maine-et-Loire experienced a "véritable revolution" when Henri Dézé, an old Parti Agraire militant friendly to Dorgères, was preferred in a secret ballot to the head of the established *syndicat agricole.*[5] In the Loir-et-Cher, Henri Brisset, head of the departmental *comité de défense paysanne* (CDP), became *syndic* when permament institutions were set up in 1942, supplanting the Radical Senator Henri Decault, prewar boss of the department's agricultural organizations and hence, at the outset, the regional chairman. A fourth department (Ille-et-Vilaine) acquired a Dorgérist *syndic* in the corporation elections of September 1943, when

Dorgères's closest lieutenant, Jean Bohuon, first president of the Comité Central de Défense Paysanne, upset the former *syndic*, the august comte Roger de La Bourdonnaye, in a secret ballot of all the local *syndics* of the department.[6]

Two departments had Dorgérist assistant *syndics:* Jacques Eynaud, in the Sarthe, and Bohuon (until his promotion in 1943), in the Ille-et-Vilaine. In a dozen departments—all but one in the north and west—Dorgérists were powerful enough to win a few places among the fifteen or so members of the departmental organizing committees.[7] The Pas-de-Calais, where CDPs had mushroomed in 1936–38 as strike-breaking devices in sugar beet and market-gardening areas, had the most: two out of fifteen, growing to four by 1943—Lucien Declémy[8]; Gabriel Tellier[9]; Ernest Pecqueur; and the influential head of the sugar beet lobby, Pierre Leclercq.[10]

After a "very violent outburst" by Dorgères, Octave d'Hespel, Dorgères's first employer, was forced under protest to increase the Nord's organizing committee to eighteen members in order to raise the Dorgérist contingent from one to three.[11] The organizing committee of the Seine-Inférieure began with two relatively new Dorgérists, Hilaire Lahalle, a mayor from the Caux, and Paul Haquet, the inflammatory editor of a farmers' newspaper that circulated in the Bray and the Caux, *le Moniteur agricole de la Seine-Inférieure.* Pierre Suplice, who had been in the shadows since the heady days of 1937, was added in the elections of December 1943, another case of a popular Dorgérist profiting from the discredit of the notables who had first taken charge of the corporation.[12]

Four more organizing committees contained two Dorgérists: Loir-et-Cher (baron Louis Goury du Roslan, one of Dorgères's major financial backers, and Clotaire Hénault, who had stepped aside as a PAPF candidate in the by-election at Blois in 1935 to let Dorgères run for the *chambre*); Maine-et-Loire (Alfred Macé and Eugène Forget, first president after the war of the FNSEA[13]); Aisne (Paul Plume and Adolphe Arduin); and Mayenne (Raymond Delatouche[14] and Marcel David). Others had one Dorgérist: Joseph Divanac'h in the Finistère; Paul Barillet in the Seine/Seine-et-Oise; Jacques Lefevre in the Oise; Abel Néel in the Pays d'Auge; Albert Mitonneau in the Charente-Inférieure;[15] and even the Bouches-du-Rhône, where Honoré Caillol, a market gardener, won a place. One might also legitimately include Henri Robichon in the Loire-Inférieure, once president of the departmental CDP but expelled by Dorgères for speaking at a rally of Doriot's Front de la Liberté. There were, finally, Dorgérist district *syndics,* such as Germain Boullot in the Calvados, and communal *syndics* at the village level, such as Jean Chalony in the Finistère. Even at their best, of course, Dorgérists were always a small minority.

A regional bias is clear: Dorgérism was strongest in the north and west. The Bouches-du-Rhône was the only department in the Midi where Dorgérism was strong enough to win a place in the corporation leadership. It was virtually absent in most of the southern, southeastern, and southwestern departments. Dorgères could mount an occasional grand spectacle there, like the mass meeting at Revel (Haute-Garonne) on 18 August 1935,[16] but he rarely established a solid footing south of the Loire. That gives us a first grid. It also suggests that Dorgérism was aided by a prior predisposition to antirepublican activism. A good test case is the Côtes-du-Nord, where Dorgères was popular in the conservative eastern part of the department but not in the more republican west; another may well be the Sarthe, where Dorgères's followers were apparently concentrated in the traditionally conservative western half.[17] The traditional attachment of farmers in the Midi and the southwest to the Radical or Socialist parties made France very different from Germany and Italy, where no farming regions were traditionally linked to the Left.

Dorgères did well where other rightwing activist peasant movements had prepared the way. He was able to absorb and build on the *cultivateurs-cultivants* in the Ille-et-Vilaine, the Entente Paysanne in the Charentes,[18] and the Masse de Combat des Paysans in the Somme.[19] He also inherited the anti-Republicans of the Parti Agraire after it split in 1936. The principal exception was Joseph Bilger's *Bauernbund* in Alsace, which flourished independently and separately, like most political movements in that province, after giving Dorgères the idea of the green shirts.

Dorgérism did not simply reflect the map of political conservatism or religious observance, however. Even in areas favorably predisposed to Dorgères's message, some farmers felt already well defended by the traditional agrarian associations: the *syndicats agricoles* and the specialized associations for particular crops, like those for wheat (AGPB), sugar beets (CGB), and wine (CGV). Even in the darkest days of 1935, large numbers of French farmers—particularly the better-organized ones—felt no need for Dorgères's drastic medicine. Even in the west and north, the spaces open to him were leftover interstices of the powerful conservative agrarian establishment. The *syndicats agricoles* occcupied far more terrain than Dorgères everywhere, even in northern and western France, and so Dorgères was never able to be the "unifier" of French agriculture.

Dorgères's talk of *jacquerie* and verbal brandishing of pitchforks might suggest that he appealed to the most backward, isolated, and marginal peasants, cynically manipulated by rural squires.[20] No simple socioeconomic criterion will identify Dorgères's followers, however. His claim to speak for the entire "peasant class" was not entirely false. He did indeed draw some support from almost every rural stratum, from day laborers through big cultivators of industrial crops[21] to *chatelains*.[22] Despite the creation of worker sections, however, when he transformed his *comités* into *syndicats de défense paysanne* in 1936 as the Popular Front approached, he recruited few poor sharecroppers and day laborers.[23] The identifiable leaders of Dorgères's movement were small to middling but independent landowners and renters.

There is evidence that many of Dorgères's listeners were "new poor," owners and employers who would tolerate no further degradation of their position. Dorgères himself—like all conservative agrarians eager for social peace—was sympathetic to the plight of renters *(fermiers)*, who clamored for reduction of their rents in the light of collapsing income and for recognition of their investments and other rights when a lease expired *(droits du fermier sortant)*. But his audiences did not always agree.[24]

As we see in our account of Salvaudon's sale, Dorgères was reluctant to take sides in the frictions that set tenants against landlords during the Depression. If he took some pains to distance himself from the narrow self-interest of landlords,[25] it was perhaps because that reproach was so plausible. The prototypical "peasant" of Dorgérist doctrine was a small or middling family farmer, preferably independent, living by his own labor and that of his wife and children—the ideal toward which he hoped all rural French society would tend. In this, Dorgères was in complete accord with the UNSA in the 1930s and its postwar heir, the FNSEA.[26] Rural grandees—whether hereditary landlords or modern industrial farmers—were happy, of course, to shelter behind the image of the independent small family farmer, all "peasants" together.

The narratives cited in Chapter 3 indicate that Dorgères enjoyed his greatest success at the margins of the cash crop market. Vulnerable modernizers clutched at him in desperation: small producers of cash crops for the city (milk and vegetables), who had borrowed and made major investments and were newly exposed to market pressures but too poorly organized to deal effectively with concentrated large buyers. Indeed market position may be a better key to Dorgérism than any other socioeconomic criterion: type of land tenure, size, subjection to rural notables, or economic backwardness.

Dorgérist areas were often politically polarized, Isigny for example. The few Dorgérist zones in the Loire seem to have been places where the Left had already succeeded in organizing some of the farmers.[27] Conservatives may have turned to Dorgères in communes where the Left seemed to be gaining. Nothing made polarized agricultural areas automatically Dorgérist, of course.[28]

It has been tempting to link Dorgérism to apple cider[29] or milk or market gardening by some kind of "crop determinism." These were all important constituencies but not universally so. Those unquenchable rebels, the *bouilleurs de cru,* or home distillers of hard apple and pear cider, were enthusiastic Dorgérists in the Calvados, but the leaders of the revolt in the Orne rejected him as a "politician,"[30] and those in the south and east ignored him.

A good leader was the most indispensable feature of a successful Dorgérist branch. Without the lucky accident of an energetic, tough, and respected local chief, a promising sector could well remain passive. Where capable young chiefs arose from genuine peasant backgrounds, like Modeste Legouez, Jean Bohuon, and François Coirre, as well as among middling farmers who cultivated land they owned or rented, like Joseph Divanac'h and Pierre Suplice, Dorgères helped them achieve regional or even national careers in a way hitherto unknown in the conservative regions of rural France.

But the Dorgérist map was not static. Above all, Dorgérism was limited in time. Fueled by fear and anger, it blazed up with the multiple crises of the mid-1930s and then subsided. Fortunately for the Third Republic, its 1935 peak did not coincide with the peak of urban antirepublican activism, the Stavisky riots of February 1934, or even with the polarization of 1936.

If the capacity to arouse an excited crowd was Dorgères's strength, his weakness was the slackening that inevitably followed. Like those other excitement-driven movements, communism and fascism, Dorgérism was vulnerable to emotional cooling off. It had the additional liability of depending on farmers' sons, who had to go home to milk the cows or put up the hay. Dorgères could draw on a far smaller reservoir of skills and free time than urban movements, whether middle class or working class. He could appeal to almost no students and few militant intellectuals. His militants were an anomaly: farmers able or willing to leave their land for sufficient periods of time to sustain the movement's tasks of speechmaking and organizing. Local CDPs had no paid officials; the national office in Paris had very few. In contrast, the *syndicats agricoles* could build their more cautious style of advocacy on a much stabler membership because these "fertilizer shops" *(boîtes à engrais)*—as Dorgères loved to call them, his contempt laced with envy—furnished commercial services to their members. Their large pool of subscribers provided numerous volunteers and helped pay for full-time staffs.

The study of any particular area, therefore, is likely to reveal wild fluctuations of membership and activity. Dorgères and his lieutenants were constantly founding CDPs and then coming back a few years later to found them again. Dorgères's home department of Ille-et-Vilaine may serve as an example. He claimed to have founded the first CDP there at a protest meeting against social security, in Pierre Morin's garage in Rennes in January 1929, and to have gathered 20,000 peasants in Rennes on 1 February 1930. In August 1934, however, the police in Rennes described it as a "skeletal organization" with only about forty members.[31] It rebounded in October 1934 with another big rally. In 1936, however, complaining that the CDP in Ille-et-Vilaine was "rudimentary," Dorgères started up with new associates.[32] In March 1937, he proclaimed that "l'Ille-et-Vilaine is awakening,"[33] although in November 1938 he complained of that department's "culpable indifference."[34] And the Ille-et-Vilaine is supposed to be a major department for Dorgères, the one that elected a Dorgérist *syndic* (Jean Bohuon) in 1943. Areas of new growth—such as the Pas-de-Calais, the Sologne, parts of the Calvados and the Finistère, and parts of the Forez in 1937–38—tended to be counterbalanced by decay in old areas like the Seine-Inférieure.

This roller coaster of mobilization and relaxation makes membership statistics meaningless. Dorgères made large claims about the size of his following, but numerical precision was never his forte. In 1937, he claimed that his movement had grown since 1935 from 35,000 members to 300,000, across forty-one departments.[35] Two years later he claimed 550,000 members in seventy-two departments.[36] Not only do these totals seem improbable, but also the impression of steady, cumulative growth is profoundly misleading. Late 1935 may well have marked the CDPs' peak; there was probably some slippage after 1936, except in a few areas of localized agitation. In August 1935, a moment of high excitement, when Dorgères addressed some of the biggest meetings of his career[37] and was sentenced to prison for advocating a tax strike, he claimed his membership had quadrupled.[38] Such a surge is not inconceivable, but a decline probably followed. By contrast, the Union Nationale des Syndicats Agricoles (UNSA) claimed 1.2 million farm families—five times the size of the CDPs at their most favorable self-estimate.

Quality, Dorgères retorted, mattered more than quantity. He liked to claim that the CDP "was by far the strongest [agricultural] organization in the country because our members were militants and not just clients of a fertilizer store."[39] If you took away the mere commercial clients from the UNSA's 1,200,000 members, he said in a Peasant Corporation meeting on 9 July 1941, it (the USNA) would have only 20,000 real militants.[40] The UNSA, he added, had filled up with veterinarians and *notaires*, who only pretended to farm. Dorgères claimed to speak for an authentic and determined peasant elite with real fighting spirit.[41]

Another way of identifying the opportunities available to Dorgères is to consider the failings of his rivals. As we see in Chapter 1, the established agricultural organizations that occupied most of the space that

Dorgères wanted to invade were deeply shaken in the middle 1930s by their failure to deal with the multiple crises of French agriculture. Their loss of legitimacy gave Dorgères his moment of opportunity. Dorgères could pull members from the established *syndicats* by offering two things that their notable leaders could not: a more intense and egalitarian form of belonging and the satisfactions of direct action, by violence if necessary.

The notable agrarian leaders recognized in the 1930s that the *syndicats'* rather disengaged form of association, founded on deference to hereditary leaders and membership in cooperative commercial services, had become inadequate in the face of economic crisis and the Left's efforts to split off a peasant proletariat. Dorgères was right, they conceded, to want to "create stronger ties between the farmers and their *syndicats.*"[42]

The *syndicats agricoles* were already responding to this challenge by organizational devices: a dense network of local *syndicats* at the base and, at the top, a new relationship to the state through corporatism. The founders of social-Catholic syndicalism in the late nineteenth century had already advocated complete coverage of the territory, broadening down to the grass roots by creating a local *syndicat* in each commune. Félix Garcin had already done this around Lyon, as had Adrien Toussaint around Dijon.

Jacques Le Roy Ladurie followed the example of these social-Catholic pioneers when he took over the Syndicat Agricole of the Calvados from the old count d'Oilliamson in the late 1920s. He crisscrossed the department, setting up branches in each commune. He wanted an activist base. In other departments, where the old *syndicats* slumbered under the leadership of remote Third Republic grandees, aggressive younger leaders built new rival federations or unions based on a dense network of communal associations and peasant ideology.[43] Vichy's Corporation Paysanne, in the same vein, tried to create a branch in each commune in order to mobilize and organize the mass of small peasants more effectively than the Left.

In their dealings with the state, conservative agrarians of the 1930s wanted to create a corporatist system within which the organized professions, instead of a faceless bureaucracy, would plan and direct the economy. Corporatism was the runaway vogue among conservative economic theorists during the Great Depression, when classical liberalism—the free market of supply and demand—was universally deemed to have failed. Almost all economists, businessmen, and farmers in 1930s France who were not socialists believed that a substitute for both liberalism and socialism must be found—the famous "Third Way"—and that the most promising solution was to let the organized professions run a planned economy themselves, under the remote supervision of a night-watchman state. A form of corporatism was to be resurrected after the Liberation as joint governance *(cogestion)* by the government together with the farmers' organization, the FNSEA. This modified corporatism was to become the way in which French agricultural policy was made and applied under the Fourth and Fifth Republics.[44] Experiments of the 1930s among the conservative agrarians, in search of new forms of mobilization, organization, and political pressure, including Dorgérism for a time, was a major way station in that itinerary.

Dorgères had the same ideas about organization (insofar as such things interested him). He wanted to create a *comité de défense paysanne* in every commune, and he was a fervent corporatist. His program departed in no way from that of the conservative agrarians. But it was not the intellectual scrutiny of a program that brought his crowds together. Dorgères offered a form of group solidarity that differed in three ways from that of the SAs. First, the basic cement was the excitement of action within a closely knitted group, something nearer to the fraternity of the Left's labor unions. Second, his groups were led by their peers rather than by paternalist notables. This meant, however, that Dorgères could no longer rely on the organic solidarity of an inherited social hierarchy, to draw my terms from Emile Durkheim. As a social conservative he did not oppose organic solidarity head-on, but as a child of his times he thought it necessary to supplement it with mechanical solidarity.[45] Hence up-to-date devices to fuse his followers into a homogeneous and obedient mass, such as colored shirts, insignia, oaths of unconditional obedience, and a motto: "Believe, Obey, Serve" *(Croire, Obéir, Servir)*.

Dorgères was distinctive primarily for the frankness and belligerency of his calls for direct action. In a world where public order was a supreme good, Dorgères put action above order. Brandished pitchforks and broken windows were his trademark. Whenever a conservative agrarian referred to these elements in the 1930s. often with disapproval, everyone knew that he meant Dorgères. In reality, Henry Dorgères was not behind all the violent peasant demonstrations that marked the Depression era. The angry farmers who destroyed the gate of the prefecture of the Eure-et-Loir at Chartres in 1933 were led by the PAPF militant Pierre Mathé; the farmers who battled the striking sugar refinery workers at Toury (Eure-et-Loir) in 1936 were also affiliated with the Parti Agraire. But Dorgères won the media battle.[46] The public identified him as the leader of all direct action by peasants in the 1930s.

Dorgères believed firmly that only force worked, and he was not afraid to say so. It was "triumphant action,"[47] and nothing else, that won concessions from the state. It was the barking dog that was fed.[48] Had not the state caved in on *assurances sociales* and provided a separate regime for farmers? Had not the CGT recoiled before the "harvest volunteers"?

Dorgères aimed his violence at two enemies: the Left and the state. He liked to give the impression that he was readier than others to do physical battle with the Marxists. Dorgères's followers found the traditional agrarians neither tough enough nor close enough to their public to repel the rising "red wave":[49] harsher times required tougher responses. As Bohuon said, "It's wimps on the Right and crooks on the Left."[50] Toughness, virility and cleansing pervaded Dorgérist language. In truth, however, it was mostly the theater of violence that the CDP provided, as in the ritual humiliation of some brave rural schoolteacher or civil servant scheduled to "provide the rebuttal" to a peasant orator. Indeed, Dorgères's friend Suplice did himself rough up Renaud Jean, the Communist party's peasant specialist, during a rally at Yvetôt in the Caux (Seine-Maritime) on 26 July 1936. The fisticuffs were minor, but both *L'Humanité* and the *Progrès agricole de l'Ouest* talked about this highly symbolic clash for weeks.

As for the state, the Dorgérists claimed that it failed to protect farmers from either the Marxists or from cheap imports, so that the peasant half of the nation could not earn a decent living from its work. If the French state did not protect French farmers from strikes, occupation, or collectivization, the farmers "would be their own policemen"[51] through direct action. If the Republic let the degradation of the peasants' condition continue, Dorgérism offered an alternative: replace the parliamentary Republic with an authoritarian, corporatist "peasant republic." Here, too, frequent invitations to the peasants to throw deputies into the manure pile was more verbal than real, though Dorgères boasted to an interviewer later that his followers had manhandled thirty parliamentarians.[52]

Dorgères's violence aroused conflicting responses among the conservative agrarian notables. Félix Garcin, the very influential leader of the Union du Sud-Est and absolute master of everything agricultural in ten departments around Lyon, repudiated Dorgères forthrightly: "Violence suits only the weak. . . . I will speak to you neither of pitchforks, nor of sickles, nor of guns."[53] Some other agrarian leaders who disagreed with Dorgères's tactics may not have been sorry to see someone else force the French state to take farmers' problems seriously. The Permanent Assembly of the Presidents of the Chambres d'Agriculture (APPCA), headed by the Radical Senator Joseph Faure, never mentioned Dorgères publicly, but it published the CAP communique of September 1935.[54] Its Executive Committee even issued a statement on 1 October 1936 (again without mentioning Dorgères by name), complaining that protesting market gardeners got arrested while striking workers did not.[55] Count Hervé Budes de Guébriant, head of Landerneau, seems to have wanted to capture

Dorgères's masses for himself. Jacques Le Roy Ladurie was ready, at least for a time, to cooperate unreservedly with Dorgères.[56]

Dorgères's capacity to draw the conservative agrarian notables into alliances was crucial to his progress from the margins toward the center of French public life. Desperate for new ways of enlisting and guiding the peasant mass, fearful of losing their followers to Left or Right, and eager to bring pressure on the state, some leading notables were attracted to Dorgères. His toughness against the Left made the attraction stronger. His actions against the state, however, tended to alienate many notables. Most agrarian notables, as we see in the next section, were to become by 1937 more interested in the joint administration with the state, which a later generation was to call *cogestion,* than in attacking the state head-on. In 1934–35, however, in the depths of the crisis, some of them were tempted to follow Dorgères even against the state. The Peasant Front was the high watermark of notable cooperation with Dorgères.

The Peasant Front

Dorgères's inclusion in the Peasant Front, founded in June or July 1934,[57] was a great step forward for him. The Peasant Front was a coalition of most French farmers' organizations of the Center and the Right for the purpose of pressing the government to solve the crisis of agricultural prices. It was made up of three blocs.[58] The "agrarian bloc," Fleurant Agricola's electoral party—the *Parti Agraire et Paysan Français* (PAPF)—seems to have proposed the front in the first place. The "professional" bloc provided the organizational bulk since it included Le Roy Ladurie's vast Union Nationale des Syndicats Agricoles (UNSA) and the specialized associations that lobbied for each of a dozen important crops, such as wheat (CGPB), sugar beets (CGPB), wine, milk, meat, flax, and so on. The "peasant defense bloc," made up of Dorgères's *comités de défense paysanne,* was dedicated to direct action.

The three elements of the Peasant Front summarize very well the different tactics that conservative French farm leaders wanted to employ in their effort to force the Third Republic to favor their interests: electoral politics, pressure group politics, and direct action. The semiofficial APPCA,[59] headed by the Radical senator of the Corrèze, Joseph Faure, did not feel free to participate in the Peasant Front, but it did draw close to its positions.

The Peasant Front was made possible by a dual convergence: the previously law-abiding PAPF and UNSA were radicalized toward direct action by the growing anger and frustration of their constituents. On the other side, Dorgères wanted respectability and recognition from the traditional notable farm leadership.

The UNSA took giant strides toward a new activism as its legitimacy was shaken in the 1930s. The rue d'Athènes, which had never been able to call on state aid for its credit and insurance cooperatives, got into trouble as soon as their distressed customers began to default on loans and drop out of the mutual-aid insurance associations *(mutuelles)*. By 1933, the Union Centrale des Syndicats Agricoles faced bankruptcy. The indefatigable Jacques Le Roy Ladurie, head of the Syndicat Agricole of the Calvados—aided by his banker brother, Gabriel—was able to assemble enough rescue capital to refloat the rue d'Athènes's structures. A new generation of more aggressive leaders replaced the courtly marquis de Vogüé and his titled colleagues in 1934.

Jacques Le Roy Ladurie became secretary-general, and a militant corporatist and avowed admirer of Mussolini, Roger Grand,[60] became the new president (1934–37). They renamed the old Union Centrale the Union Nationale des Syndicats Agricoles (UNSA). They changed far more than the name, moreover. Both leaders had a more active political agenda. Because they doubted that a parliamentary republic was adequate to French national needs, they wanted to replace it with something with more authority, better capable of defending traditional French values. They also wanted to replace the discredited market economy with some kind of corporatism, in which the great economic interests—agriculture, industry, and commerce, organized into powerful self-governing associations—would take over from incompetent parliamentarians and civil servants the business of managing a regulated, autarkic economy. Proud of farming his land personally and claiming peasant identity, Le Roy Ladurie changed the name of the UNSA journal in 1937 to *Syndicats paysans*.

Roger Grand set the new tone at once with an inaugural speech that called for "a great new breath" of "national union" and a regime that would give the family and the organized agricultural profession a greater role.[61] He made no secret of his admiration for Mussolini[62] and for his belief that corporatism had been the salvation of other European states in trouble, including "our hereditary enemy Germany."[63] On the other side of the barricades, he also found good things to say about the Swedish cooperative movement.[64] In any event, for Roger Grand, "now Liberalism and Individualism have had their day."

Radical elements of the PAPF were also moving toward direct action, after disappointing electoral results in 1932. Vice-president Pierre Mathé was using more and more intemperate language. He was often at Dorgères's side at meetings, such as the immense Peasant Front rally (possibly as many as 10,000 people) at the Salle Wagram in Paris on 28 November 1934. On that occasion they covered the parliament with insults, and Dorgères threatened to bring the Republic to its knees by a tax strike and the withdrawal of peasants' savings from public savings institutions. The audience then took to the streets of Paris, where they battled with the police in a minor agrarian replay of the riots of the previous 6 February.

Dorgères claimed to dominate the Peasant Front (a claim that his colleagues doubtless disputed) and, through it, to speak for two million French farmers.[65] At the least it meant that the conservative agrarian establishment was willing to give him its blessing.

The Peasant Front's minimum program, published in December 1934, covered the points on which the three blocs could agree. The front's basic purposes were to unify French agriculture, to enunciate a propeasant farm policy, and to mobilize enough mass demonstrations to oblige the government to adopt its program. It opposed the reigning economic policy of deflation and urged an increase in agricultural prices and the defense of "national labor." It advocated "professional organization of the national economy." It called itself "Republican," but it conditioned its loyalty to the Republic on a "reform of the State based upon the family and the craft."[66]

In 1935, the Peasant Front moved more decisively toward Dorgères's brand of activism. This was the moment when the usually cautious, established, conservative agrarian leaders of France came closest to direct action against the Republic. Indeed conservative rural notables were more disaffected under the conservative Premier Pierre-Etienne Flandin in 1934–35 than under the Socialist Premier Léon Blum in 1936, out of phase with industrial and commercial notables. Not only did 1935 mark the nadir of farm prices, but also Flandin failed to consult the established farmers' associations when he redirected wheat policy back toward the free market in December 1934. The ongoing price collapse exposed cruelly the farm leaders' inability to help their constituents within the existing constitutional system. It was therefore their moment of maximum disaffection from that system, when many of them were ready to try Dorgères's way.

Dorgères had been advocating a tax strike since at least late in 1932.[67] In 1935 he and his colleagues in the Peasant Front planned a more comprehensive form of economic resistance to the French state. They created an action arm within the Peasant Front, the Comité d'Action Paysanne (CAP). The CAP asked the entire peasantry of France to sign a petition affirming that, if the government did not take action on peasants' problems by 15 September, they would, upon receipt of a "command for action" (*mot d'ordre*) from the CAP, cease all purchases and break off all contact with French public authorities (including the tax collectors). The CAP leaders, convinced that the French government was willfully ignoring the central importance of a healthy peasantry for the French economy, wanted to demonstrate to French business and to the treasury the weight of peasants' purchasing power. It was thus more an educational enterprise than massive civil disobedience, though it teetered on the brink of illegality. The French tax collectors understood it as the tax strike Dorgères had been threatening for some time.

The petition, accompanied by a draft text of the "command for action," was widely circulated. It appeared in most of the local agrarian press, and there are traces in many departmental archives. It was said to have been signed by 100,000 people in ten days, including 70,000 in the Finistère alone.[68] In the Seine-Inférieure, 15,000 people were reported to have signed in the first few days.[69] The Peasant Front implemented its "command for action" in slightly moderated form (the tax strike became a "moratorium," and the boycott of public officials was omitted) on 16 September 1935.[70] The peasants' purchasing and taxpaying strike was, however, a fizzle, and the CAP quietly went to sleep after its one bold initiative. In 1936, it is true, it was in the CAP's name that Adolphe Pointier asked peasants to come to the Somme and help break the agricultural strikes of that summer.[71] But that was, apparently, a personal gesture. By then the CAP was moribund.

We can follow the fate of the CAP petition in the Calvados, one of the departments where it was most vigorously promoted, for there the heads of the two most powerful agricultural organizations were close to Dorgères. One was Jacques Le Roy Ladurie, head of the departmental agricultural association, the Union des Syndicats Agricoles du Calvados, as well as secretary-general of the nationwide union of agricultural syndicates; the other was André du Boullay, head of the main farmers' organization of the hard cider country, the Syndicat des Agriculteurs du Pays d'Auge.

Le Roy Ladurie had his organization mail the CAP petition to every local *syndicat agricole* and every rural mayor, with a personal letter from him that urged all peasants to sign: "It is high time that [French agriculture] defend itself, if it wants . . . to keep everyone that lives from the soil from becoming extinct."[72] André du Boullay's organization not only distributed the CAP petition but also, a few months later, collected money to help pay Dorgères's legal expenses. Du Boullay handed Dorgères a check for 5000 francs before 600 members of the Syndicat des Agriculteurs du Pays d'Auge during its annual meeting at Lisieux on 19 October 1935, an action for which the Republic attempted to prosecute him.[73]

According to the prefect of the Calvados, about 10% of the department's population and about 30%–40% of those subject to the tax on agricultural profits signed the petition, but it seemed to make no difference in tax receipts during the fall and winter of 1935. Very few of the signers actually made good on their threat not to pay the tax on farm profits *(bénéfices agricoles)*. By early in the following spring, the tax collector of Isigny reported only three or four who still refused to pay. The tax collector of Grandcamp had a little more difficulty since twenty-seven farmers, including a number of *conseillers municipaux,* were refusing to pay. In spite of this antitax campaign, tax receipts in 1935 were running a little ahead of 1934, 97.5% of the tax on land and buildings *(contributions directes)* and 97% of the income tax *(impôt général sur le revenu et les impôts cédulaires)* having been received.[74] This result was typical of Dorgérism: a lot of theater and verbal fury but meager concrete results.

Outside the Calvados, the "command for action" produced some protest gestures but resulted in major effects only locally. Generally, enforcement of the tax moratorium depended on a supportive local mayor. Officials in the Seine-Inférieure reported that 90% of the villagers of Pierre Suplice's commune of Bourg-Dun (whose activities as Dorgères's main lieutenant in that department are discussed in Chapter 3) did not pay their taxes in 1935.[75]

The giant Office Central des Associations Agricoles du Finistère et des Côtes-du-Nord at Landerneau (Finistère) was reported to have been sent 92,209 unpaid tax forms, weighing a total of ninety-eight kilos.[76] Landerneau was deeply involved in Dorgérism by this time. Count Hervé Budes de Guébriant, its president and absolute ruler of agricultural organizations in western Brittany, showed up in person when Dorgères whipped 5000–6000 people into excitement at Quimper (Finistère) on 1 February 1936 to block the sale of Joseph Divanac'h's cattle for unpaid taxes. Asked later about what Dorgères had meant to him, de Guébriant said, "Dorgères was my Minister of War."[77]

But if the "command for action" had any measurable impact on the national level, we have not been able to find any evidence for it. It is quite likely that many of the farmers who sent in their tax forms limited themselves to that one gesture of protest and then quietly paid up later.[78]

The ministers of the interior and of finance took the threat to the government's revenues very seriously, however. The Ministry of Justice was already prosecuting Dorgères and several of his colleagues for impeding the collection of taxes following an incendiary speech in Rouen on 22 February 1935, even before the CAP had been formed. It was thus with full knowledge of Dorgères's legal troubles that prominent notable rural leaders like Jacques Le Roy Ladurie, André du Boullay, and Adolphe

Pointier joined him in the Peasant Front and its action arm, the CAP, and that some of the French conservative agrarian elite helped finance Dorgères's actions against the Republic.

Where Did the Money Come From?

Dorgères's enemies on the Left liked to claim that he was funded by wealthy, noble landowners from the Vendée, or the intransigently royalist *(chouan)* country of Brittany, and that Dorgères was himself the vicomte d'Halluin. Dorgères himself claimed that his movement was funded by small contributions from the peasants' proverbial wool stocking. In fact, the profits of the newspaper, CDP dues, and other sums collected from within the movement probably met much of its modest costs. Dorgères's movement required relatively little money. It had very few paid employees and depended mostly on local volunteers.

The CDPs were capable of generating a good bit of cash from their own membership. In addition to individual dues,[79] local branches sent funds to the central office.[80] The PAO kept up a more or less perpetual appeal for special contributions and published each week the names of contributors and the amounts each contributed.[81] Beyond that, the movement charged entry fees to meetings,[82] sold insignia[83] and photographs,[84] and took up collections during meetings.[85]

These internal sources were never enough, however, and Dorgères constantly exhorted his supporters to contribute more. The prefect of police in Paris believed that Dorgères also received money from wealthy supporters, but it was common for the police and the public to underestimate the sums of money that mass movements of the New Right could generate from within.[86] Some big landowners in the west, in addition to the duc d'Harcourt, such as the marquis de Kérouartz and the conservative Deputy Etienne Le Poullen, were believed to contribute money to the movement.[87] It is certain that wealthy businessmen outside the west, such as the baron Louis Goury du Roslan, an insurance executive with a big estate in the Sologne,[88] and Jacques Lemaigre-Dubreuil, the head of Huiles Lesieur, the giant vegetable oil company, contributed money. These big contributors were grouped in a shadowy Rural Alliance, which Dorgères never mentioned publicly before 1940.[89]

On two occasions in 1935, Lemaigre-Dubreuil seems to have lent Dorgères an airplane: on March 24, the day of the first round of voting at Blois, when Dorgères had promised to speak at Josselin (Morbihan) on behalf of Joseph Cadic, and again on October 21, when he was speaking in the Eure and needed to reach Quimper in a hurry because the cattle of the president of the CDP of the Finistère, Joseph Divanac'h, were being seized for auction by the tax authorities.[90] When Dorgères buzzed the crowd for effect upon arriving over Quimper, he had attained the technological glamor of the better-known urban demagogues of his era. But such contributions by the wealthy should not blind us to the reality of popular support for the *comités de défense paysanne* and their capacity to raise at least part of their own funds.

The Republic against Dorgères

The French Republic had no doubt that Dorgérism was a genuine threat to public order and perhaps to the stability of the regime. The ministers of the interior and of finance began to take note in 1929 when Dorgères was opposing social security in the west. When he managed to mobilize enough angry farmers to block a judicial sale against Valentin Salvaudon in 1933, the state prosecuted him. In all, the Ministry of Justice was to open nearly twenty files on Dorgères.[91] The government prosecuted him eight times between 1933 and 1939 and convicted him six times. Two of these convictions resulted in jail terms, the other four in fines.[92]

Cabinet ministers dealt in person with the Dorgères problem. In May 1934, Minister of Justice Henri Chéron had already declared Dorgères "a dangerous agitator" and informed the Public Prosecutor *(procureur-général)* at Rennes that "if he has violated a law, do not hesitate to prosecute him."[93] In June a Justice Department official wrote that Chéron "was upset by the campaign led by this Dorgères . . . who is exciting the peasants against the government and organises demonstrations that are sometimes violent." Chéron wrote "approved" in the margin and ordered his staff to "follow this case with the greatest attention."[94]

Georges Pernot, Chéron's successor as minister of justice in the government of Pierre-Etienne Flandin, personally saw to it that Dorgères was prosecuted for the 22 February 1935 speech in Rouen. Pernot peppered his subordinates with demands for greater speed: "Please see," he wrote the chief magistrate in Rouen in April, that there is "no unjustified delay."[95] Indeed, even before the Rouen meeting, Pernot had been making notations in the margins of papers concerning Dorgères. In December 1934 he had urged Rennes to "watch" Dorgères "very attentively" after the PAO had insulted Flandin and boasted of the CDP's "secret plan." On 18 January, even before the Rouen speech, the Director of Criminal Cases and Pardons was telephoning Rouen to open an investigation of Dorgères.

In February 1935 Pernot brought Dorgères to Prime Minister Flandin's personal attention.[96] Dorgères's tax strike came close to the state's jugular vein, and the state reacted vigorously. Prime Minister Flandin had good reason to be interested. He had gotten off to a very bad start with the agrarian notables, first by cutting the bread price for Christmas 1934, then by failing to consult them before issuing a new grain law that same month. Even the usually staid *chambres d'agriculture* reached their peak of anger and opposition in December 1934. The Assembly of Presidents held a special meeting in early December that they called "the Estates-General of Agriculture." There Joseph Faure accused the government of "improvisation" and "contempt for the legislators' will" and published a Peasant Front communiqué of 17 December that threatened a purchasing strike as an example of the "harmful" effects of government ineptitude.[97] As 1935 opened, the assembly wrote Flandin an angry letter, accusing him of showing disrespect for all of French agriculture.[98] Flandin was eager to prosecute Dorgères because he wanted to pick off the most conspicuous leader of peasant rebellion before it could contaminate the notables any further.

The records of this trial bear the marks of government anxiety. The examining magistrate had Dorgères's home and offices searched, as was to be expected; he also ordered a search of the home of the powerful comte Roger de La Bourdonnaye, president of the Chambre d'Agriculture of the Ille-et-Vilaine, whom the authorities suspected of backing Dorgères. They found nothing incriminating, and the government was then interpellated by the monarchist and anti-Semitic Deputy Xavier Vallat for subjecting the count to this indignity.

On 11 July 1935, the Tribunal Correctionnel of Rouen found Dorgères and several of his associates (two of whom, the rural mayors Pierre Suplice and Jean Chalony, were featured in Chapter 3) guilty of "collective refusal to pay taxes."[99] It sentenced Dorgères to eight months in prison (later reduced on appeal to six months, suspended). While his case was being appealed, Dorgères exploited the victim's role skillfully. His powerful allies organized rallies to protest his conviction. In Normandy, a protest meeting drew over a thousand people in a meadow near Bény-Bocage (Calvados) on 25 July. Among the speakers was Jacques Le Roy Ladurie, secretary-general of the UNSA, who declared that they should use "every means" to keep Dorgères out of prison.[100] On 18 August at Revel (near Toulouse), Le Roy Ladurie said before an audience of some 15,000, "In order to emprison him, they will first have to pass over our bodies."[101] Adolphe Pointier, president of the AGPB and agrarian leader of the Somme, called a protest meeting at Amiens.[102] Somewhere between 6,000 and 20,000 people gathered in Rouen on 25 August to try to influence the sentence about to be handed down.[103]

Justice Minister Pernot was now so eager to finish off Dorgères that he forced the prosecuting magistrate at Rouen to postpone his August vacation until Dorgères's appeals had been denied and final sentences were handed down.[104] On 29 August 1935, Dorgères was sentenced to six months in prison, suspended; his secretary, Lefèvre, received two months, suspended; and the others were acquitted. These reduced sentences did not persuade the government to let Dorgères alone. In the fall of 1935 he was being watched closely by the Sûreté Nationale.[105]

The Popular Front, the Left government that came to power under Léon Blum in June 1936, had its own reasons to find Dorgères alarming. They feared him less as a danger to the treasury than as a branch of French fascism, alongside the urban-based antiparliamentary leagues. Interior Minister Salengro ordered the prefects on 20 August 1936 to keep a close watch on Dorgères's *comités de défense paysanne,* as well as on Colonel de La Rocque's new Parti Social Français. The authorities also acted quickly and decisively when Dorgères threatened to become the "starver" of Paris in the market gardeners' strikes of the fall and winter of 1936.[106] Dorgères was charged with attempting to rig prices *(action illicite sur le marché)* and provoking disorder *(provocation à des attroupements)* following the 29 September strike; he was arrested at Les Halles in the predawn hours of 20 October (with Suplice) and detained again by the police on 18 December.[107]

The Popular Front government never thought it necessary to dissolve the Greenshirts, however, as it did such city-based leagues as the Action Française and the Croix de Feu in June 1936. On 16 August, Dorgères published a defiant editorial in PAO, as if to remind the authorities of his actions, in case they had forgotten him: "We entrust Cambronne with replying to those who want to dissolve our movement."[108] In fact, the government never proposed to dissolve Dorgères's renamed *syndicats de défense paysanne.* Although the prefect of the Seine suggested dissolution in late December 1936 and early January 1937, after the market gardeners' three brief strikes,[109] that step—perhaps to Dorgères's chagrin, considering the impetus that dissolution gave to Colonel de La Rocque—never took place.

By 1936, however, the steam was clearly going out of Dorgères's movement. Agricultural prices had begun to improve at the end of 1935 and continued upward in 1936, removing the most universal source of anger among farmers. There were indeed areas of new growth, where some energetic local chief played on some major local issue: family support payments *(allocations familiales)* in the Sologne and strikebreaking in the Pas-de-Calais. Germain Boullot founded new sections and multiplied financial contributions by 2.5 in the Calvados in 1937–38.[110]

On a national level, however, Dorgères's mass meetings became rarer. He claimed one mammoth audience of 30,000 in 1936,[111] but after 1936 only once did he even claim to exceed 10,000.[112] Most Dorgérist rallies now gathered only a few hundred participants, poor by the standards of the time. The Greenshirts had slipped to a handful in Brittany; they never held a second annual convention. After the Paris Congress of Peasant Unity in September 1937, Dorgères held only regional congresses in 1938. He seemed to be losing that quality most precious for a demagogue: momentum. Whereas Dorgères had absorbed local peasant newspapers in 1935, in 1937 the *Défense paysanne du Massif Central* (Aurillac) and the *Action paysanne* of Toulouse were swallowed up by Alain de Chantérac's fast growing *Effort Paysan,* linked to Le Roy Ladurie and the UNSA. Graver still, by late 1937, Dorgères had lost many of his notable allies. By that time, he clearly seemed less useful to the grandees.

The Notables Drop Dorgères

It became clear in 1937 that relations were cooling between Dorgères and some of his notable supporters. The clearest sign was that Dorgères wasn't even invited to the great Peasant Congress at Caen on 5–7 May 1937. There the leading conservative agrarians of the UNSA declared publicly for corporatism at the invitation of Dorgères's former ally Jacques Le Roy Ladurie, under the influence of the two leading theoreticians of agrarian corporatism, Rémy Goussault and Louis Salleron.

We know at least the public reasons for Le Roy Ladurie's break with Dorgères.[113] Their association had been close in the near insurrectionary days of 1933–35. On 27 September 1936, following the Greenshirt strikebreaking action at Isigny (discussed in Chapter 3), Le Roy Ladurie told his Norman followers to have "limitless confidence in their great leader Dorgères."[114] He appeared (uncharacteristically taciturn) on a platform with Dorgères as late as 5 December 1937.[115] But the disagreement had already been made public in a September 1937 editorial, which claimed that the *syndicats agricoles* were "less noisy" but "more efficacious" than other kinds of agricultural organizations (i.e., the *défense paysanne*).[116]

It was not that Jacques Le Roy Ladurie had lost his taste for a good fight. He was arrested in June 1938 at Castres—in the company of his new activist ally, Alain de Chantérac, of the Tarn[117]—for violating the mayor's ban on a peasant rally at the War Memorial. But Le Roy Ladurie wanted to invest his main energy in building local corporatist organizations, which would take over from the state the task of regulating the agricutural economy. His preference for supplanting the state through precorporatist construction, rather than attacking it frontally, was even more explicit in an editorial of May 1939. Some, said Le Roy Ladurie, (without doing Dorgères the honor of naming him) want to "tear everything down before beginning to build." As for the notables, "It is better to make your voice heard" than to give in to "noisy agitation . . . it is better to build than to tear down."[118]

Dorgères's campaign against the way family support payments *(allocations familiales)* were to be applied to peasant families deepened the break with Le Roy Ladurie and the notables of the USNA. When the French Republic decided in 1932[119] to establish a system of salary supplements to families according to the number of their children, in an effort to increase the birthrate and equalize the burden of child rearing, the special character of farm families delayed its application to agriculture.

It was relatively easy to extend this benefit to wage laborers on large farms on terms similar to those of workers in industry, as the Popular Front did in August 1936.[120] But that affected only a few large farms, mostly in the northern plains. What of small farmers who received little or no salary to be supplemented? What of renters and sharecroppers or small landowners, who cultivated their own couple of acres and worked at times for neighbors or their own fathers to round out their income? It was not until the spring of 1938 that family support payments were extended to sharecroppers *(métayers)* and only in June 1938 that they were extended on a voluntary basis to independent small farmers and rural artisans.[121]

The problem was how to pay for family support. Salaried workers paid for part of this program with regular payroll deductions *(cotisations),* like those of social security. Once more, with a new social program, the French state was proposing to add to the paperwork and cost of farming and was interfering in personal relationships on the farm. Dorgères probably believed that the peasants' opposition would revive the heady days of 1933, when he led a genuine mass resistance against social security. He urged his followers to boycott the system entirely until peasants received the same benefits as anyone else and until the state paid all of the peasants' *cotisations.*

The extension of family support to tenants, some family members, and (under special conditions) some independent farmers gave Dorgères a tricky problem. Many small farmers, in fact, wanted to receive the new benefits. Dorgères's demand was "family allocations equal for all and paid by the state"; that is, farm families should receive the same benefits as, say, the families of civil servants but without paying a *cotisation*.

Here and there some rural populations responded to Dorgères's boycott. Resistance spread in 1937–38 in the Sologne area of the Loir-et-Cher, where Dorgères's meetings persuaded many peasants who had enrolled in family support accounting offices *(caisses d'allocations familiales)*, founded by the departmental *syndicat agricole,* to withdraw from them.[122] Thousands of peasants protested in front of the courthouse at Angers (Maine-et-Loire) in the spring of 1939 when some Dorgérist and Parti Agraire militants were tried for obstructing the family support system.[123] But the opposition to family support was much weaker than the opposition to social security had been.

Dorgères also found his position on state interference becoming ambiguous. He was no longer trying to keep the state out of peasants' affairs but to increase state aid. His approach to family support, simultaneously statist and confrontational, also widened his differences with the notables. The notables, in contrast, saw an opportunity to strengthen their organizations by adding family support accounting offices to their already elaborate empires.[124]

The UNSA, led by Le Roy Ladurie, was particularly hostile to Dorgères's tactics. It had campaigned for the extension of family support to peasants, and it wanted the *syndicats agricoles* to profit financially and institutionally from setting up the accounting offices *(caisses)* to administer it. They saw an opportunity to begin building elements of a protocorporatist self-administration of farmers' affairs, from the ground up. They wanted to become the liaison between the peasants and the state, as was indeed the main function of notables. Dorgères wanted to fight the system until the state agreed to pay for it. Since the most advanced corporatist agrarian leaders would not follow him, he was left on the margins of rural life.

The rupture with leading notables in 1937 was no doubt a painful blow to Dorgères. He put the best face on it he could by calling his own Congress of Peasant Unity in Paris in September 1937, a relative failure (even he claimed only 15,000 people).[125] In compensation, he grew more strident in 1938 and 1939. Although his intransigent activism won a following in a few new areas (the Pas-de-Calais, the Sologne, the Maine-et-Loire, a few spots in the Forez) and continued expansion in the Calvados, his shrillness was partly a function of his isolation. He accused the UNSA and its network of *syndicats agricoles* of being mere "shop-keeping organizations" and "fertilizer stores," unfit for leadership and more interested in clients than in political action. Some agrarian activists were drawn to Colonel de La Rocque's Parti Social Français, which made a particular appeal to farmers after 1937 and which appeared to have more future at that point as a genuine catchall party, capable of appealing to all classes.

Dorgères's other main new theme at the end of the 1930s was the danger of war. Starting with Ethiopia in 1935 and growing more insistent with each successive crisis by which Hitler and Mussolini dismantled the 1918 settlement, Dorgères reminded rural families that farm boys would once again bear an unfair burden if France fought for the Spanish Republicans or the Bolsheviks. Here Dorgères tapped a deep visceral feeling,[126] but so many of the rural notables were saying the same thing that he lost his distinctiveness. Jacques Le Roy Ladurie proposed that in the coming war, skilled workers should alternate with peasants in spending time at the front.[127]

The government was no longer alarmed by Dorgères's campaigns. On 11 April 1938, Minister of Agriculture Georges Monnet urged the minister of justice to take sanctions against Dorgères's CDP for the circular it was sending to farmers that explained how to avoid paying *cotisations* for their employees' family support.[128] But even though the two ministers followed Dorgères's campaign against the family support program in 1938 and 1939, and although they gathered evidence on fifteen more cases[129] and prosecuted him successfully in two of them[130] (plus a suit by the Deputy Robert Mauger for "blows and injuries" during a meeting in Romorantin on 26 March 1939), they agreed in June 1939 that "by now" Dorgères's articles "were no longer of great interest."[131] The government also hesitated to arouse sympathy for Dorgères and to give his declining movement publicity. For these reasons, the Ministry of Justice closed without action twelve of the fifteen dossiers opened against him in 1938–39.

Dorgères had failed to make himself indispensable to the conservative farm leaders of France. They found that they could fight the Left, recruit the small peasants, keep order in the countryside, bring pressure on the state, and even share administrative authority with it by themselves without having to call on the likes of him. The future lay with conservative agrarian organizations in France, not with a radical-rightwing peasant activism. The *syndicats agricoles,* federated in Jacques Le Roy Ladurie's UNSA, were the principal base on which the Vichy Peasant Corporation was to unite all French farmers in a single association and on which, in turn, the main postwar French farmers' association, the FNSEA, was to develop a modified form of corporatism (rebaptised *cogestion*). Another base was the Jeunesse Agricole Chrétienne (JAC), which offered a Christian-social framework for ordering peasant society in a less confrontational way than did Dorgères; it was rapidly becoming the most important intellectual force among conservative farmers in the 1940s and after. But Dorgères's form of direct action certainly had a future whenever the established agrarian organizations seemed to have compromised too deeply with the state. Moreover, he had made a part of the French peasantry skeptical of the Third Republic and ready for something else.

Triumph and Disappointment: Dorgères at Vichy

The outbreak of war in September 1939 realized Dorgères's somber prediction: the peasants would once again have to pay a "blood tax." Dorgères's patriotic reflexes and relish for a fight were as strong as his pacifism, however. Volunteering at the age of forty-three for the active military service he had missed in World War I, Dorgères saw combat in Alsace and on the Somme in May and June 1940 as a corporal in a commando unit *(corps franc)* of the Fifteenth Regiment of Alpine Infantry. On 12 June, as General Weygand's effort to form a final defensive line along the Somme failed, Corporal D'Halluin was taken prisoner with his unit near the English Channel at St.-Valérie-en-Caux (Seine-Maritime), not far from his friend Suplice's home village. He managed to escape while being transferred to a prisoner-of-war camp. As he said in his postwar trial, he did not want to undergo a second German captivity. He was awarded the Croix de Guerre.

Returning to Paris, Dorgères found that he could not resume publication of his newspapers there (he later claimed that the German occupation authorities prohibited it, but the severe newsprint shortage was more likely responsible). So he went to Lyon and managed to relaunch his weekly *Cri du sol* in a greatly reduced format, at first on only one side of a single sheet of white newsprint. The first postarmistice issue appeared in Lyon on 23 August 1940.

The replacement of the Third Republic by the new Etat Français under Marshal Pétain promised to open a brilliant career for Dorgères. Everything he had struggled for seemed realized. The hated regime of parliament and political parties had been swept away, and the liberal market system with it. The peasants' enemies—the Left, the politicians, the intellectuals—were cowed. Now that food was scarce, city people humbly begged for the peasants' help. A National Revolution was setting up an authoritarian state based on the values of family and *métier*. At its head was an old war hero, who proclaimed that "the peasant must be highly honored because he continues, with the soldier, the essential guarantees of the existence and safety of the country."[132]

Dorgères could expect to be called on, for the new Etat Français would need new kinds of links with the population, especially with its agrarian half.

On 26 July 1940, Dorgères began pressing his claims on the new government in a letter to Dumoulin de Labarthète, who (he later claimed) had given him advice in 1935 and who was now the head of state's chief of staff. In a follow-up letter on 15 October he wrote, "I believe that I am, at this moment, the man who has the closest contact with the Peasantry, and also with the population of country towns, thanks to my organizations in the Unoccupied and Occupied Zones."[133] Dumoulin may well have replied in some encouraging way, for Dorgères wrote again on 5 December, suggesting himself, Bernard Faÿ, and Thierry Maulnier as an ideal team to set up "the movement that you want to create."[134]

Dorgères's efforts to find a place in the new regime were rewarded in a modest way on 24 January 1941, when he was made a member of the Conseil National, the assembly of notables charged with helping Pétain draft the new constitution. Dorgères was also an early recipient of Pétain's new civic decoration, the Francisque, as Number 153.[135] The most important arena of action for any ambitious farmers' leader in 1940–41, however, was the Peasant Corporation (Corporation Paysanne), created by the law of 2 December 1940. The Peasant Corporation was supposed to give French farmers the three things that their antiparliamentary leaders had been demanding since 1934: parity with workers and the urban middle class, a single united organization, and self-governing structures to administer their own conditions of work and life.[136]

Although Dorgères had been a conspicuous proponent of corporatist self-government during the 1930s, he had nothing to do with drafting the law that set up the Peasant Corporation. That was primarily the work of the jurist and corporatist theoretician Louis Salleron and of Rémy Goussault, a former official of agrarian pressure groups and now the director of the UNSA's newspaper *Syndicats paysans,* who had gained particular notoriety in 1935 by attending the Nazi Peasants' Day *(Bauerntag)* at Goslar.[137] Dorgères could hardly be left out, however. He was made one of the corporation's nine directors-general, with particular responsibility for propaganda, when the corporation's organizing committee, Commission d'Organisation Corporative (COC), was set up by the ministerial order of 21 January 1941.[138]

When the Peasant Corporation's local structures were finally established, in a laborious process of consultation with local agrarian notables that lasted into 1943, Dorgères himself and his *comités/syndicats de défense paysanne* played a relatively limited role. The UNSA's "shopkeeper *syndicats,*" which Dorgères had so despised, were to form the real backbone of the Peasant Corporation.

Dorgères worked hard to fight the UNSA's emerging dominance within the corporation and to win a larger place for his people. In a "very violent outburst" on 9 July 1941 in the COC, Dorgères insisted that the UNSA's numbers were inflated: if you deducted the passive commercial clients, one would find hardly 20,000 real militants. His *syndicats de défense paysanne,* he maintained, were actually "the strongest [farmers'] organization in the country" because they were made up of authentic militants.[139] Dorgères and some of his most powerful allies at this time, such as Pierre Leclercq, head of the sugar beet lobby, intervened often in the multiple local struggles for predominance in the process by which organizing committees were set up within each department. As we saw earlier, they actually succeeded in expanding the number of Dorgèrists in the organizing committees of departments like the Pas-de-Calais and the Nord. Dorgères was not satisfied with this limited representation, of course, and tried to intervene in a number of other cases, without much success.[140] In the end, the Dorgèrists played only a minor role in the Peasant Corporation, confined to areas where local leaders were too solidly entrenched to ignore.

We can follow Dorgères's efforts to establish his own authority at the top in the minutes of the meetings of the COC.[141] Dorgères spoke less than his more experienced and polished colleagues on the commission, and he seemed constrained by the formality of the meetings. He started well: at the April 1941 meeting, after his "lively success" in communicating enthusiasm for the corporation to 500–600 farmers at Bourges, de Guébriant congratulated "dear Dorgères" for his work. (De Guébriant always addressed him familiarly as "Dorgères," but he spoke to the others more formally as "Monsieur".)

Dorgères reported in November 1941 and January 1942 on the orators' schools he had set up in two zones, which were, in reality, merely three-day documentation sessions for about forty young speakers. The commission praised him for this "gratifying initiative."[142] His repeated proposal for a Peasant Corporation insignia had little effect, however. He proposed a Francisque, Pétain's personal decoration based on the gallic two-headed ax, with a superimposed bunch of grapes or sheaf of wheat, claiming that he had sold 600,000 of his own CDP insignia of crossed pitchforks superimposed on a sheaf of wheat with very positive effect before the war. The others clearly had no intention of letting Dorgères appropriate the corporation's symbolism.[143]

Sometimes Dorgères showed a little of the old fire. When someone objected that he was straying from the agenda, the minutes record his blunt "I don't give a. . . ."[144] When the issue of whether Masonic ties were incompatible with positions in the Peasant Corporation (it was decided that they were), he said, "Take the Jews out, too."[145] The trouble was that while the others spoke of grand general principles, Dorgères tended to focus on detailed complaints he had picked up in some rural café: for example, in Normandy, Belgian renters *(fermiers)* were snapping up all the leaseholds and pushing rents up.[146] He took an increasingly negative tone: peasants were being left to "stew in their juice" instead of being confronted by peasant orators who "get themselves shouted at for two–three hours" and could then "drain the abcess," "deflate" the crowd, and let the bad humor out.[147] To Dorgères's disappointment, the corporation had not authorized him to name a propaganda delegate in each commune—that is, to place clones of Jean Bohuon or François Coirre in every village and thus complete the work the CDPs had begun. He began to predict that "the fine enthusiasm is going to be extinguished easily."[148]

The matter that divided Dorgères most bitterly from his colleagues on the COC was control of the corporation's press. Dorgères seems to have assumed that his position as delegate-general for propaganda would give him authority over the agricultural press, which was, after all (as he reminded his colleagues on 20 November 1941), the *métier* he had exercised without a lawsuit for twenty years.[149] But at the September meeting of the commission, one of the many Dorgères missed, the corporation's press activities had been assigned to the central staff, under Jean de Blois and Rémy Goussault. De Guébriant refused to change his decision and asked Dorgères to cooperate anyway. Said Dorgères: "I won't until I get authority over the press."[150]

Subsequently Dorgères felt free to complain (quite effectively, given the evolution of opinion) that the agrarian press was not working well and that peasants were being turned away by the corporation's "statism" and its failure to address the concrete concerns of the smallest peasants. For their part, the top officials of the corporation were exasperated by Dorgères's habit of playing the lone wolf. Even André du Boullay, who once collected funds to help pay Dorgères's legal bills and was now the corporation's regional delegate for the Pays d'Auge, complained in August 1941, in a letter to de Guébriant, of Dorgères's "discourteous tone . . . toward us" and his criticism of his colleagues. Du Boullay thought Dorgères wanted to use his position in the corporation "for his own personal ends."[151]

Dorgères's failure to exert the influence he felt was rightfully his within the corporation has two explanations. Personally, he was much more skillful in the market square than in the committee room. His talents for administrative maneuvering were more modest than those of agrarian grandees like the comte Hervé Budes de Guébriant, the first president of the corporation's organizing committee, and the seasoned officials like Goussault who surrounded him. More fundamentally, the *défense paysanne* was structurally weaker than the "shopkeeper *syndicats*," which Dorgères claimed to despise. Zeal and authentic calloused hands counted for less than administrative skill and structural solidity when the Peasant Corporation was built.

The builders of the corporation constructed it as if for eternity, patiently seeking local "living forces" in each of the 30,000 rural communes on which to root a network of active peasant *syndicats*. Initially their work was welcomed in conservative regions and accepted in Republican regions with more or less willing acquiescence. By 1943, however, the corporation had become distorted into a hated state machine for gathering foodstuffs for the hungry cities and for the grasping Germans. But that is another story. The important thing for our purposes is that two important elements of the peasant utopia of the 1930s had been realized: unity of every farmers' organization, including insurance offices, credit agencies, and cooperatives, within a single system[152] and the assignment of public functions to the organized agricultural profession. But the unifier was not Dorgères; it was the UNSA, and the corporatist design was increasingly subverted by the centralized direction necessary to meet ever-swelling German demands for food deliveries.

On trial in 1945–46, Dorgères insisted that he had left the Peasant Corporation at the end of 1942 because he had seen the hand of Marcel Déat in the appointment of Max Bonnafous as minister of agriculture.[153] In fact, the entire organizing committee offered its collective resignation in December 1942, not because of the Allied landing in North Africa a month earlier, followed by the German occupation of the formerly unoccupied zone of southern France, but because its work was done and the permanent structures were ready to be set up. In those permanent structures, the *défense paysanne* was to become slightly stronger than in the temporary ones, as grass-roots disgruntlement with the Peasant Corporation discredited some of its first leaders.

Dorgères's departure was somewhat counterbalanced by the presence in the Peasant Corporation's National Council of Pierre Leclercq, the sugar beet lobbyist and Dorgères's ally, and the arrival in September 1943 of Jean Bohuon, which "marks a very great day."[154] The new *syndic national,* moreover, was Adolph Pointier: an old ally of Dorgères from the Salvaudon sale in 1933 and from the Peasant Front and its *comité d'action paysanne* of 1935. But Pointier represented the big wheat and sugar beet growers of the Paris basin and had little time for Dorgères in the affairs of the Peasant Corporation.

Even before he left the corporation, Dorgères found other resources that permitted him to play the independent role that suited him best. The *Cri du sol* continued to appear every week until July 1944—occasionally censored at first for striking too militant a tone[155]—supported by 20,000 francs a month from Marshal Pétain's staff. He also seems to have received support, as early as 1941, from the Secretariat of Peasant Propaganda at the Ministry of Propaganda, under Paul Marion, who had admired his pugnacious style in 1935.[156] Although the Syndicat Central de Défense Paysanne had been closed down in the name of peasant unity, along with all other prewar farmers' organizations, Dorgères remained in touch with his faithful in the provinces and dreamed of reviving his movement. Encouraged by the election of Bohuon as *syndic* of the Ille-et-Vilaine and some increased representation in the Pas-de-Calais, he sent a circular to his supporters in September 1943, hinting that it was time for the *défense paysanne* to become active again.[157]

Meanwhile he submitted ten private reports on peasants' opinions to Marshal Pétain between February 1943 and July 1944.[158] Although Dorgères's secretary testified at Dorgères's postwar trial that some of these documents were designed to cover him in case Laval or the Germans searched his offices, Dorgères made no such defense himself. We can assume that his wartime writings honestly reflect his feelings about the Vichy regime.

Dorgères never wavered in his faith in "the Pétain miracle, the equivalent five centuries later of the Jeanne d'Arc miracle."[159] He enjoined his readers to "work without asking questions" with a "blind faith" in Marshal Pétain.[160] The defeat had permitted France to "make an orderly revolution," which would produce "a peasant France" with fertile families where peasants could work without fear of overproduction,[161] liberated from the influence of Jews, Freemasons, and Communists.[162] The peasants had realized their dreams of peace and prosperity.[163] Collaboration opened up the possibility for French peasants to produce for export: "France must and can become the garden of Europe."[164] Even the draft of workers for German war plants had special virtues for peasants: for once, there was parity between workers and peasants in the "blood tax."[165] After the Allies landed in North Africa, the peasants' duty was to "listen only to one voice, that of Marshal Pétain" and "follow him blindly."[166] After D-day, with Allied armies ashore in Normandy, Pétain was still the "only one chief," obedience to whom was the only way to avoid civil war.[167]

Dorgères felt rising doubts, however, about the Vichy government and administration. Many other French people drew a similar distinction between the good Marshal Pétain and the bad advisors and administrators who deformed his message. Dorgères's particular disillusion with Vichy was colored by his own failure to play the role he expected in the Peasant Corporation. By October 1943, after he had ceased to play any role in the corporation, Dorgères denounced it as the "take-over of all of agriculture by one group" (i.e., the UNSA) and "the slave of the administration."[168]

Dorgères's disappointment with Vichy also reflected a general shift in agricultural opinion from hopeful expectation about the corporation in 1940 to irritation and, finally, to anger at the corporation's role as enforcer of the rationing, requisitions, and government regulations of the occupation regime. The parity that Dorgères expected between peasants and city people in the "new peasant order"[169] turned sour as urban Frenchmen accused the peasants of growing fat by starving the cities.[170]

Dorgères understood the trend of Laval's government in 1943 as a move backward toward the old regime. On the one hand, the corporatist experiments of the first days turned more and more to outright statism under the exigencies of war government. On the other hand, Laval surrounded himself more and more with former parliamentarians and other cronies, including Agriculture and Food Supply Minister Max Bonnafous, whom Dorgères considered (erroneously) a protégé of Marcel Déat, the "most anti-peasant" journalist of prewar France.[171] Dorgères's public quarrel with Déat in October 1943 helped Dorgères in his postwar trial.

Even Pétain's gift of peace receded in 1943 as the tide of war turned and an invasion drew near. Dorgères warned Pétain by 1944 that most peasants would side with the Allies in an invasion and that they were not sure whether the "terrorists" and "bandits" of the Resistance who menaced their crops were patriots or pillagers.[172] Although he urged Pétain to show more independence from the Germans, he found nothing good in the prospect of Liberation at Allied hands.[173] He told Pétain that the peasants feared it would mean the end of autarkic Europe and a renewed invasion of foreign wheat.[174]

The Vichy years were probably Dorgères's most comfortable, materially. After the defeat, he lived in his Paris offices at 10, boulevard du Montparnasse until 15 July 1941. Then, officially established as the delegate-general of propaganda of the Peasant Corporation, he brought his wife, Cécile, and their two boys from Rennes to Paris, to a comfortable but not luxurious apartment at 4, rue Albert Semain (XVIIe), whose rent was 15,000 francs a month. When the Germans requisitioned his Maison du Paysan at 10, boulevard du Montparnasse in January 1944, he was able to move his offices to a six-room apartment at 30, boulevard Sébastopol. He also had a pied-à-terre in Lyon, where his weekly *Cri du sol* was still published; it was never authorized to appear in Paris.

At the end of July 1944, it was clear that the noble experiment was over. Well ahead of the Liberation of Paris, in late July 1944, Dorgères moved his family to the relative safety of Cormery (Indre-et-Loire). Now, like so many other French people, he was a refugee.

Building on Jacques Le Roy Ladurie's *syndicats agricoles* rather than Dorgères's *défense paysanne,* the Vichy regime had established permanently some long-lasting patterns in agricultural affairs. The long-sought unity of peasants' organizations had at last been achieved in the Peasant Corporation. The corporation, dominated by UNSA, would be strongly represented in the leadership of the postwar FNSEA. The ideal of an organized profession managing its own affairs would reappear in the *cogestion* of agricultural affairs in the Fourth and Fifth Republics by the government and the FNSEA.

As for Dorgères's effort to turn the French peasantry away from the Republic toward an authoritarian and corporatist regime based on the family and the *métier,* isolated from the world market and devoted to sufficiently high food prices to keep France half peasant, it had failed. But the image of a "peasant France" that Dorgères had helped to popularize had not lost its resonance in French national identity.

After the war, farmers would not use direct action as an assault on the very principle of the parliamentary Republic. But direct action was not dead. Postwar French farmers used it often after the war, sometimes led by Dorgères's disciples, on occasion even by Dorgères himself. It would be a mere instrument of pressure, however, designed to force the government to favor some specific agricultural interest. And it would not stop the transformation of French agriculture after 1960 into the powerful engine of world trade that it has become, operated by a mere 5% of the population. Were these farmers still peasants? We take up this matter in Chapter 5.

five
. . .

AFTERMATH, LEGACY, MEANINGS

Dorgères after the War

THE LIBERATION OF France meant emprisonment for Dorgères and the end of much he had worked for. Although his punishment was light, he never regained his prewar influence. Nevertheless, his tactical example and traces of his agrarian values are still powerful today.

On 18 August 1944, Resistance units arrested Dorgères in the Indre as he bicycled toward Vichy, intending, he told the court, to intercede with Marshal Pétain for an associate who had been arrested.[1] As a former Vichy official, he faced a charge of treason *(atteinte à la sûreté extérieure de l'Etat)*. The local Cour de Justice in Chateauroux began to hear his case in November 1944, but in early December he succeeded in having jurisdiction transferred to Paris.[2] There his case was investigated throughout 1945, while he remained in Fresnes prison. Dorgères spent nineteen months altogether in prison during 1944–46 awaiting trial.[3] After lengthy indictment hearings, he was finally tried on 3 February 1946. Not even François Tanguy–Prigent, who had helped wrestle him to the ground at Bégard (Côtes-d'Armor) in January 1936 and who now, as minister of agriculture, wrote to urge the prosecution forward—believed that Dorgères had served as an agent for the German occupiers.[4] The court acquitted him of the treason charge.

The Paris Cour de Justice then sent Dorgères's dossier to the Chambre Civique de la Seine, which condemned him on 20 october 1946 to ten years of "national indignity" (deprivation of civic rights).[5] It immediately relieved him of this sentence, however, for services rendered to the Resistance. Those services were modest at best. According to the friendly witnesses who testified on Dorgères's behalf, they consisted mainly of helping a few friends and supporters cross the demarcation line, assisting a few young men to avoid the German Labor Service (STO), and ordering his people to stay away from the Vichy regime's hated paramilitary corps, the Milice, and Marcel Deat's collaborationist Rassemblement National Populaire (of course Dorgères was always jealously forbidding his people to join rival movements).

Dorgères was not yet finished with the justice of the Liberation, however. Although he faced no further personal charges, the Cour de Justice of Lyon had on its calendar the case of his *Cri du sol,* published there during the occupation. That court pronounced on 19 December 1946 the dissolution of Dorgères's Société de la Presse Paysanne and the confiscation of its property.[6] Dorgères was free, but his modest press empire was gone, his movement evaporated, and his career under the cloud of his faith in Marshal Pétain—which he never ceased to proclaim, even in the courtrooms of the postwar purge.

Dorgères seems to have lived quietly in Paris in 1947, selling advertising space in farmers' newspapers. By the end of the year, the old itch to speak and write could no longer be denied. In December he addressed a crowd at Saint-Lô (Manche).[7] In January 1948 he took charge of a struggling prewar farmers' weekly, the *Gazette agricole,* trying to raise money from his old friends in the north and west to pay its debts.[8] On 10 October 1948, at Landivy (Mayenne), Dorgères summoned an audience of about 200 farmers to unite around his *comités de défense paysanne* to fight economic *dirigisme,* taxes, and the regime of parties, instead of joining the official Confédération Général de l'Agriculture, headed by his old enemy Tanguy-Prigent. Marshal Pétain's government was, he concluded, "in agricultural and family matters, an example to follow."[9]

Dorgères's exploits lingered in rural memories. When postwar scarcity turned into surpluses and farm prices began to soften in the early 1950s, demonstrations began again. The Comité de Guéret, which coordinated the first wave of postwar protests in 1953 in the south (where the CDP had not been strong), remembered the Peasant Front's idea of massive withdrawals of peasants' savings from the state's savings agencies (*caisses*).[10] Dorgères's influence was more direct in the west. In the Calvados, Germain Boullot, former head of the Greenshirts, who now cultivated a farm in the Caen plains, was still an active speaker and organizer. He and Dorgères aroused 20,000 listeners at Lisieux on 1 August 1953, mainly *bouilleurs de cru* threatened with the abolition of their rights to distill by their old enemy Pierre Mendès France.

Just after this meeting Dorgères's *Gazette agricole* was fined 25,000 francs for calling the riot police, the Compagnies Républicaines de Sòreté (CRS) "those thugs [*voyous*] in uniform."[11] In 1955 a group of *bouilleurs* sacked the tax collector's office, the Recette des Contributions Individuelles at Pont-L'Evêque, an action for which one of Dorgères's disciples, Camille Voivenel, received a sentence of eight months in prison.[12] The most important department after the Calvados was the Sarthe, where Dorgères's followers were strong enough to generate broad resistance to the establishment of the departmental social security agency, the Mutualité Sociale Agricole.[13]

Dorgères was elected deputy from the Ille-et-Vilaine on 2 January 1956. His list of candidates won 11% of the vote, doing best in the least populated and poorest communes in the northeast (around Fougères), the west (Montauban and Saint-Méen), and the southwest (Bain-de-Bretagne and Grand-Fougeray) of the department.[14] Although his electoral campaign had enjoyed the support of the populist leader Pierre Poujade and the rightwing leader Jean-Louis Tixier-Vignancourt against their common enemy, the Christian Democratic Mouvement Républicain Populaire (MRP)—Dorgères called it the "movement to trick the people" *(mouvement pour rouler le peuple)*— he remained unaffiliated in the Chamber of Deputies with any group.

Long-running negotiations with Poujade's Union de Défense des Commerçants et Artisans and with Paul Antier's Parti Paysan to form a new Rassemblement Paysan came to nothing in the end since Dorgères, never willing to be subordinated to anyone, asked for too many positions on any joint committee. He spoke only rarely in the chamber, mainly to complain of police action against peasants' demonstrations or of state regulations and taxes. In any event, his parliamentary career was brief. He was defeated in the Gaullist landslide of 1958.

After losing his parliamentary seat, Dorgères was left with the *Gazette agricole* and the *Syndicat agricole de défense paysanne,* which he had reconstituted after the war. Their small size and financial difficulties did not prevent him from stirring up trouble. The Algerian war offered a momentary opening, and he participated—along with militants of the paramilitary group defending the French presence in Algeria, the Organisation de l'Armée Secrète (OAS)—in bloody street fighting in Amiens in early February 1960.[15] But Amiens was his last action. The Fourth and Fifth Republics offered him far less space than the late Third. That seems curious, for the demonstrations mounted by French farmers in 1959–61, as France began to adjust to membership in the Common Market, were bigger and more widespread than anything achieved by Dorgères during the 1930s.[16]

Their meaning, however, was quite different. They were pressure tactics rather than antiregime protests.

The greatest difference was that the agrarian notables now paid no attention to Dorgères. He was almost entirely isolated, without real influence or even contact with the powerful, now-unifed agricultural organizations: the Fédération Nationale des Syndicats d'Exploitants Agricoles (FNSEA), whose roots were in the prewar UNSA via the Peasant Corporation,[17] and its affiliated young farmers' movement, Centre National des Jeunes Agriculteurs (CNJA), whose roots were in the interwar Catholic young farmers' association, the Jeunesse Agricole Chrétienne (JAC). These dominant postwar organizations were committed to modernization humanized by cooperation and association, an approach quite foreign to Dorgères's high-price solution. Moreover, Dorgères was tainted by his association with Vichy and prewar fascism. The farmers no longer wanted to change France's constitution; they simply wanted to get more from it. Dorgères was the same, but the setting in which he operated had been altogether transformed.

Gradually Dorgères's political activity ceased, but he faced a long old age. He lived in the Paris suburb of Antony (Hauts-de-Seine), where in December 1936 his militants had blocked truckloads of vegetables on their way to Les Halles in Paris. His old friends occasionally corresponded, and in 1971 some of his early backers, including the duc d'Harcourt, signed an appeal to help the old man raise the funds to pay his debts.[18] Dorgères died in Antony on 22 January 1985, at the age of eighty-eight.

A Village Fascism?

We cannot evade the issue of fascism. Rural fascism is particularly important because both Mussolini and Hitler had their first success with farmers. It was the agricultural crisis that gave Mussolini his first powerful allies and Hitler his first electoral victories. Once Mussolini and Hitler had established important local power bases among farmers, they were able to persuade influential conservative leaders that they were inescapable forces who must be courted; protected from the state's efforts to make them obey the law; and even, when conservatives could no longer rule alone, brought into the government. We cannot understand how Italian fascism and German nazism came to power without understanding their initial success among Italian and German farmers.

That being the case, no study of the successes and failures of fascism in France can afford to neglect the countryside. In a curious failure of historical imagination, no one has ever explored rural fascism in that country. The abundant works on French fascism deal, without exception, with urban movements and intellectuals. The fault lies with the writers' overestimation of their own kind and with insufficient attention to comparison. If it was agricultural crises that gave fascism its first local footholds in the rest of Europe, we cannot understand the strengths and weaknesses of fascism in France without studying its course in the countryside.

The need to study French agrarians in the fascist era is even more pressing because France had a higher proportion of farmers than any other European great power. France was still almost half agricultural in the 1930s. No regime could survive without the support of at least a plurality of the farm population, and no new regime could be established against the farmers' will. The Republic had not been fully established in France until it was implanted in the villages.[19] Was fascism, in its turn, implanted in French villages in the 1930s? Can we speak of a "village fascism"?

But, first, was Dorgères himself really a fascist? He boasted of it in 1933: "Wherever [fascism] is installed, dictatorship has placed the peasant in the first rank. In France, on the contrary, the peasant has been placed in the nation's lowest rank."[20] Mussolini was his ideal: "Peasants, if you only knew what Mussolini has done for the Italian peasants, you would all demand a Mussolini for France."[21] As for Hitler, while Dorgères described in a positive tone the Nazi measures of September 1933—which established controlled agricultural markets (the *Reichsnährstand*) and guaranteed that a hereditary family farm (*Erbhof*) could not be foreclosed for debt or bankruptcy—Dorgères admitted that his methods "may not accord with French tastes."[22]

As late as the spring of 1934, he asserted that "for my part, I believe in the development of a movement of the fascist type."[23] After that, however, he grew much more reticent. His rare later references to Italy found Mussolini's version of corporatism too statist; Nazi Germany was even more so. When he began to be attacked as a fascist in the aftermath of the February 1934 riots, he dismissed it as a Marxist smear, refuted by the desire of most French people for a change of regime.[24] Even when, by 1936, he rejected the fascist label, he also refused to criticize fascism: "neither fascism nor anti-fascism."[25]

When Dorgères praised a foreign regime after 1934, it was more likely to be the authoritarian and ruralist Portugal of Salazar[26] and (with reservations born of fear of Spanish agricultural exports) the Spain of Franco.[27]

Allied with conservative agrarians in the Peasant Front after the summer of 1934, Dorgères was committed by the front's platform to a qualified defence of the Republic, subject to "reform of the State based upon the family and the profession [*métier*]." But like many French conservatives of the 1930s who found the actual Republic inadequate, he was looking for a "third way": "neither fascism nor communism."[28] He never stopped affirming his aim to cleanse the Republic of parliament, palaver, and party politics. "We defend the Republic," wrote one of Dorgères's lieutenants in 1939, "but a cleansed Republic."[29]

Dorgères was less attracted to the Nazis' peasant policy than were some of the grandees and agrarian technocrats. Rémy Goussault, a corporatist theorist and official of several specialized associations and later secretary-general of the Vichy Peasant Corporation, attended the Nazi Peasant Assembly (*Bauerntag*) at Goslar in November 1935; he found the Germans "like our peasants at meetings" except they were "taller, cleaner, younger, and in uniform." He was impressed by the assembly's fervor and by the Nazis' commitment to defend "a way of life," to make rural existence "agreeable and even gay," and to restore rural landscapes and festivals.[30] Even Jacques Le Roy Ladurie, who was to turn away from Vichy after having served as minister of agriculture in 1942 and participate actively in the armed Resistance in 1944, found some good things to say about Nazi support for the family.[31]

Dorgères's visceral nationalism made him cool to foreign regimes in general, and his experience of German occupation and prison in World War I left him with both a solid anti-Germanism and a compensatory patriotism. Although right up to 1939 he passionately opposed the war against Hitler as a Leftist maneuver for which the peasants would pay the "blood tax," once war was declared Dorgères volunteered for active duty at the age of forty-three and fought in Alsace and on the Somme. If fascism is defined by overt sympathy for the regimes of Mussolini and Hitler, Dorgères was too nationalistic to fit.

Nevertheless, to search in the 1930s for new political solutions along antisocialist and nonliberal lines placed one squarely within the "magnetic field"[32] of fascism at its most successful moment. Despite his tactical denials, Dorgères's language and rhetoric make him appear tempted by fascism. He was passionately antiparliamentary. He had only scorn for democratic institutions. The world had gone wrong, he thought, with the individualism of the French Revolution and the collectivism of the industrial revolution. He rejected the liberal market system in economic matters, preferring a planned and managed economy run by the organized professions—that is, corporatism. He was frequently and crudely anti-Semitic and occasionally anti-Islamic.[33] He said he wanted revolution, but it was public authority and morals he wanted to change, not the social and economic hierarchy. He placed little value on due process and legal remedies, preferring to intimidate his enemies by force.

It is also tempting to see the influence of fascism in Dorgères's style: the greenshirts; the insignia; the slogans ("Believe, Obey, Serve"); the oaths;[34] the theatrically staged rallies, with their banks of wheat sheaves and massed pitchforks for effect. It must be admitted, however, that groups on all points of the political spectrum used these devices of "mechanical solidarity" in the 1930s, including the Socialist Red Falcons (Faucons Rouges). More subtly, one hears echoes of fascism in Dorgères's exaltation of toughness and physical hardness; in his constant appeals for action, cleansing, sacrifice, unity, and heroism; and in his taste for humiliating his enemies.

But are we so sure that fascism is best defined by its programs and by its stage settings? As a quest for a unique national essence on which to construct an obligatory solidarity, fascism varies profoundly in its key symbols and images from one national context to another: Mussolini's *Romanità* was unlike Hitler's *Blut und Boden* in rhetoric and symbolism. The two movements and regimes had quite similar functions, however.

The most useful definition of fascism may be a functional one, based more on how it works than on what it says.[35] Both Mussolini's fascism and Hitler's nazism offered a system of authority and regimentation that promised to reinforce the unity, energy, and purity of a community that had fallen prey to decline and division. To reach these goals, they sought not to enlighten a public of free citizens by a coherent discussion of intellectual principles but, rather, to carry a crowd along by passionate sentiments. Marc Bloch, writing for an underground newspaper in 1943, went to the heart of the matter when he compared a constitutional democracy's "people governed by laws" to fascism's "tribe which a collective passion welds to its leader."[36]

Dorgères's preference for community duties over individual rights, authority over debate, and force over law place him on the fascist side of this great divide. His promise to eliminate class conflict in the countryside had more in common with fascism than it did with either the liberal model of representation, based on the individual citizen, or the socialist model, based on economic class, although in the term "peasant class" Dorgères betrayed his latent fascination with socialist models.

Yet Dorgères differed in important ways from the fascist leaders of the 1930s. His commitment to the family and the profession as organic social building blocks places him closer to authoritarianism than to fascism.[37] Authoritarians seek a self-regulating, organic society managed by natural elites; fascists supplement or even replace traditional social authority by a new "mechanical solidarity," leveling and egalitarian and embodied in the party.[38]

The frontiers between authoritarianism and fascism are at best imprecise, however. They were never more fluid than in the 1930s, when fascism was ascendant. In that decade a continuum ran from the clerical authoritarianism of a Franco, Salazar, or Dollfuss—all colored to some degree by fascist borrowings in their decor and one-party systems—through the incomplete fascism of Mussolini, who shared power with Italian conservatives, to the most integrally fascist regime of all, Nazi Germany. But even Hitler shared power with conservatives.[39] No regime in 1930s Europe was 100% fascist, although many authoritarian leaders had taken a few steps in that direction. Dorgères belongs somewhere along that continuum of fascist-authoritarian mixtures. He was authoritarian in his organic conception of society, but he leaned toward fascism in his glorification of action, his uniformed young men, and his cult of the "chief."

Dorgères departed most fully from the fascist model in defending one sector of the population—a "peasant class"—against the urban middle class. He failed to grasp the genius of the successful fascist leaders, who appealed "across classes" to the whole population in order to become a national unifier. He was too exclusively a peasant chief to rise above being simply the leader of a pressure group. One senses that Dorgères would have cooperated with a fascist authority that gave an adequate place to peasants' self-administration and kept food prices high and a large rural population intact. Dorgères's real foreign parallel is Walther Darré, Hitler's peasant leader; and, like Darré, he must have noticed that both Hitler and Mussolini eventually sacrificed their early propeasant policies to the necessities of national military expansion and the heavy industry it required. Triumphant fascism subordinated peasant society to industrial growth, just as liberalism had done and as Soviet communism was doing, in a far more bloody manner, at the same time.

Dorgères came closer than any other rural leader in France (except for his sometime associate and rival Josef Bilger in Alsace[40]) to detaching large numbers of French peasants from the Third Republic and making them potentially available to some new regime, which would be authoritarian, populist, autarkic, anti-Semitic, and corporatist. His rivals who came closer to fascist models, such as Doriot's Parti Populaire Français[41] and the Solidarité Française, had almost no success among farmers. In contrast, his rivals who were most successful among farmers distanced themselves from fascism. Colonel François de La Rocque, who turned closer to authoritarianism than to fascism after he replaced his banned Croix de Feu with the more moderate Parti Social Français (PSF) in 1936, made a serious effort to recruit farmers after 1937. In fact, he made serious inroads into Dorgères's constituency after the rural notables began to find Dorgères too negative. Dorgérist activists and sympathizers began to show up in PSF meetings after 1937.[42]

The most successful new movement of the 1930s among conservative farmers was the Jeunesse Agricole Chrétienne (JAC), which was looking for organic alternatives to liberal democracy in the 1930s but overtly rejected fascist racism and violence. Dorgères was not mistaken to see in progressive Catholics his most serious rivals and enemies. Despite an imperfect fit with fascism, he remains the French farmers' leader who came closest to occupying the niche of French rural fascism, at the moment of maximum fascist success in Europe.

My attempt to measure Dorgères against the programs, style, and functions of fascism has been inconclusive, as are most attempts at political labeling. It may well be that the most important differences between Dorgères and successful rural fascism lay less in the personal qualities of Dorgères himself and his Greenshirt movement than in the circumstances: the political space available and the allies and accomplices who found Dorgérist lawlessness useful enough to tolerate it. The French New Right movements of the 1930s resemble their German and Italian colleagues quite strongly if one limits oneself to studying their language and gestures.[43] The most important differences appear when one examines the society in which they functioned and the political crisis that offered them opportunity.

That being the case, we need to understand with precision the spaces and allies that were available to Mussolini and Hitler in the Italian and German countryside and the exact nature of the political openings they were able to exploit. There were two scenarios of fascist success in rural Europe in Dorgères's day: the delegitimation of the traditional notable agrarian elites, as they faced economic depression and political blockage (as in the German state of Schleswig-Holstein), and the rescue of big planters from labor disorders (as in the Italian Po Valley).

At the beginning of 1920, Italian fascism was on the verge of failure. Mussolini had wanted to create a movement based on war veterans that could be simultaneously radical and nationalist, combining such reforms as the abolition of the monarchy and the upper house, confiscation of war profits, workers' rights, and the vote for women with an aggressively nationalistic foreign policy. In the parliamentary election of 16 November 1919, however, his Fascist candidates in Milan received only 4,793 votes out of a total of 270,000. An urban radical nationalism was not viable, for lack of room between more plausible radicals on the Left and more plausible nationalists on the Right. At that point, agrarian fascism came along to "rescue the town-based fascism of Mussolini from extinction."[44]

In alliance with the landowners of the Po Valley, the black-shirted *squadristi* helped break the power of socialist unions of farm workers that had forced the landowners after 1919 to adopt social policies that the landowners found both expensive and humiliating. Thus the Fascists became the de facto local government in the Po Valley in 1921–22. The landowners of the northeast of Italy and the local bosses (*ras*) of the Fascist movement became so strong a local force that conservative political leaders in Rome, such as Giolitti and Salandra, concluded that they were obliged to include Mussolini within the ruling political establishment to restore the order that Mussolini and the Left together had helped destroy.[45]

The German National Socialist Party, for its part, had made little headway by 1928. In the agitated elections of May 1924, it received 6.5% of the parliamentary vote, only to fall to 5% in the calmer elections of December 1924.[46] In 1928, the Nazi party strategists decided to give more attention to farmers and less to the urban working class, which up to then had responded little to their propaganda. This was a fruitful strategy. Aided by a revival of nationalism provoked by the Young Plan and by the stock market crash of 1929, the Nazi vote grew—and it grew especially rapidly in farm areas. In the parliamentary elections of 1930, it displaced the local agrarian leagues that had so far garnered the votes of farmers disillusioned with traditional Liberal and Conservative parties. In the two elections of July and November 1932, German farmers were more likely to vote for the Nazis than for any other party.[47] Protestant farmers voted even more readily for the Nazis than Catholic farmers since Catholic parish life gave Catholic parties a solid social base that Nazism failed to shake.

The one German state where the Nazis won an absolute majority of the vote in the parliamentary elections of July 1932 was Schleswig-Holstein, where the Nazis persuaded Protestant cattle raisers and dairy farmers suffering from the Depression that neither their traditional leaders nor the new local leagues that sprang up in the 1920s could help them. The Nazis never won a majority vote on the national level, however, and it was the effort of conservative leader Franz von Papen to harness the Nazi following to his own leadership that persuaded him to rescue Hitler—whose popular vote had begun to slip in November 1932—and make him chancellor.

There were situations in rural France analagous to those in which Italian fascism and German nazism struck root. The strikes of 1936–37 and the notables' loss of legitimacy in the Depression opened genuine possibilities for some kind of French rural fascism in the 1930s. Dorgères found and exploited some of these openings, with at least momentary and partial success. But he failed to establish a power base in the countryside sufficiently strong and durable to force the rural notables to come to terms with him or to try to coopt him. The French agrarian notables were not sufficiently shaken in their rule for them to find Dorgères's help indispensable for their political survival.

Rural France was potentially receptive to fascism in some respects: the peasantry was numerous; not always well integrated into the Republic or even into the farmers' organizations; ready for a demagogue; and prepared to take direct action when crisis seemed fatal, as in 1935. In other ways, however, rural France lent itself less readily to a rural fascism than did certain regions of rural Germany or Italy.

It has sometimes been claimed that France had no indigenous fascism or that the French were "allergic" to this particular political virus.[48] But there was no mysterious antibody to it in French political culture. Indeed no Western country was exempt during the periods of fascist glamor and success, and France was not exceptional in this point. On the contrary, France produced one of the most luxuriant growths in the Western world of fascist or near fascist intellectual expressions. But there were concrete social, cultural, and political obstacles in French rural society to Dorgérism.

A first major obstacle was the vigor of the French state. French agriculturalists never felt as deserted by the state as the Po Valley landowners did in Italy. When agricultural laborers went out on strike in the plains of the Paris basin in the summers of 1936 and 1937, the state—even the state of Léon Blum—sent the gendarmes. In contrast, when the landless laborers (*braccianti*) of the Po Valley brought pressure on the large landowners by organizing and striking, the Italian state was not very helpful to the latter. The landowners turned to their own devices, the most effective of which were the squads of young fascists spoiling for a night of union bashing.[49]

A second major obstacle lay in the political space available. France was unusual in the extent to which the political Left was already rooted in its countryside. Much of the Mediterranean slope had already turned republican in the early nineteenth century, and the wine areas became radical or socialist in the later nineteenth century.[50] In the Midi, only market gardeners were available to be recruited by Dorgères in any numbers. The very limited development of Dorgérism in the lower Rhône Valley was limited to market gardeners around Cavaillon and in the Var and Vaucluse. The most important Dorgérist leader on the Mediterranean coast—Honoré Caillol—was a small market gardener in Aubagne, and his followers were mostly similar. In a crisis, suffering farmers in historically republican areas of France tended to look to the Left for help—hence the phenomenon of small-farmer communism, nearly unknown in Germany and limited to landless laborers in Italy.

A third major obstacle was the power of the notables in the French countryside. They did not lose power to new organizations. They hung on to their clientel remarkably well. Some of the notables supported Dorgères for a while, but even some of the conservative ones were too firmly rooted in the concept of a state of law to lend themselves to "direct action." One thinks, for example, of the mayor of Caen, Camille Blaisot, who, though a conservative, wrote articles against Dorgères's demagoguery. Blaisot was arrested by the Germans for his resistance and died in deportation. It seems clear that the agrarian notables in Germany and Italy supported nazism and fascism much more wholeheartedly than the French agrarian notables supported Dorgérism, for reasons of history and political culture. The deep legitimacy in France of the Republican regime and the rule of law were not matched in Weimar Germany or in the liberal Italian monarchy. The legal order was not seriously shaken in France until foreign armies had occupied its soil in 1940.

A fourth major obstacle was the power and solidity of the agricultural organizations already in place. Only a minority of French farmers felt isolated, without some kind of organization to turn to. These organizations were powerful and successful. They were not all pro-Republican in the late 1930s, but they worked fruitfully with the existing state and they were reluctant to embark on adventures. When the Peasant Corporation was formed under Vichy, it built on these existing organizations which perpetuated notable rule, although slightly leavened by the new blood of the 1930s (a few Dorgérists and many more followers of the Catholic farm youth, the JAC). The traditional organizations continued to occupy the terrain through thin (the Depression) and thick (the German occupation).

A fifth important obstacle was that the crisis of the 1930s, serious as it was in France, was less catastrophic there than in Germany or even in England and the United States. The peasants' anger was volcanic, but it peaked in 1935, a year before the Popular Front carried middle class panic to its height. That spread of nearly one year between the peak of rural anger in late 1935 and the peak of urban-industrial effervescence in the summer of 1936 helped the Republic weather the storm of the mid-1930s. And there was something in the argument that French socioeconomic balance kept the unemployed salaried sector smaller in France than elsewhere.

More fundamentally, the Third Republic, though it was in serious difficulties in the 1930s, did not suffer the outright political blockage that the Weimar Republic did or even the Italian liberal monarchy. It is true that the French notables felt threatened. It is true that the Republic worked badly, particularly in the years of revolving-door governments between 1933 and 1936. But the Republic did not cease to function. The Weimar Constitution ceased to function normally in the spring of 1930; almost three years of stop-gap government under emergency decrees ensued before Hitler was called to power. In Italy, the state had failed to protect property and it had failed to protect itself from the Blackshirts. It could not form an effective government capable of maintaining its monopoly of armed force in 1921–22. Weimar Germany and liberal Italy had left a yawning hole into which fascism moved; the Third Republic was even solidifying itself in 1938 and 1939.

Finally, successful fascism needed a synthesizer, whose momentum toward rule gave the movement's militants the hope of booty and power. What would have happened to the peasants of Schleswig-Holstein, converted to nazism after a dozen other nostrums, if Hitler had not taken power at the crucial moment and frozen their new local leaders in place? The same question applies to the landowners of the Po Valley. The local power of Dorgérism was occasionally complete for brief moments, but without someone at the top to link that local power to a new regime, the local mobilization soon subsided.

If at the peak of the peasants' agitation in the fall of 1935, allied for a moment with the rural notables, the Third Republic had faced simultaneouly the disaffection of other large parts of the population; and if the government had been deadlocked; and if some national figure had managed to unite all the strands of anti-Republicanism into a powerful single movement—four big "ifs"—Dorgérism would no doubt have furnished the rural element to a French fascism. However, those are not only big "ifs" but also counterfactual statements: interwar France fitted none of these conditions. A sober and realistic estimation of effective fascism in France in 1935—as groups prepared to take and exercise political power, not simply journalists and pamphleteers—leaves us with only the fragments of an anti-Republican coalition that never formed. We must remember that nazism and fascism succeeded in collecting a "bundle" of disaffections and acting as "gatherers" of multiple rebellions on their way to power. No one was capable of doing that in interwar France.

In the 1930s, the success of Hitler and Mussolini and their skillful use of the press and radio prepared people to expect vigorous and ambitious demagogues to succeed everywhere. But such a comparison rests on a faulty understanding of how Hitler and Mussolini came to power. They did not come to power by fanning discontent and making speeches; they came to power by becoming indispensable to power brokers within the conservative leadership—the Papens and the Salandras and the Giolittis. For a time, important conservative rural notables offered Dorgères a place in their world: they tried to coopt his forces (just as Papen tried to coopt those of Hitler). But Jacques Le Roy Ladurie and the others had turned away from Dorgères by 1937, so he received only a minor role in 1940. By then, the conservative elites had created an authoritarian France, not a fascist France, and they kept Dorgères to the margins.

It would be wrong, therefore, to consider Dorgères's failure merely a personal one. Personal inadequacies played a part, to be sure. Dorgères was neither a solid builder of organizations nor a master strategist. His strategy was erroneous, especially in that he tried to speak only for peasants. Except for a time in 1935, when he was running for parliament at Blois, he did not try to address the middle class. He spoke for the "peasant class," as the Socialists and Communists spoke for the "working class," and so, like them, he narrowed his audience. Hitler created the first "catchall" party in German history. Dorgères never even imagined such a political exploit. He wanted only to speak for France's peasant half. But even within French farming circles, Dorgères's appeal was a narrow one. He was a master of the market-day crowd in conservative country towns, but he was less skilled in building a durable political power. He could not make himself indispensable to the rural grandees.

The tough farm boys of the Calvados whom Germain Boullot led against the Popular Front and the strikers of Dupont d'Isigny may not have been very different, in their truculence and in their readiness to fight communism, from the tough farm boys of the Po Valley in 1921 or of Thuringia in 1932. But the relative political health of the French Third Republic left them with little room to usurp the collectivity's monopoly of force. It was the circumstances more than any qualities of their own— any love for the Republic's due process or any willingness to compromise with the Left in the French countryside—that kept them from being the action squads of a fully developed rural fascism.

Let us put the issue of fascism behind us, for at worst it can easily degenerate into facile name-calling that generates more heat than light. I wanted to use comparison of the national variants of rural fascism to bring out the differences between Germany and Italy, where it succeeded, and France, where it failed. The exercise confirms the specificity of France in the 1930s, with its strong state (even when it was shaken) and its powerful conservative elites who were not sufficiently delegitimized by the crisis of the 1930s to share power with radical demagogues. It also helps us to understand that the Vichy regime was closer to an authoritarian-clerical model than to a fascist one, at least until its last desparate days, and that its agrarian ideology helped make it so.

The Dorgérist Moment

Dorgères's actions were not merely the personal exploits of one man. They fit into a particular time in the western and northern French countryside when there was a public for them and when they received the acquiescence, or even the support, of influential rural notables.

French rural society in the 1930s presented a demographic paradox. It had suffered the full psychological shock of a rural exodus without actually shrinking into silence. The French rural population had reached its historic apogee around 1860.[51] Certain regions of poor soil had begun to drain slowly as early as the 1830s. Then, between 1862 and 1892, a quarter of the rural population abandoned the countryside for the glamor and opportunity of towns and cities. Between 1900 and 1914, another 7% (400,000) left, and 800,000 more departed during 1919–29.[52]

In comparative perspective, however, the French rural exodus was the slowest in western Europe. A higher proportion of the people continued to work the land in France than in any other industrialized nation. In 1906, the proportion of the active French population engaged in agriculture had declined only to 43%. That level had been passed in 1882 in Germany, in 1849 in Holland,[53] and in Britain even before the first census in 1801[54]—though not until about 1900 in the United States.[55] In the 1930s, furthermore, there was actually a small "return to the soil,"[56] as the Depression drove some of the unemployed back to the refuge of the ancestral farm. Thus a reversal of the rural exodus seemed plausible for those who dreamed of it. The Vichy government was to try to make a virtue out of that necessity.

Rural decline seemed particularly threatening in France because it reinforced a fear of systemic national decadence. Defeat by Germany in 1870 and economic depression in the 1880s had been followed by the discovery, with the census of 1891, that the French birthrate had become the lowest in Europe. Compared to Germans, British, or Americans, French people were each year becoming older and relatively less numerous. Many came to believe that French identity and strength depended on maintaining the size and health of its fertile rural population.

Thus French farmers and their supporters felt threatened with disappearance in the 1930s, and yet they remained numerous enough to react noisily and forcefully to the three crises considered in Chapter 1. Their outcry was shrill and marked by a vivid sense of rural-urban incompatibility—urged on by Dorgères—because rural society in the north and west of France had become isolated from the rest of French society.[57]

The economy of the polycultural family farm, in Dorgères's day, was more purely agricultural than it had ever been before or was ever to be again. Disindustrialization had eliminated such rural manufactures as spinning, weaving, and ironwork, which had rounded out many peasants' incomes well into the nineteenth century. That meant that rural populations had nothing but agriculture to keep them afloat. Their best remaining cottage industry was distilling—hence the passion with which the *bouilleurs de cru* fought for their freedom to make and sell apple and pear brandies. Thus French farmers stood or fell with farming. They had been reduced to a "peasant ghetto." [58]

Another link that had once knitted together rural and urban society was labor mobility. Seasonal work, part-time work, temporary migrations to the city, the return of retirees—all these human contacts between town and country diminished in the late nineteenth century. As seasonal labor migrations ceased, both urban and rural work forces became increasingly full time and specialized. They saw each other, in mutual incomprehension, only when city people embarked on a rural holiday.[59] During France's long relative stagnation between two periods of growth (roughly from the 1860s to the 1950s), all but the biggest French farmers borrowed as little as possible, bought as little as possible in the towns, and lived mostly on what they produced themselves. French peasants became "a world apart." [60]

The agrarians, far from regretting the isolation of rural society, gloried in it. Agricultural life, they said, was a distinct and superior social order, based on natural rhythms and organic communities, irreconcilable with individualistic and contractual urban society. Jacques Le Roy Ladurie called this difference "the peasant fact":

> Between man and his soil, there is the bond of a natural law. There is no social contract. On the contrary, between the capitalist and his debtor, between the proletarian and his boss, between the civil servant and his State, there are contractual ties, collective and individual agreements, negotiated, concluded, or revised according to the wishes of the contracting parties, or else a legal statute.[61]

While the agrarians wanted rural society to become as prosperous as urban society, they did not wish it to be contaminated. They wanted urban society to adapt to rural needs, not vice versa. They were not to get their wish.

French city dwellers, for their part, also felt detached from peasant society. The new accessibility of agricultural imports by the 1870s freed them from dependence on French farming for food. The two economies could henceforth follow divergent rhythms of prosperity and dearth. Before the era of agricultural imports, a crisis in French agriculture (as in

1846–48) had meant expensive bread—and social unrest—in French towns. The steamship and the railroad snapped that link. Cheaper bread was available outside of France than within. And French farmers could still not feed all of their fellow citizens except in good years; the self-sufficiency in temperate zone products fully achieved after World War II was only on the horizon in the 1930s. Rural prosperity and urban prosperity came to seem a zero-sum game. Thus French city dwellers felt no particular obligation to limit their consumption to the more expensive food their peasant neighbors produced, and they felt free to cultivate a host of negative stereotypes about peasants: dolts, boors, and (more recently) whiners and tax dodgers. Dorgères's vivid sense of country-town antagonism had some basis in fact. Economic, social, and cultural segregation between the two had reached its apogee in his time.

Dorgères worked at a formative moment in farmers' responses to their isolation and degradation within French society. The two principal strategies still being pursued by aggrieved French farmers were, in fact, developed and tried out in the 1930s: direct action and *cogestion,* or management by partnership between farmers' organizations and the state.

Rural direct action could take several forms in Dorgères's day. One kind centered on labor disputes among the masses of hired hands who worked the great wheat and sugar beet farms of the northern plains. Labor-intensive extensive agriculture no longer exists in France,[62] and we will not see any more "hot summers" like those of 1936 and 1937, accompanied by the big growers' frantic search for some counterforce to discipline the workers. A large, concentrated agricultural work force can never again serve as a battleground in France between conservative agrarians and the Left and open a space for vigilantes like the Greenshirts. That part of the Dorgérist moment is closed.

The other kind of rural disorder was the peasant demonstration: angry gatherings of farmers who meant to force the government and city people to alleviate rural problems. Violence by angry peasants belongs to a millenial tradition, but Dorgères only rarely claimed that ancient lineage by calling his movement a *jacquerie.*[63] Journalists commonly explained Dorgères by the same medieval imagery. In many respects, however, Dorgérist direct action was innovative behavior. Dorgères brought it to the rural north and west of France for the first time since the French Revolution. The endemic peasant violence of the old regime had lasted longest in the Midi, where it found modern expression in the insurrections against Louis Napoleon in 1851[64] and in the revolt of the wine country in 1907. The north and west, in contrast, had been orderly (even if dissatisfied) since the "Great Fear" of 1789 and the royalist insurgency *(chouannerie)* of 1793–1800 in Brittany. Dorgères cleansed the use of violence of its revolutionary taint and made it legitimate again among farmers in the conservative regions of France.

So it is mistaken to perceive Dorgérism in the 1930s as a last desparate spasm by the poorest and most retrograde farmers. Dorgères did indeed speak for them, for he proposed to refloat all peasant homesteads—even the most inefficient—with high prices. Many of those Dorgérist activists whom we can identify, however, were disappointed and frightened would-be modernizers, neophytes in the food market caught by the Depression with debts and without experience or support structures. Dorgères's direct action fit their desperation and their inexperience. These eruptions by the Greenshirts recall the intermittent bursts of anger of the early labor movement. Just as Luddism, machine breaking, and unplanned explosions of violence by industrial workers were to be replaced by more sustained and calculated forms of pressure within mature labor organizations,[65] so farmers' violence was later to move toward more routinized forms of planned pressure (a matter to which we return subsequently).

Dorgères appealed in the 1930s less to a historic tradition of peasant revolt than to a desire to catch up with the working class. He never claimed descent from the *chouans* (it was the Left press that constantly made that connnection); in the Vendée the CDP was only "a marginal movement."[66] He referred only rarely to historical precedents. On his one venture into the Haute Garonne, at Revel, on 18 August 1935, he did claim a link with Marcellin Albert and the angry *vignerons* of 1907,[67] expressing pride in sharing the platform with Cambriels, a veteran of that insurrection. But his usual model was the contemporary Left. "*La Défense Paysanne* is the CGT of the peasants," he liked to proclaim.[68] Peasants must acquire the solidarity and discipline of a "peasant class."

Dorgères fought not to restore ancient peasant rights but to gain "parity" with workers and civil servants; the word appears only after the war, but the idea is already there in the 1930s. Economic parity might undermine some of the specificity of the rural economy, but Dorgères was not concerned about this inconsistency. He reflected the profound belief of peasants that they were the principal victims in the inflationary spiral that had begun in 1914. In a world where the stable "Napoleon franc" no longer kept the social order in its place and where costs had risen at variable rates in different sectors of the economy, peasants believed that they had suffered the most serious loss of status. No Dorgérist speech was complete without a litany of "coefficients"—the amounts by which different prices and costs had multiplied since 1914. Peasants sold their produce at a coefficient of two or three; the cost of living was at five; workers' salaries had reached six; and public expenditure had soared to nine.[69] Dorgères did his best to fan peasants' resentment, especially after the reforms of the Popular Front, toward the "privileges" of workers and civil servants. Many peasants were ready for violent action to reverse what they perceived as a severe decline relative to the city, caused by city-based policies.

This kind of Dorgérist direct action left an enduring legacy in French rural politics. We saw how Dorgères's tactics, his disciples, and even he personally reappeared in the even greater peasant demonstrations in 1953 and 1961–62. But long after Dorgères had ceased all activity and his memory had faded among French farmers, direct action reappeared when, in 1984, the European Community introduced quotas to reduce its sea of surplus milk, following the long slide in farm incomes that began after the oil shocks of 1973 and 1979.[70] It was further provoked by the entry of Spain and Portugal into the European Community (EC) in 1986 and by the plans for removal of some land from cultivation (*gel de terres*) that was announced by Brussels in 1988. The shrinkages forced on EC price supports in the 1990s by the growing financial burden of the Common Agricultural Policy (CAP) and by American pressure to include agriculture in the Uruguay Round of GATT provoked the Coordination Rurale to make two highly publicized attempts to besiege Paris in June 1992 and September 1993.

French farmers have continued to employ direct action because it works. During the Fourth Republic, peasant activists were able to change national policy. They forced the Fourth Republic to return to market management in the early 1950s and to index farm prices against inflation in 1957.[71] The Fifth Republic was less easily influenced by such pressures, and indexation was repealed in December 1958.[72] De Gaulle's basic decision to open France to the European and world markets was never seriously placed in doubt by farmers' opposition. Nevertheless, farmers' actions received a compensatory reward in the form of increased subsidies and assistance to distressed sectors. It became an annual ritual for the minister of agriculture to respond to major demonstrations by announcing new reductions in tax burdens and social charges and new forms of aid.[73]

The other enduring strategy shaped during the 1930s was the participation of agricultural organizations in public administration: *cogestion,* as it is called today. In the late Third Republic, French agriculture's "turn inward upon itself"[74] had the further effect of persuading agrarian leaders that they alone were competent to understand and manage the farming business of France. The corporatist concept of organized "professions" that directed their own affairs—ubiquitous among agrarian leaders in the 1930s—reflected their sense of incompatibility with the urban economy and their conviction that neither the market nor electoral politics could help them.

It would be hard to find a nonsocialist economic thinker in France in the 1930s who still believed in a market economy overseen by parliament. Corporatism's key concepts—a managed economy operated by professional organizations empowered by the state, with a minimum of either bureaucratic control or abstract lawmaking—are found everywhere in the agrarian speeches and newspapers of that decade. The convergence that was to permit the union, at last, of French farmers in the Vichy Peasant Corporation and the postwar FNSEA was already taking shape in the 1930s through this corporatist consensus.

Dorgères missed the turn in the road that was to lead through corporatism to *cogestion* because, although he was a corporatist like everyone else, he saw it as a weapon against the state, whereas the agrarian notables saw it as a way to emerge from isolation and to share power with the state. Perceiving that they could play a major role in managing a corporatist system if one were instituted, the agrarian notables accepted the welfare state (such as family support payments) and market management (such as the Wheat Office) on the condition that their organizations would administer them. After the most agitated days of the price collapse of 1934–35, therefore, the French conservative agrarian elite preferred power to confrontation and left Dorgères out in the cold.

The first generation of leaders of conservative agrarian organizations had always seen their *syndicats agricoles* as more than mere economic agencies. From the beginning, in the 1880s, they engaged in the moral and social guidance of their peasant clientele in competition with the godless Republic's cooperatives and mutual associations. Their heirs in the 1930s reinforced that social role in their renamed *syndicats paysans,* but they stopped trying to work outside the Republican state and tried to assume administrative responsibility in partnership with it (without ceasing to hope for something better). Their claim to a public role was most clearly expressed in Jacques Le Roy Ladurie's great Peasant Congress in May 1937 (from which Dorgères was exluded). The assembled leaders, Le Roy Ladurie later recalled, "oriented our syndicalism definitively toward the Corporation" and asked the state to "give official recognition to our *syndicats,* already virtually peasant and corporatist."[75]

Cooperation between the state and professional organizations raised to quasi-state functions was to be a major line of continuity in French agrarian politics. It eventually culminated in the form of *cogestion,* institutionalized in 1961–62 by regular meetings between Agriculture Minister Edgar Pisani and FNSEA President Michel Debatisse. Under their successors over the next thirty-five years, agricultural policy was formed in close joint consultation between the government and a single farmers' organization (the FNSEA and its affiliated youth organization, the CNJA), and administered by those organizations endowed with a quasi-state function.[76]

Although *cogestion* has always been challenged by dissidents, the principal partners have always managed to preserve the system, which was of mutual benefit. The payoff for the government has been relative social peace in the countryside and, for the FNSEA/CNJA leadership, official recognition as the sole legitimate farmers' organization. This settlement has enjoyed the acquiescence, at least, of a majority of French farmers for the last thirty-five years.

Although Dorgères took the other road, that of forcing policies on a hostile state by direct action, he did have an impact on this emerging partnership. He played a major role in transforming agrarian organizations through revolt of the "calloused hands" against the "white hands" that had traditionally run them. Some of Dorgères's ablest followers led the first seizures of power—fully accomplished today—by middling practicing farmers. The ascent of Jean Bohuon, one of Dorgères's chief militants and first president of the Comité Central de Défense Paysanne, is a splendid example of this process.

Bohuon's election in 1943 as *syndic régional* of the Ille-et-Vilaine made this quiet revolution stunningly clear to everyone. Count Roger de La Bourdonnaye, who, in a way typical of notable leadership in the countryside, had accumulated the offices of president of the Chambre d'Agriculture and president of the Syndicat Agricole of the Ille-et-Vilaine before the war, more or less automatically became the regional delegate of the Peasant Corporation there, charged with setting up the corporation in his department. He assumed that he would automatically become the regional syndic when the local officers of the corporation were confirmed by the vote of delegates in a departmental assembly on 23 September 1943. He could barely comprehend what happened to him that day.

Jean Bohuon, a small farmer with a "long past as an agitater,"[77] was the son of a small renter (*fermier*) and himself the owner and cultivator of eighteen hectares (about forty acres) at Montreuil-sur-Ille. He was elected by the assembled local *syndics* of the Ille-et-Vilaine—by 161 votes to 136— to the office that the count de La Bourdonnaye regarded as his by a kind of divine right.

After the election, a long impasse ensued. The count, incredulous at his defeat by a small farmer, waited for two weeks and then asked for advice from Paris, suggesting that there had been irregularities in Bohuon's campaign. The central authorities of the Peasant Corporation in Paris, apparently uncertain about what to do, told the count to continue to exercise his powers on an interim basis. Dorgères urged Bohuon to assert his claims, and Bohuon warned both Paris and the count that the "peasants" were losing patience. Finally, nearly a month after the vote, on 20 October, Adolphe Pointier, the national *syndic* of the Peasant Corporation, sent a telegram confirming Bohuon in office as the regional *syndic* of the Ille-et-Vilaine.[78]

One reason for count de La Bourdonnaye's defeat was the growing unpopularity of all officials of the Peasant Corporation when it was transformed by the pressures of the occupation into a bureaucratic agency for the requisition of foodstuffs. But Bohuon's election campaign evoked explicitly the issue of notable rule versus peasant rule. He wrote to all the communal *syndics* (the voting delegates) that "I want . . . the *syndics* of this Department to face up to the choice between an aristocrat *[châtelain]* and a real farmer *[cultivateur]*."[79] Count de la Bourdonnaye, addressing the assembled *syndics* before the vote, spoke as a long-suffering natural leader, one of those who had "paid dearly for devotion to the public good." The count's fellow notables found it inappropriate that Bohuon had introduced "the worst electoral morals of the old days" into what should be simply the ratification of a natural leadership.[80] They considered that Bohuon had injected issues of "class" into what should have been a seamless and hierarchical rural community.[81]

Part of the behind-the-scenes negotiations that seem to have accompanied Jean Bohuon's confirmation as regional *syndic* was Bohuon's agreement to subscribe to a family benefits office and pay his back fees, thereby abandoning years of adamant opposition to this social program. Accepting a role as administrator meant renouncing at least part of his war against the administration. As for Dorgères, he wrote his supporters that Bohuon's success "marks a very great date" and that "the *Défense paysanne* is not dead."[82]

Since the war, it has become unthinkable for someone to preside over agricultural associations who does not farm with his own hands and who does not call himself a "peasant." Indeed it is easier today for a woman than for a noncultivating man to occupy such a position.[83] Long gone are the days of inherited notable leadership, when the arrival of the first active farmers in the highest positions in the agrarian world caused a stir. Authentic farmers even serve as ministers of agriculture, for example, François Guillaume, minister of agriculture in the Chirac government, 1986–88, who assured an interviewer shortly before assuming office that he did not farm "by telephone" but returned to his cattle in Lorraine each weekend.[84]

Both strategies pioneered in the 1930s—direct action and *cogestion*—are still employed today, but their social and economic contexts have been profoundly transformed since Dorgères's day. Peasants' direct action in

France today is no longer meant to "change the state," as Dorgères sought to do in his fundamental challenge to representative democracy. Even the Coordination Rurale, Dorgères's indirect successor as a movement dedicated to action rather than to organization, intends only to make the government respond to particular grievances. It conducts pressure politics by tractor.

Action has become a matter of routine, calculated and applied when necessary by the leadership. Here is how François Guillaume, as president of the FNSEA, described the routine application of peasants' demonstrations to negotiations with the government in 1984 (a year of high tension, it is true, because of the European Community's new milk quotas):

> I warned Rocard [the Minister of Agriculture], I told him that I would in any case play the role that I had to play, and that if his agricultural policy diverged too much from that advocated by the FNSEA, if we didn't get the means that seemed to us indispensable, we would carry out the normal demonstrations.[85]

This "normalization" of protest from explosions of anger to calculated pressure, a process completed by industrial labor between the world wars, has now come close to completion among farmers. The process remains unfinished, however, for the price of *cogestion* is that the agrarian leaders are held responsible by the rank and file for government policy and its inevitable compromises. Those farmers who feel that the FNSEA has "sold out" and is failing to protect the weaker half of France's remaining farms from the rural "genocide"[86] caused by U.S. pressures and EC cutbacks, reject *cogestion* in favor of a confrontational stance. For them, direct action offers more emotional satisfaction and more likelihood of compelling the government to act than does trying to influence policy from within. So a functional equivalent of Dorgères's direct action finds a clientele in the 1990s among angry farmers, who quite possibly have never even heard of Dorgères, in the Coordination Rurale[87] and among the unorganized who carry out wildcat destruction of foreign produce trucks. Their actions require the FNSEA/CNJA, in turn, to mount demonstrations in order to prove their militancy.[88]

But the social context of direct action has changed radically between Dorgères's day and the 1990s. The social basis for Dorgères's style of market-day harangues has disappeared totally, as recreation as well as group self-expression. Its setting and its audience are gone. Rural markets still thrive, but more for the delectation of summer people than as a key element in rural sociability. The Coordination Rurale functions quite differently. It does not try to build a network of activists around a weekly newspaper nor to mobilize a crowd by public debates on market day. Its public is not small farmers isolated and undefended in a collapsing market but substantial farmers heavily indebted in the capital-intensive production of industrial crops, terrified of a reduction in their subsidies.[89] It assembles its crowd by telephone and fax and attempts to demonstrate to a television audience the justice of its cause, the excesses of government overreaction, and the costs of antagonizing French farmers.

As we see in more detail in the next section, French farmers have declined in the present century from nearly half the working population to only about a twentieth of it. Most marginal farmsteads have disappeared. Self-sufficient agriculture exists now only among a few "1968-ers" who seek rural utopia. Rural society is linked to urban society by new currents of social interchange. "Parity" is now explicit national policy,[90] and French farmers now look and act like well-tanned examples of the entrepreneurs that they have become.

But that transformation may have come at the cost of mortal damage to France's identity as a "peasant nation." Even as the socioeconomic basis for it has disappeared, the imaginary universe into which Dorgérism fit—along with its conservative agrarian allies—has survived. It still shapes the debate today about how many peasants France should have and what sacrifices are appropriate to support them.

France as a Peasant Nation

Dorgères thought that France could fulfill its true destiny only by becoming a "peasant state."[91] He considered farmers the only true creators of wealth, but, unlike the eighteenth-century Physiocrats, he did not value them primarily as economic entrepreneurs. "The peasantry, by the economic, social, and moral values that it represents, must take the first place in the restored order of French values."[92] Dorgères accepted all the implications of giving agriculture "the first place in the country."[93] To be a peasant state, France must be autarkic. It must not foster industrial exports at the price of accepting agricultural imports. It must not allow the pressures of a world market to deform its society. Peasants' purchasing power, not exports, must drive the economy of the peasant state. Even though bread might thereby cost more in the city, a prosperous peasantry would compensate by buying the city's products more abundantly than before.

A peasant-based political economy could not be put into effect by an unregulated market, however, or left to the vying of particular interests within a representative democracy. Some kind of authority was required to override the pressures of industrial lobbies, trusts, and commercial interests and to fend off foreign dumping. But the Dorgérists were allergic to state intervention. To them, a statist economy meant the dictatorship of civil servants ignorant of rural realities. They wanted each profession—and most important, the agricultural profession—to unify and organize itself and, in tandem with the other organized professions, to plan and run a managed economy. An authoritarian state must provide the ultimate enforcement, of course, but it should leave the conception and the application of economic policy to the organized professions. Above all, it should leave farm policy to farmers, for the economic laws of agriculture are irreconcilable with those of industry and commerce.

Dorgères wanted France to be a peasant state because he thought it would be stronger, more fertile, more economically resilient, and more moral than an urban, industrial France. The latter path, chosen by Britain, Germany, and the United States, had led them, he asserted, to a rootless citizenry and an unbalanced economy subject to violent fluctuations. Dorgères did not invent these ideas himself, of course, nor was he their only expositor in the 1930s. As we have seen, conservative agrarians generally agreed with all of them.

The economic and moral primacy of agriculture is not part of some universal and self-evident "common sense," even if Dorgères and his conservative allies thought so. It is an intellectual construction. The West draws on both Christian and classical sources for idyllic visions of the original garden, but each Western nation has developed Arcadian and agrarian imagery in its own way. Agriculture as the foundation of national wealth and power was a theme particularly well developed to Old Regime France, from Sully to the Physiocrats. Social and moral arguments for a strong agriculture were strengthened after the French Revolution in the search for a stable society rooted in rural property. Conservatives prized agriculture as the source of social stability during the years of urban effervescence (1848–71). Even "liberal" French political economists rejected the British model and sought a social "balance" without the economic and political turmoil that inevitably accompanied unbridled industrialization and a swollen working class. The decision to retain a large agriculture became official French policy in the 1870s. The infant Third Republic chose stability over growth. It revoked Napoleon III's free-trade policy and adopted a series of measures that protected local production, both agricultural and industrial, culminating in the Méline tariff of 1892.

A further virtue was attributed to the peasantry after the census of 1891 revealed that the French population was barely reproducing itself. French natalists, believing that a low birthrate meant a loss of national vitality, placed their hopes in fertile peasant families. World War I further persuaded agrarian conservatives that peasant vitality was a necessary precondition of national defense. "At the darkest times," recalled Marshal Pétain in 1935, "it was the calm and decided look of the French peasant that sustained my confidence."[94] Although peasants were indeed overrepresented in the trenches, as many skilled industrial workers were assigned to armaments production, no persuasive evidence proves that they fought better than anyone else—even though agrarians liked to think so.

The ideal of the peasant nation could not acquire its full emotional force until the word "peasant" had been rescued from opprobrium. We see in Chapter 3 how Dorgères worked, with many others, to hasten this revolution in meaning. He and his allies succeeded to the point where, today, it has come to be one of the most positive French words for a farmer. A peasant is not merely one who cultivates the soil; a peasant embodies all the virtues associated with a healthy, rooted, traditional rural culture.

By the 1930s, the peasant virtues of social stability, military vitality, and economic balance played a large role in the imagination of French conservatives. Dorgères never tired of calling the peasantry "the healthy, serious, and solid base of this country."[95] France must "give the priority to the peasant economy." Once unified and organized, the peasantry would be able to oppose both communism and capitalism, and to "defend Western Civilisation against asiatic corruption."[96] Jacques Le Roy Ladurie wrote in *Mait' Jacques* in June 1937 that "the hour of the peasantry . . . is near." Amid the increasing anarchy created by the illusory pursuit of urban prosperity, France would soon have to call on its peasant core. Then the peasantry would fulfill its "historic mission" to "guarantee social peace" and "reestablish economic stability" in "balance and peace."[97] "France needs happy peasants," said Marshal Pétain in 1939, "to get back to the source of its vitality and its balance."[98] For many agrarian conservatives at the end of the 1930s, France was most fully itself as a peasant nation, with a mass of independent family farms as its principal socioeconomic base.

Similar thinking permeated even the leadership of Republican agricultural organizations, such as the permanent Association of Presidents of the Chambres d'Agriculture (APPCA) and the netork of cooperative and credit organizations linked to the boulevard Saint-Germain. Other perspectives on the agricultural economy were rarely expressed. The opposing side was limited mostly to socialists (who had little influence in agricultural circles) and free-trade liberals (a declining species in the 1930s). Agricultural specialists between the world wars who gave a higher priority to rationalizing French agriculture than to keeping all farms afloat through higher prices—the ubiquitous price increase *(révalorisation)* demanded by Dorgères and the conservative agrarians—were the exception. The best known was René Dumont and his mentor, Jacques Duboin. Horrified by the deliberate creation of scarcity by crop destruction and industrial cutbacks as a Depression remedy, they affirmed that a rural society could have both abundance and ease if farms were larger and more mechanized. Their ideal was farms large enough and modern enough to produce enough in eight-hour days to feed all of France and compete in the world market, while consuming more industrial products (such as farm machinery and fertilizer). They accepted the disappearance of small, inefficient peasant holdings.[99] Dumont's priorities were to influence policy only after the Liberation.

World War II played a pivotal role in the perception of France as a peasant nation. Vichy policymakers were divided on this issue. The traditionalists among them, dominant in the first shock of defeat, fostered the return to the soil that was occurring anyway. They imposed a long-sought unity on agricultural organizations and granted them quasi-state functions within a new public authority designed to give farmers the principal responsibility for nurturing and managing agriculture, the Peasant Corporation. As technocrats and modernizers grew more powerful at Vichy in 1941 and more French industrialists began working for the Nazi war machine, Admiral Darlan and such of his associates as François Lehideux and Jean Bichelonne began preparing France to play an industrial role in a united continental Europe, capable of competing with the Americans and the British. The collapse of Vichy discredited the first school of thought; the second school was quietly integrated into postwar reconstruction when the Commissariat Général au Plan took over some of its projects and absorbed some of the younger staff members of the Vichy Ministry of Industrial Production.[100]

The defeat of 1940 made it harder to argue convincingly that France could best ensure its future by closing in on itself as a peasant nation. It was easier to believe, with Marc Bloch, that what had been defeated in France was its rural charm[101] and, with Jean Monnet, that the future lay with full participation in the world economy as an efficient producer, both of agricultural and of industrial products. Dorgères—ever a sponge of ambient ideas—had his first glimpse of France's future as an agricultural exporter in 1941, under the influence of the collaborationists' vision of a "new Europe": "France must and can become the garden of Europe."[102]

That is exactly what France began to do after the Liberation. It is important to remember what a central place agriculture had in the vision of Jean Monnet and his Commissariat au Plan. But the planners meant to encourage Dumont's kind of mechanized farmers capable of producing at world prices, not a peasant nation. Immediately after the Liberation, the Planning Commission's efforts to modernize French agriculture were driven by two immediate needs: first, to feed the French population, half starved by fourteen years of agricultural disinvestment and four of pillage; and, next, to restore a positive trade balance, urged on by the eagerness of the United States to be relieved of its aid burden. They were terrified by the prospect of a peasant France caught in a descending spiral of trading low-value-added products for high-value-added ones, like the less-developed world today. So they explicitly recognized that the most marginal farms must disappear.[103] The plan of 1948 added a more ambitious long-term goal for French agriculture: to produce surpluses for export.[104] Farm products have never since lost their prominence in French economic thinking as a way to earn foreign exchange.

President De Gaulle turned France decisively toward agricultural competitiveness in 1958 by accepting entry into the Common Market. He took a calculated gamble on France's potential dominance of European food production. Entering the Common Market, however, meant accepting profound social and economic adjustments. The most productive sectors of French agriculture must compete with the most efficient farmers of Europe, such as the Danes and the Dutch. The least efficient farms must disappear. This triage must be made on economic criteria alone, social considerations coming into play only in the assistance given to those farmers who leave the soil. The surviving farms, those capable of competing abroad, would then receive aid. Economic triage became even more urgent when France began to export beyond Europe. Meeting world prices required export subsidies, and neither French taxpayers nor the European Community could be expected to subsidize inefficient farms.

Two agricultural orientation laws, in 1960 and 1962,[105] set up machinery to forward this rapid adaptation of French agriculture to world market standards. At the same time, laws were framed to retain the social texture of the family farm through retirement benefits to hasten overdue departures, collective structures[106] to help family farmers pool their marketing arrangements and their ownership of expensive machinery, the systematic reassemblage of small dispersed plots into larger units (*remembrement*), restrictions on the sale of farmland to prevent speculators from removing it from cultivation and pushing up its price,[107] assistance to young farmers starting up, price subsidies, and a promise to raise living standards for small and medium farmers to parity with the urban middle class—all in return for the family farmers' willingness to produce as much as possible.

The gamble succeeded. Within twenty years, France had become the second agricultural exporter of the world (after the United States) and the first agricultural producer of Europe. France was not just "the garden of

Europe," as Dorgères had dared to hope in 1941, but "the great agricultural power of Europe."[108] Transformed French farm products go around the world under labels like Dannon and Yoplait. France subsidizes massive exports of vegetable oils and frozen poultry and has seized a large share of world agricultural sales from the hitherto dominant United States.[109] Rouen has surpassed Duluth as the world's largest wheat-exporting port.[110] French farmers have also acquired the sad distinction of being among the world's heaviest users of fertilizers and chemical pesticides and herbicides.[111] Family farmers in Canada, the United States, and New Zealand have learned to fear the French colossus.

This trade-driven transformation of French agriculture has had shattering social effects. Small farms, long dwindling slowly, have now crashed. Where four peasants still tilled the soil in 1950, there is one farmer today.[112] What is left of French agriculture is more homogeneous. Since day laborers,[113] sharecroppers, and small renters have become far fewer, and since the social power of the great proprietors has vanished, French farmers are increasingly grouped around two social types: the independent family farmer and the industrial-scale cultivator. It has become easier to unite this narrowed social range within one semiofficial farmers' association, the FNSEA, and its affiliated organization for those under thirty-five, the CNJA.[114]

Moreover, farmers are now fully reintegrated into French society. This is partly the result of the economic parity that Dorgères and his conservative allies advocated. Farm families generally have television and kitchen appliances. Some of them even take vacations. Most of them sell their produce to a giant cooperative or processing company and provision their own tables at the supermarket. The ancient stigmata of peasant difference—weather-beaten bodies, coarse dress, regional dialects (*patois*)—have been largely erased. Insecurity, the grimmest aspect of peasant difference, has been reduced to urban dimensions as the Fourth and Fifth Republics extend the welfare state to agriculture. That task had already been started in Dorgères's day, and he bet wrong about it. When he chose family benefits as his main issue in 1938, it was already apparent that what most peasants wanted was parity, not difference. It has become harder to speak, as did Dorgères and Jacques Le Roy Ladurie, of a separate and distinct peasant civilization. The postwar planners aimed explicitly to assimilate peasants into French society as full citizens. They have largely succeeded.

Thus agricultural society is no longer a "ghetto," a world apart. Exchanges of population between farms and cities, achieved in preindustrial times by seasonal labor migrations, have now been revived in new forms: the return of retirees, the visits of children, the establishment of light industry in rural villages, and more part-time work in towns for many farm family members. Electronic networks permit growing numbers of business and professional people to perform their work in pleasant rural surroundings.[115] The rural population (as distinct from the farm population) has ceased to decline. It has even turned slightly upward.[116] The rebirth of a new rural society is at hand, although it will never again be as purely agricultural as in Dorgères's day. That "peasant ghetto" was, after all, a brief and exceptional moment of rural isolation.

All these postwar developments seem, at first glance, to make Dorgères as archaically remote as Jacquou le Croquant. Yet, subtle but insistent echoes persist in France today of a mental universe in which Dorgères would have felt entirely at home. France has become conscious of a peasant identity in inverse proportion to the number of its farmers. The very disappearance of traditional peasant society has permitted its harshest features to be forgotten and its beauties to be romanticized—an attitude already apparent at the turn of the century. "All townspeople must be like that," mused the peasant organizer and author Emile Guillaumin in 1904:

> They see only the pleasures that the country can give. They dream about the meadows, the trees, the birds, the flowers, the milk, the butter, the vegetables and the fruit. They have not the least idea of the sufferings of those who work there, the peasants. And we are in exactly the same position, when we speak of the advantages of the towns.[117]

We need to be reminded today how grim living conditions still were on most French farms in Dorgères's day. As late as the 1930s, hired hands often slept with the animals in stables, without any sanitary facilities or even a bed;[118] poverty, disease, illiteracy, malnutrition, and mental disorders were more prevalent in the countryside than in the town.

A very large number of French people today can connect idealized images of peasants' happiness to authentic early memories because there were so many peasants a mere two generations ago and because they have disappeared so recently. Many people have peasant grandparents, and the homestead is the seat of nostalgia for more of them than for other, comparable European nations. That gives the mental universe in which Dorgères flourished an immediacy in France that is unique among urban, industrial nations in the West. It persists, even a generation or two after the socioeconomic world that it reflected has vanished.

The very intensity of the debate in France about the proper place of agriculture in the nation reflects that immediacy. Other countries have indulged in nostalgic regrets about the declining family farmer. But they did so earlier; and in most cases such plaints were swept aside long ago by the rush to economic development. The most radical decline of the family farmer in Britain came before the nineteenth century. When Cobbett, Blake, and Coleridge lamented "deserted villages" and "dark satanic mills" in "England's green and pleasant land" in the early nineteenth century, it was already too late. Having already sacrificed its peasantry to sheep raising in the sixteenth and seventeenth centuries, Britain gave up agricultural protection almost without a murmur in 1846.

Germany, like France, protected its agriculture after the 1870s for explicit reasons of social harmony and balance. The Depression's epidemic of farm foreclosures and a longing to rescue a traditional peasantry from modernization helped bring the Nazis to power in 1933. Subsquently, however, Hitler favored industry and a rural exodus in order to feed his rearmament drive, supposing perhaps that he could redeem his pledges to German peasants later by gifts of rich, Ukrainian black earth. In the United States, many family farms in the earliest-settled parts of the country, especially the Appalachians and hills of New England, were abandoned when the western frontier opened up in the mid-nineteenth century. For Americans, it is the frontier and the wilderness that serve as reservoirs of moral values. These images attached to land are the product of a different national experience. In the United States, the land is most sacred where the individual is most unfettered. In France, the land is most sacred where the human community is most intact (an altogether admirable value, but one that may require active support and heavy expenses).

The particular experience of France, with its dense fabric of peasant society right up to 1945 and the agrarian dreams fostered by the Depression and German occupation, have left powerful residues in the French imagination. Four echoes of those agrarian dreams have become axiomatic in France today. They are so ubiquitous, even among city dwellers, that it is hard to grasp that they are historical constructs, neither "natural" nor eternal. They contain elements of myth, rooted firmly in the era when it seemed plausible to perceive France's identity as a peasant nation.

The first axiom is that France is not itself without a large peasantry. France is exceptional today for the number of its citizens who are unwilling to decide on purely economic grounds how many farmers France should have. It is not, for them, a simple calculation of how many farmers it takes to feed the French population, plus producing some specialties for export. The proportion of peasants in the French population, they believe fervently, is also an issue of fundamental national identity. They resurrect the conviction common to Virgil, Rousseau, and Chateaubriand—relatively muted in the middle and late nineteenth century before its revival in the twentieth—that peasant society is the seat of special virtues lacking in urban society. They believe France is losing essential moral and social values as its farm population, once a major mark of French exceptionalism, dwindles to levels close to those of other industrial nations.[119]

These social and moral imperatives dictate a second axiom: that even areas not particularly suitable for agriculture should be farmed. This position is defended by the Confédération Paysanne, the principal farmers' organization to the Left of the FNSEA, on social grounds: "disfavored regions," where climate or topography make agriculture difficult, need compensatory assistance to prevent agriculture from declining there. Total cultivation is defended even at the highest levels of government. French agriculture, said Agriculture Minister Jean Puech in January 1995, "has two complementary missions": to produce foodstuffs in "intensive and competitive" fashion and to "occupy the territory."[120] This second mission argues strongly against letting any poor land go out of cultivation, whether to reduce agricultural surpluses or because of the human, economic, and environmental costs of wresting a crop from it. No one expects, of course, to continue to make wine on Montmartre except for tourists, but in this view every inch of France that was brought into cultivation in the expansionist days of the 1960s and 1970s ought to so continue.

This leads to the third axiom, that the land is not beautiful unless it is cultivated. In the eye of the "peasant nation," land without the shaping hand of man becomes "desert." "Bare idle land *[la jachère nue]* is a scandal," declared a recent minister of agriculture.[121] "Farmers shape the landscape."[122] The danger of "desertification" is evoked today ubiquitously in France, from *L'Humanité*[123] to the National Front. The word "desert," once a neutral or even favorable term for thinly inhabited country (as in the fantastical pleasure park built west of Paris in the eighteenth century and called "le désert de Retz"), has been debased to frighten people who know little about the countryside into accepting the social sacrifices needed to keep every inch in cultivation.

The scarecrow of desertification conceals the extensive tracts of marshes, moors, heaths, wet meadows, woodlands, and hedgerows that were destroyed during the years of all-out agricultural expansion between 1960 and 1980—and continue to be. It also conceals the potential benefits of restoring some of these lost treasures Frence's natural patrimony. Just as Prosper Mérimée and others taught in the 1830s that the built patrimony, up until then heedlessly destroyed, should be protected and restored, the same discovery is overdue for the natural patrimony. The EC's new requirement that land be taken out of cultivation to reduce unmanageable surpluses is now perceived only as a loss. But it should be seen as a positive opportunity to reverse the impoverishment of France's flora, fauna, and variety of landscape, now lost to the exotic new monocultures of corn, colza, and sunflowers. Instead of lamenting the supposedly idle "fallow," France could rejoice in increased game, the recovery of rare plants and animals, more recreational possiblities; and more natural beauty in marshes, brushy edges, and moorlands.

The fear of desert is further encouraged by the long French preference for the cultivated landscape. Of the two forms of Arcadian myth, the wild and the cultivated, Americans, who felt a mission to build a new society in virgin land, have always been more drawn to the wild.[124] They find inspiration in "wilderness," a word for which there is no exact equivalent in French. The French, in their millenially worked land, are at the other extreme in their stress on the cultivated. "Unlike the United States," recalled former Agriculture Minister Edgard Pisani, "we are a country that does not like desert or overgrown fields *[la friche]*."[125]

But the belief that any cultivation at all is better than none can be used to justify egregious assaults on the French natural patrimony and landscape. The real "desert" consists of miles of sunflowers drenched in chemical pesticides and herbicides, uninhabitable by authentic French flora and fauna. The habit that triumphed in the 1930s, with the Peasant Front, of subsuming all of agriculture under the term "peasant" permits high-tech cultivators to claim the nation's emotional and financial support as "peasants" while sweeping the land bare of hedgerows and marshes and copses, soaking it with chemicals, and producing on an industrial scale exotic crops such as soybeans, unknown to their grandparents.

Dorgères would have approved all these axioms. He did not use the word "desert"—it is a new discovery—but he believed entirely that every parcel must remain cultivated. He never had occasion to imagine any other use of rural land, and he never imagined it. Each farm that went out of cultivation—even a marginal one of inescapable misery—was for him a tragedy. A departure for school and the city was never, for him, a liberation but a soul lost.

A final axiom holds that French farmers are authentic peasants, whereas other nations' farmers are soulless entrepreneurs who cultivate the soil only for immediate profit or, worse still, vast impersonal agribusinesses. The personification of French agriculture as the family farmer of ancestral acres does bear some relation to reality. As small renters and sharecroppers have diminished, the substantial family farm has become a larger percentage of total farms. The family farm worked by two "UTH" (*unités de travail humain*) was the basic type of farm set out as the ideal in the orientation laws of 1960–62, the basic charter of post–Common Market French agriculture.

But the independent family farm that fully and solely occupies a husband, a wife, and their children is not, in practice, today's norm. Many farms occupy only part of the family's time, while the rest is spent in outside work.[126] An increasing proportion of farm wives work in town. Then there are the great industrial farms, which are never mentioned in agrarian rhetoric but which play a very large role in French production and exports. This sector of French agriculture receives the largest share of state subsidies, too;[127] it includes the large cereal and sugar beet farms of the north, which even in Dorgères's day, were sometimes run by industrial concerns rather than by families.[128] Even when these are owned and inhabited by a family, they are not worked by the family as a group. In Dorgères's day they were worked by masses of hired hands; today they are worked by machines and offer employment to part of the family.

French agrarian values are more thoroughly committed to the preservation of community in rural society than in most Western countries because the young farmers' allegiance in the 1930s was won mainly by the Catholic Farm Youth, Jeunesse Agricole Chrétienne (JAC), which carried forward a strong communitarian tradition. The defeat of Dorgères's more confrontational policy, which stressed private rights and high-price solutions, was in fact a significant turning point in rural values. The JAC was more effective with young farmers in Catholic regions of France than Dorgérism in the 1930s because the parish gave it a more solid structure, because it encouraged technical progress, and because its advocacy of social action appealed more effectively to the conservative young farmers' apoliticism than did Dorgères's form of direct action. After the war, the JAC succeeded in mobilizing much of the younger generation of French farmers in conservative areas of France.[129]

The most influential post-1960 agrarian leaders, such as Michel Debatisse and François Guillaume, came up through the JAC, which helps explain why French agricultural policy tries more than that of other modern nations to keep the rural social texture alive and to promote collectivity in rural settings. This is entirely admirable and has so far persuaded most French people to support this policy in the national budget. It is good to preserve rural society where it can have sufficient density to function as an economcically viable community—a praiseworthy goal of the JAC's heirs.

Since World War II, a contradictory element has entered the mental landscape of French agriculture, one unknown to the "peasant nation": agricultural exports as an instrument of state economic power—what former President Valéry Giscard d'Estaing liked to call "green oil" (*le pétrole vert*). In Dorgères's day, there was scarcely an inkling of this new mission for French agriculture. In the 1930s, France could mostly—not every year and not in every commodity—feed itself, but agrarian conservatives wanted to soak up the occasional surplus at home. Their emphasis was on protection and price supports. Since 1945, and with redoubled energy since 1960, the emphasis has been on productivity and exports.

Dorgères first grasped the idea of exports in 1941, as we saw. The post-1945 planners made consensual the idea that a modernized French agriculture could earn foreign exchange and serve the interests of national economic prosperity. Around 1968, France became fully self-supporting in foodstuffs (except for a few tropical products) and a major exporter in the 1970s. Now it is with real pride that spokesmen like Agriculture Minister Philippe Vasseur proclaim that "we have every intention of affirming our capacity as a great productive and exporting nation."[130]

The race for agricultural grandeur changes everything. When the "peasant nation" becomes a world-class exporter, it can no longer avoid the pressures and forces of the international market from which Dorgères and his notable allies wanted to shield an autarkic agrarian France. It also provides a justification for all-out productivity extended to the maximum, without concern about surpluses or about damage to the natural environment. And it creates a new motive for persuading the French public to subsidize agriculture.

Yet there are powerful internal obstacles to continuation of the 1960s dash toward productivity at all costs, and it is a grave error to suppose that all the objections come from outside France: the EC, GATT, and the United States. The mass of surplus products, and the growing cost—France no longer has a net gain from the Common Agricultural Policy (CAP)[131]—are powerful domestic incentives to accept the economic and environmental imperatives of agriculture in the twenty-first century. Healthy steps are being taken in that direction: France finally, in 1989, stopped subsidizing all farmers through high prices—a Dorgérist model—and shifted to income support.

So, caught in a three-way tension among the dream of a peasant nation, success as a world agricultural power based on mechanized productivity, and the limits imposed by the costs of that very success, France still wonders how to maintain a large peasant population, what it will cost, and how it might be accomplished. An overwhelming percentage (74%) of the French public supports subsidies to agriculture, "for we must maintain rural France no matter what it costs." The 19% who disagree (mostly on the Left) believe, contrary to the values of a peasant nation, that agriculture "is an economic activity like any other."[132] Dorgérism gave a rather crude but powerful impulse to the vision of France as a peasant nation without, to be sure, being solely responsible for its current persistence. His kind of perspective lingers in the French national consciousness today, troubling the people's sense of their priorities and of their identity as they adapt in the short space of one lifetime to world competition in agriculture.

NOTES

AN   *Archives Nationales,* French National Archives

AD   *Archives Départementales,* French departmental archives, followed by the name of the particular department

CAC   *Centre des archives contemporaines,* annex of the French National Archives for contemporary papers, at Fontainebleau

OURS   *Office Universitaire de Recherche Socialiste*

PAO   *Progrès agricole de l'ouest,* Dorgères's newspaper in Brittany

PCO   *Paysan du Centre-Ouest,* Dorgères's newspaper in the Loire Valley

PP   *Préfecture de Police,* Paris

INTRODUCTION

1. Paris: Les Oeuvres Françaises, 1935.

2. Dorgérist orators sometimes closed their speeches by shouting it. Cf. PCO, 12 September 1935. It was also the title of the monthly newspaper of Dorgères's action squads, the Greenshirts.

3. Pierre Barral, *Les Agrariens français de Méline à Pisani* (Paris: A. Colin, 1968), p. 238. It is better in French: "plus formé à l'art oratoire qu'à l'art aratoire."

4. Called *Le Cri du paysan* after 1937.

5. For example, *La Défense paysanne de la Charente-Inférieure* (1935–37), *La Défense paysanne de la Seine-Inférieure* (1935), and *La Provence paysanne* (1938–39). *L'Action paysanne* supported Dorgères in Toulouse in 1935–37 but then was absorbed by a rival.

6. *Le Cri du sol,* 16 October 1943.

7. For example, 7000 at Montbrison (Loire), 18 September 1938, the biggest meeting in 100 years of farmers' organizations in that department. Jean Vercherand, *Un siècle de syndicalisme agricole: la vie locale et nationale à travers le cas du département de la Loire* (Saint-Etienne: Centre d'Etudes Foréziennes, Université de Saint-Etienne, 1994), p. 67.

8. This once utilitarian, indoor grain market has been remodeled by the city of Blois into a sleek auditorium and exhibition space.

9. Paul Marion, "Le Paysan veut vivre: D'Halluin est mort, vive Dorgères!" *Vu*, No. 366, 20 March 1935, p. 342. Marion's taste for this kind of show fitted him to administer Vichy France's propaganda efforts, from February 1941 and January 1944, first as *secrétaire-général*, then as *secrétaire d'etat à l'information*. He testified in Dorgères's postwar trial, on 25 April 1945, that he helped finance Dorgères's propaganda services (AN: Z⁵ 127).

10. Raymond Triboulet, *Un Gaulliste de la IVᵉ* (Paris: Plon, 1985), p. 29.

11. *La Voix socialiste,* La Rochelle, 9th year, No. 143 (23 March 1933).

12. Fédération Nationale des Syndicats d'Exploitants Agricoles (National Federation of Farmers' Associations). The first president of the FNSEA was, however, an old sympathizer of Dorgères from the Loire Valley, Eugène Forget.

13. I borrow this apt phrase from Philippe Burrin, "La France dans le 'champ magnétique' des fascismes," *Le Débat,* No. 32 (November 1984).

14. *Le Progrès agricole de l'ouest* (PAO), 2 May 1937.

15. AN: Ministry of Justice, BB¹⁸–2914, M.

16. Isabel Boussard, "La Mort d'Henri Dorgères," *Le Monde,* 26 January 1985.

17. In addition to *Haut les fourches* (1935), *Au XXᵉ siècle: dix ans de Jacquerie* (Paris: Editions du Scorpion, 1959) and *Au Temps des fourches* (Paris: Editions France-Empire, 1975).

18. Henri Michel, "Histoire de la résistance française," *Revue historique,* No. 498 (April-June 1971), 484.

19. The law of 3 January 1979 that regulates access to French archives established a thirty-year rule, but the sixty-year restriction on archives that concern national security and private life has been extended in practice to cover most government records, including all prefectoral and police reports.

20. This probably accounts for the absence of monthly prefectoral reports in the Ministry of Interior files after 1935, for example.

21. Thousands of Sûreté Nationale files (including some concerning Dorgères), seized by the Germans during the occupation and then by Soviet troops as war booty in 1945, were being returned by the new Russian authorities to France as this book was being completed.

22. Some departmental archives, such as those of the Aisne, were fought over in two wars.

23. For example, part of the archives of Rouen.

24. The Ministry of Labor stopped compiling strike reports in 1935, just before the social explosion of 1936. Thus the agricultural strikes of 1936–37 have to be studied locally. In some departments (e.g., Ille-et-Vilaine), departing prefects seem to have taken their papers with them as late as the 1930s.

25. A barge loaded with archives sank during evacuation from Paris in 1940. Isabelle de Richefort, "Les Archives du Ministère de l'Agriculture," Institut d'Histoire du Temps Présent, *Bulletin trimestriel,* No. 23 (May 1986), 17.

26. Jean-Luc Allais, "Dorgères et ses hommes: la défense paysanne en Basse-Normandie," Mémoire de maîtrise, Université de Caen, 1992–93, consulted papers belonging to Germain Boullot, the national leader of the Greenshirts. The most

important private archive of a notable supporter of Dorgères, that of Jacques Le Roy Ladurie, remains closed.

27. Clifford Geertz, *The Interpretation of Cultures* (New York: Basic Books, 1973), p. 313.

CHAPTER I

1. Pierre Hallé, "La Politique du blé: le point de vue des producteurs," report to the Conseil National Economique 10 June 1931, p. 2 (AN: F^{10} 2180).

2. Lucien Romier, quoted in *La Revue des agriculteurs de France,* 67th year, No. 7 (July 1935), 247: "Only in France, cutting the bread remains a mealtime ritual even in the humblest households."

3. Direction des Services Agricoles to the prefect of the Somme, 29 March 1934 (AD Somme: M126).

4. Some proprietors of restored farms in the war zone, men of ambition and drive who knew how to get help from the French state and came to expect it, play an important role in this story. Such was the case with Adolphe Pointier of the Somme—head of his departmental *syndicat agricole,* then after 1934 president of the General Wheat Growers' Association (AGPB), and finally national chairman *(syndic)* of the *Peasant Corporation* of the Vichy regime—an early backer of Dorgères.

5. Hallé, "Politique du blé."

6. A quintal is a metric unit of weight amounting to 100 kilograms (about 220 pounds).

7. Letter of Martin, a farmer of the Tours region, to André Tardieu, 10 August 1930. André Tardieu papers (AN: 324AP 64).

8. "Révision des baux ruraux. Loi du 2 juillet 1935," Archives of the Ministère des Finances (AN, CAC Fontainebleau: B43235).

9. The Special Commissioner [of police] of Toulouse to the Director of the Sûreté Nationale, 17 October 1933 (AN: F7 13629, "Haute-Garonne").

10. A classic account of one Beauceron peasant's resourceful improvisation to avoid purchases during the Depression is Ephraim Grenadou and Alain Prévost, *Grenadou, paysan français* (Paris: Seuil, 1966), pp. 171–77.

11. *Journal officiel,* Débats, Chambre des Députés, 1 January 1936, p. 2938.

12. According to Gilles Postel-Vinay, "L'Agriculture dans l'économie française," in *Entre l'etat et le marché: l'économie française des années 1880 à nos jours,* ed. Maurice Lévy Leboyer (Paris: Gallimard, 1991), p. 83, the increased farm debt of the 1930s, reaching about 10 billion francs, was well below pre-1914 levels.

13. Postel-Vinay draws this distinction. Ibid., p. 66.

14. Letter of Joseph Caillaux to Henri Queuille, 18 May 1934, Henri Queuille papers (B12, "Correspondance"), Musée Henri Queuille, Neuvic d'Ussel (Corrèze).

15. AD Eure-et-Loire: 1M 21. The Entente Paysanne did the same in the Charentes.

16. *Police spéciale,* Caen, No. 1168, 26 June 1935 (AN, CAC Fontainebleau: No. 1–8-2304, Box 940451/28).

17. (PCO), 29 August 1935.

18. Ministry of Agriculture, "Table analytique des lois, décrêts, et arrêtés concernant le blé du 1er décembre 1929 au 15 mars 1934." (AN: F^{10} 2170).

19. André Tardieu described the world economic crisis as "born outside our country, for which we are not responsable." Speech at Giromagny, 17 April, n.d. (probably 1932) (AN: 324AP 58).

20. M. Beaumont, League of Nations, "Le Probléme du blé en France," General Assembly of the General Association of Wheat Producers (AGPB), 14 March 1932 (AN: F¹⁰ 2169).

21. *Admission temporaire* was the duty-free import of foreign wheat to be milled into flour and then reexported. The big flour millers, always looking for ways to use excess capacity, fought hard to keep this practice legal; peasant leaders denounced it uniformly and passionately, for they were convinced that a flour of foreign origin remained fraudulently in France. Even Left deputies elected in farm regions, like Pierre Mendès France of the Eure, wanted to abolish *admission temporaire*. Tardieu decreed that the flour must be exported within three months.

22. Like most conservative agricultural spokesmen, Dorgères dated the French state's subordination of agriculture to industry to Napoleon III and the Cobden-Chevalier free-trade treaty of 1860. The Commercial Treaties of the 1920s were, along with taxes and the infestation of France by civil servants, one of Dorgères' favorite targets. See *Haut les fourches* (Paris: Les Oeuvres Françaises, 1935), pp. 32–34, 47, 71.

23. For those who believed in the sanctity of wheat, these processes were "crimes of *lèse-humanité*." See letter of Raoul Lemaire to André Tardieu, n.d., André Tardieu papers, "Correspondance" (AN: 324AP 9).

24. Law of 10 July 1933, *Journal officiel*, 10–11 July 1933, pp. 7198ff.

25. *Journal officiel*, 29 December 1933.

26. Law of 15 August 1936, *Journal officiel*, 18 August 1936, p. 8866. (still in existence as the *Office National Interprofessionnel des Céréales*).

27. "Renseignements divers et situations de la Trésorerie fournis aux parlementaires et membres du gouvernement, janvier-octobre 1935," Archives of the Ministry of Finance (AN, CAC Fontainebleau: B33193).

28. Ibid., November 1935–October 1936 (AN, CAC Fontainebleau: B33194).

29. Dorgères never ceased to ridicule the farming abilities of Georges Monnet, who, he claimed, had gone bankrupt twice on some of the richest land in the Aisne.

30. Adolphe Pointier, supporter of Dorgères and president of the all-powerful AGPB, quit the board of the Office du Blé on 31 August 1936 because he thought it had set the price of wheat too low, but he did not try to have the office abolished. Dorgères attacked the office consantly, but more for its costs, its numerous "budget-eating" *(budgétivore)* employees, and its nonagricultural members than for the principle of its existence. He wanted an Office du Blé run entirely by the agricultural profession.

31. AN: 324AP 9, "Correspondence." Tardieu had sent Hallé a copy of his pamphlet "Alerte aux Français" (Paris: Flammarion, 1936).

32. AD Seine-Maritime: 1Z 6. See more fully in Chapter 2.

33. "Le Problème du blé: la politique du blé," Note sur la réunion du Groupe des "Agro" de l'Alimentation, 30 November 1934 (AN: F¹⁰ 2169).

34. Hallé, "Politique du blé," p. 42.

35. PAO, 18 December 1932. See more fully in Chapter 2.

36. M. de Mirepoix, president, Confédération Générale des Vignerons, report to the Conseil National Économique, 1 December 1930. (AN: F¹⁰ 2180).

37. André Tardieu used this figure in a speech he made as minister of agriculture at the Salon des Vins, Foire de Paris, 20 May 1931 (AN: 324AP 54).

38. AN: 324AP 58.

39. AN: F^{10} 2180.

40. From 147,000 hectares in 1907 to 399,512 hectares in 1939, much of it in large estates. Georges Chappaz, inspecteur honoraire à l'agriculture, "L'Organisation du marché de vins de consommation courante," report to the 3e section professionnelle, Conseil National Economique, 1939 (AN: F^{10} 2182).

41. Ibid., p. 14.

42. Laws of 4 July 1931, 8 July 1933, and 24 December 1934.

43. Chappaz, "Organisation du marché de vins," p. 18.

44. "Le marché français du vin—II," *Revue des agriculteurs de France,* 68th year, No. 3 (March 1936), 113.

45. The Service des Alcools bought eighteen million hectolitres of the 1934–35 production (ibid., p. 18). Distillation was also the safety valve for the sugar beet producers. Some was used for automobile fuel, the so-called *carburant national.*

46. Chappaz, "Organisation du marché de vins," p.29.

47. This was also true in Germany: J. E. Farquharson, "The Agrarian Policy of National Socialist Germany," in *Peasants and Lords in Modern Germany,* ed. Robert G. Moeller (Boston: Allen and Unwin, 1986), p. 235.

48. "Viande et animaux vivants," Conseil National Economique (AN: F^{10} 2180).

49. Rudolf Heberle, *Landbevölkerung und Nationalsozialismus: Eine soziologische Untersuchung der politischen Willensbildung in Schleswig-Holstein 1918–1932* (Stuttgart: Deutsche Verlags-Anstalt, 1963) is the classic work, prepared in 1932. In exile, the author published a much-abridged English version, *From Democracy to Nazism* (New York: Grosset and Dunlap, 1970); see p. 71.

50. For example, in a speech at Le Neuborg (Eure), 28 May 1934 (AD Eure: 1M161; PAO 3 July 1938). See also, independently of Dorgères, a resolution against the importation of frozen meat voted by the Municipal Council of Mamers (Sarthe) and forwarded by the prefect to the minister of agriculture in January 1935 (AN: F^{10} 2168).

51. Henri Girard, former president of the Confédération Générale des Producteurs de Lait, report to the Conseil National Economique, 15 January 1931 (AN: F^{10} 2180).

52. "Comptes rendus de la commission contre la vie chère," 31 May 1934 (AN: F^{10} 2168).

53. Achard report to the minister of agriculture, reprinted in *Mait' Jacques,* 27 May 1934. A liter is a little less than a quart.

54. This was, at least, the claim of the Confédération Générale des Producers de Lait, General Assembly, 15 March 1934 (AN: F^{10} 2168).

55. Arthur Boursier, *Histoire de la betterave* (Paris: Editions SEDA, 1983), gives CGB's perspective on its own history.

56. Law of 31 March 1933.

57. Law of 8 August 1935. This was called the Commission Poulle, after its chairman, a high magistrate.

58. For example, Jacques Le Roy Ladurie, *Mait' Jacques,* 22 April 1934 and 17 September 1937. Le Roy Ladurie overlooked the fact that the system was not self-

regulating: the French state kept it going by purchasing and distilling the surplus in years of overproduction.

59. Boursier, *Histoire de la betterave,* pp. 78–80. Modeste Legouez should also be counted among the Dorgériste sugar beet growers: in 1935, he organized a *syndicat betteravier* at Neubourg, in the plains of the Eure; he had come to Dorgérism earlier, during the price collapse. Ibid., p. 188.

60. PAO, 13 June 1937.

61. François Mévellec, *Le Combat du paysan Breton à son apogée* (Rennes: Imprimerie "Les Nouvelles," 1974), pp. 178, 338.

62. Jacques Chevalier. "Bouilleurs de cru et manifestations paysannes, 1934–36," *Le Pays Bas-Normand,* 73rd year, No. 3 (1980), 33.

63. Postel-Vinay, "L'Agriculture dans l'économie française," p. 82.

64. Ronald Hubscher, *L'Agriculture et la société rurale dans le Pas-de-Calais du milieu du XIXe siècle à 1914,* Mémoires de la Commission Départementale des Monmuments Historiques du Pas-de-Calais, XX, nos. 1–2, Arras, 1979–80, is particularly rich on the many kinds of farmers' complaints and actions in the 1880s that foreshadowed those of the 1930s.

65. The French census takers defined as "rural" those living in a commune with fewer than 2000 inhabitants.

66. About 51,000 males who had engaged in agriculture left the land each year in the prosperous years 1906–11, about 40,000 a year in 1921–26, but only 19,000 a year during the 1930s crisis. Since the exodus affected part-time and seasonal workers more than small owners and full-time workers, the number of farms declined by a lesser amount. Departures swelled to 70,000–80,000 a year in 1949–68. Postel-Vinay, "L'Agriculture dans l'économie française," pp. 75, 85.

67. Pierre Alphandéry, Pierre Bitoun, and Yves Dupont, *Les Champs du départ: une France rural sans paysans* (Paris: La Découverte, 1989), pp. 61–62. Cf. Dorgères, *Haut les fourches,* p. 28.

68. Out of the 3,700,000 farmers mobilized in 1914–18, 673,000 were killed. Louis Marin, *Journal officiel,* Chambre des Députés, Documents parlementaires, III, No. 633 (29 March 1920), 51–52.

69. *Revue des deux mondes,* Vol. 6 (1935), 758. This speech furnished ubiquitous quotations later: for example, the deputy Vincent Inizan in *Journal officiel,* Chambre des Députes, Débats, 3rd session (17 December 1935), p. 2684; and in *Syndicats paysans,* the newspaper of the Union Nationale des Syndicats Agricoles 15 December 1939.

70. Speech at Giromagny (Territory of Belfort), 17 April (probably 1932), André Tardieu papers, "Discours hors parlement" (AN: 324AP 58).

71. Speech to the *Société des Agriculteurs* of the Somme, Amiens, 16 May 1931 (AN: 324AP 54). The president of this association was Adolph Pointier, one of Dorgères's most powerful supporters, later head of the wheat growers' association (AGPB) and during Vichy national chairman *(syndic)* of the Peasant Corporation.

72. Review of Henri Queuille, *Le Drame agricole,* in *Le Figaro,* 4 July 1932.

73. Quoted by Jacques Le Roy Ladurie in *Mait' Jacques,* 17 April 1938.

74. AD Eure: 1M 162, "Commissaire de Police de Vernon, 1935–37."

75. Eugen Weber, *Peasants into Frenchmen: The Modernization of Rural France* (Stanford, Calif.: Stanford University Press, 1976); Roger Thabault, *Education and Change in a Village Community: Mazières-en-Gâtine, 1848–1914* (New York: Schocken, 1971).

76. Agrarian corporatists in the 1930s wanted farming to be considered a profession, and they referred increasingly to organized agriculture, with which they intended to replace the republican state in the management of agricultural affairs, as "la Profession," with a capital P. See Armand Frémont, *Paysans de Normandie* (Paris: Flammarion, 1981), p. 190.

77. Maurice Barrès had already assailed this view in *Les Déracinés* (Paris: E. Fasquelle, 1897).

78. For the *ecole d'agriculture* at Le Nivot, see Mévellec, *Combat du paysan Breton,* pp. 218–19, 237. The Vichy government was to establish a separate rural curriculum on 14 August 1941.

79. Dorgères to P. Le Floc'h, 18 November 1933 (AN: BB^{18} 2914, "Perquisition chez Henry Dorgères").

80. The Prefect of the Finistère to the Minister of the Interieur, 23 January 1935 (AD Finistère: 1M 133).

81. PAO, 5 May 1936. Darius Le Corre was later a Communist deputy of the Seine-et-Oise, 1936–40.

82. Ibid., 10 October 1937.

83. Ibid., 26 December 1937.

84. *Le journal de Neufchâtel,* 14 February 1939.

85. PAO, 5 December 1937.

86. Cf. Albert Mathiez, *La Vie chère et le mouvement social sous la terreur* (Paris: Payot, 1927).

87. Minutes of the sessions are in AN: F^{10} 2168.

88. *Journal officiel.* Débats, Sénat, 30 March 1933 (AN: F^{10} 2174, "Bourse de Commerce").

89. André Tardieu papers (AN: 324AP 54).

90. Joseph Faure, president of the Assemblée des Présidents des Chambres d'Agriculture, May 1936: reestablishment of peasant purchasing power is "the essential foundation of the whole economic structure of the country" (*Les Travaux des chambres d'agriculture,* 10 June 1936). The Chambre d'Agriculture of the Côtes-du-Nord, 23 May 1935: the whole national economy depends on "the farmers' purchasing power" (AD Côtes-d'Armor: 7M).

91. "When peasants don't buy, cities like Chartres die." PCO, 1st year, No. 1, 15 December 1932.

92. UNSA communiqué: "Rural purchasing power is the primordial element of the French economy." *Les Travaux des chambres d'agriculture,* 19 May 1935.

93. For example, the title of his Ambassadeurs speech of April 1935 was "The Peasant Will Save France."

94. Farquharson, "Agrarian Policy," p. 245.

95. Le Roy Ladurie, *Mait' Jacques,* 7 March 1937.

96. This was the thesis of the Russian economist Alexander Chayanov, whose work influenced a school of Western theorists who viewed a "peasant rationality" as distinct from a market rationality. See Teodor Shanin, ed., *Peasants and Peasant Societies* (New York: Penguin, 1971), and Gregor Dallas, *The Imperfect Peasant Economy* (Cambridge: Cambridge University Press, 1982), pp. 27–39.

97. See Steven Laurence Kaplan, *Le pain, le peuple, et le roi* (Paris: Perrin, 1986) and other works.

98. Richard Cobb, *The Peoples' Armies: The armées révolutionnaires: Instrument of the Terror in the Departments, April 1793 to Floréal Year II* (New Haven, Conn.: Yale University Press, 1987).

99. *L'Humanité,* 14 December 1936; 4 March, 28 April, and 19 June 1937; among others.

100. *Les Travaux des chambres d'agriculture,* 10 January 1935, p. 3.

101. Speech at Alençon, 28 September 1930, André Tardieu papers, "Discours hors parlement" (AN: 324AP 54).

102. André Tardieu, *La Révolution à refaire: le souverain captif* (Paris: Flammarion, 1936), and *La Profession parlementaire* (Paris: Flammarien, 1937).

103. PCO, 18 January 1934.

104. PAO, 16 December 1934.

105. Ibid., 13 January 1935.

106. Dorgères charged Mauger with assault for allegedly hitting him with a chair after a meeting at Romorantin (Loir-et-Cher) on 28 March 1939; the case was dropped. "Résumeé des affaires Dorgères contenus dans le présent dossier," No. XVI (AN: BB^{18} 2915).

107. See Chapter 2 for more detail.

108. "Aux chiottes les députés!" PAO, 8 September 1935.

109. A typically pungent epithet by Jacques Le Roy Ladurie, *Souvenirs 1902–1945* (Paris: Flammarion, 1997), p. 83.

110. Chéron failed to be elected deputy of his own city of Lisieux, of which he was mayor; he was deputy for Caen I, 1906–13, and senator of the Calvados, 1913–36. The Radical Party, once "radical" against Napoleon III in the 1860s, was now a moderate party devoted to civil liberties, secularism, and the interests of provincial small property.

111. The "Chéron law" of 12 March 1920 authorized farmers' cooperatives to operate commercial enterprises, a right that store owners had opposed.

112. See later in this chapter for a fuller discussion of that curious feature of the French Third Republic: its twin networks of farm organizations, one "republican" (moderate Left and anticlerical) and the other Catholic and cool (if not worse) toward the Republic.

113. Ernest Labrousse, "Avant-propos," in Maurice Lévy-Leboyer, *Le Revenu agricole et la rente foncière en Basse-Normandie: étude de croissance régionale* (Paris: Klincksieck, 1972), p. viii.

114. Le Roy Ladurie, unpublished memoirs.

115. "A nos lecteurs," PCO, 1st year, No. 1, 15 December 1932.

116. Nicholas Varin, "Le Parti agraire et paysan français (1928–36)," Mémoire préparé pour le DEA, Institut d'Etudes politiques, Paris, 1995; Marc Leclair, "Le Parti agraire et paysan français, 1928–39," Mémoire de maîtrise, Université de Paris X, Nanterre, 1974. The PAPF also managed to elect a few *conseillers généraux* and *conseillers municipaux* in 1935 and 1937, especially in the Loire Valley, the Côte d'Or, and Haute Loire.

117. The Subprefect of Dieppe to the Prefect of the Seine-Inférieure, 25 March 1933 (AD Seine-Maritime: 1Z 6, "Parti agraire").

118. Boursier, *Histoire de la betterave,* pp. 64–65.

119. PAO, 14 June 1936.

120. A useful study is Mark C. Cleary, *Peasants, Politicians, and Producers: The Organization of Agriculture in France since 1918* (Cambridge: Cambridge University Press, 1989). See also Paul Houet, *Coopération et organisations agricoles françaises—bibliographie* (Paris: Editions Cujas, 1970); and Louis Prugnaud, *Les Etapes du syndicalisme agricole en France* (Paris: Editions de l'épi, 1963).

121. For example, Soissons, founded in 1850, "sometimes inactive" but vigorous on Sunday, 9 July 1933 (AN: F7 13629, Aisne).

122. For example, Châteauneuf (Maine-et-Loire). Dorgères saluted "my friend" Eugene Forget, later first president of the FNSEA (1947), for organizing the centennial celebration of its *comice* in 1935. PCO, 3 October 1935.

123. PAO, 15 October 1933.

124. See Suzanne Berger, *Peasants against Politics: Rural Organization in Brittany, 1911–1967* (Cambridge, Mass.: Harvard University Press, 1972).

125. Henri Mendras, "Les Organisations agricoles," in *Les Paysans et la politique dans la France contemporaine,* ed. Jacques Fauvet et Henri Mendras (Paris: A. Colin, 1958), pp. 231–51.

126. *Le Matin,* 28 January 1936; the Public Prosecutor of Rennes to the Minister of Justice, 27 January 1936 (AN: BB[18] 2915, 31A34/36F: "Poursuites c/Dorgères pour action illicite sur le marché et provocation à des attroupements"). Dorgères claimed an attendance of 6000, the Prefect thought 3000, the Public Prosecutor 2500—a fairly typical spread of estimates.

127. Its first president, Eugène Forget, had been a Parti Agraire candidate for parliament and a sympathizer of Dorgères in the Maine-et-Loire in the 1930s.

128. Le Roy Ladurie, *Souvenirs,* pp. 34–35.

129. This is the definition of rural notable in Henri Mendras, *La Fin des paysans,* 2nd ed. (Paris: Actes-Sud, 1984), pp. 18, 59, 70.

130. The CGPT and the PAPF cooperated in a demonstration against a judicial sale in the Côtes-du-Nord in June 1934. The Prefect to the Minister of the Interior, 25 June 1934 (AD Côtes-d'Armor: 1M 264).

131. The Prefect of the Corrèze to the Minister of the Interior, 20 March 1934. (AD Corrèze: 1M 76).

132. Ibid., 9 January 1935 (AD Corrèze: 7M 22).

133. Ibid., 26 February 1935. The Prefecture of Chartres was occupied on 14 January 1933 by activists of the Parti Agraire; Dorgères was not involved. A vivid eye-witness account is found in Grenadou and Prévost, *Grenadou* pp. 178–80.

134. The Subprefect of Brive to the Prefect of the Corrèze, 10 October 1935. (AD Corrèze: 7M 22).

135. The indispensable account is by Heberle, *Landbevölkerung und Nationalsozialismus.*

CHAPTER 2

1. For Dorgères's early years, we have drawn on Clément Lépine, "La Naissance du mouvement Dorgériste (1926–1930)," Mémoire de maîtrise, Université de Paris Nord, Paris XIII, 1993.

2. Ibid.; Cour de Justice de Châteauroux, Renseignements sur Henry Dorgères. 8 November 1944. AN: Z[5] 127. No. 5815.

3. Cour de Justice de l'Indre, Chambre d'Instruction, Procès-verbal d'interroga-toire, A. Boulade-Périgois, Juge d'Instruction, 10 November 1944 AN: Z^5 127. No. 5815.

4. PAO, 10 October 1937.

5. In the issues on 3, 8, 11, and 17 March 1919. These notes were discovered by Lépine, "Naissance," p. 13.

6. Parquet de la Cour de Justice de la Seine, Citation directe contre D'Halluin, dit d'Orgères [sic], AN: Z^5 127. No. 5815.

7. Pascal Ory, "Henry Dorgères et la 'Défense Paysanne' des origines à 1939," Mémoire de maîtrise, Faculté des Lettres et Sciences Humaines de Nanterre, 1970, p. 30; Lépine, "Naissance," p. 17. In a rare interview near the end of his life, Dorgères was reticent about the circumstances of his move to Rennes and his entry into farmers' journalism. Régis Fricot and Pierre Genaitay, Dorgères et le mouvement paysan, Mémoire de maîtrise, Université de Rennes, 1972, pp. 8–10.

8. Le Sillon, a Catholic laymen's movement and newspaper that sought to recon-cile the church with political democracy, had been condemned by Pope Pius X in 1910.

9. Pierre Barral, "Les syndicats Bretons de cultivateurs-cultivants," Le Mouvement social, No. 67, April–June 1969.

10. Speech to the UNCA General Assembly of 1926, quoted in Pierre Barral, "As-pects régionaux de l'agrarisme français avant 1930," Le Mouvement social, No. 67, April–June 1969, p. 156. The Marquis de Vogüé was also president of the Suez Canal Company.

11. Some think the archbishop wanted to separate his agricultural activities from the Nouvelliste after the papal condemnation of the Action Française in December 1926.

12. In a letter of 4 November 1933 to a M. Paillière, Dorgères said he was willing to accept associates of any political persuasion except those "who would like to make religious influences predominant in the government of this country" (AN: BB^{18} 2914). He probably meant Christian Democracy, one of his lifelong hatreds.

13. The Minister of the Interior to the Minister of Justice (Garde des Sceaux), No. 15.637, 21 December 1934 (AN: BB^{18} 2915, "Dorgéres—Annexe"). Pascal Ory reached the same figure by consulting the feuilles de dépôt légal. See Ory, "Henry Dorg-ères," pp. 200–1; and Pascal Ory, "Le Dorgérisme: institution et discours d'une colère paysanne (1929–39), Revue d'histoire moderne et contemporaine, XXII, No. 2 (April–June 1975), 172.

14. The Minister of the Interior to the Minister of Justice 21 December 1934 (AN: BB^{18} 2915). The duc d'Harcourt sat in the Chamber of Deputies as a Républicain Indépendant.

15. L'Avenir du Bessin, 1 January 1936, p. 2; 5 February 1936.

16. The Public Prosecutor of Rennes to the Minister of Justice (Garde des Sceaux), 29 January 1935: "The prosecutor's office [parquet] believes that Dorgères is a royalist agent" (AN: BB^{18} 2915).

17. The list of subscribers is found in a letter of the Prefect of the Ill-et-Vilaine to the Minister of the Interior, 21 December 1934 (AD Ille-et-Vilaine: 1M 147a). The duc d'Harcourt had 350 of the 560 shares, possibly, the prefect suggested, as a front man for a group of investors. Dorgères admitted to a judge that the duc originally

held a majority of the shares, but he had diminished his holdings and was not "master of this newspaper." Interrogation of Dorgères, 11 April 1935 (AN: BB^{18} 2915, "Dorgères—Annexe").

18. *Regards vers un passé* (Paris: Robert Laffont, 1989).

19. Fricot and Genaitay, *Dorgerès*, p. 43, and annex XXIII. The police found no evidence of La Bourdonnaye's connections to Dorgères, however, when they searched the Count's home in 1935 during Dorgères's prosecution for encouraging nonpayment of taxes. The Public Prosecutor of Rouen to the Minister of Justice (Garde des Sceaux), 4 March 1935 (AN: BB^{18} 2914). The real shareholders were mostly middling farmers and rural mayors who held only a share or two.

20. The smaller *Mait' Jacques* (circulation 8000), the paper of Jacques Le Roy Ladurie's Syndicat Agricole du Calvados, earned an average of 36,000–40,000 francs per year from advertising before the war, while the larger *Ar vro goz* (50,000), the paper of the Office Central at Landerneau, earned 80,000. These papers devoted roughly the same proportion of pages to advertising as did the PAO. See "La Presse Syndicale Paysanne (1941) Questionnaire" (AN: F^{10} 5080). The PAO was no longer publishing in 1941, and Dorgères does not seem to have replied to this questionnaire for *Le cri du sol*.

21. *Mait' Jacques*, which had become a weekly in March 1934, was forced to cut back to three issues a month on January 1935, and then to every other Sunday on 17 November 1935, because of reduced advertising.

22. PCO, 3 October 1935. The archives of the *dépôt légal* indicate a circulation of only 2900 in 1938. Ory, "Dorgères," p. 203.

23. Jacques Le Roy Ladurie claimed as much in the 1980s in a tape recording of his reminiscences.

24. Dorgères's letter (undated) to Juge d'Instruction Zousmann, Parquet de la Cour de Justice de la Seine, Citation Directe contre D'Halluin, Henri, dit d'Orgères *(sic)*. No. 5815 (AN: Z^5 127).

25. Ministry of Justice, Le Procureur de la République près le Tribunal de 1ère instance du Département de la Seine, Réquisitoire définitif (undated, but 1938) (AN: BB^{18} 2914, Dorgères—Annexe). Dorgères was not indicted in this case.

26. Report of Inspector Regerat, Direction de la Police Judiciaire, Préfecture de Police, No. 5815, 10 October 1945 (AN: Z5 127).

27. Letter of Henri D'Halluin to Juge d'Instruction Zousmann, 13 September 1945 (AN: Z5 127). No. 5815.

28. Fricot and Genaitay, pp. *Dorgères*, 31–34, 68, 111. The minister of the interior thought that Dorgères gave about 200 speeches in 1930. The Minister of the Interior to the Minister of Justice No. 15.63, 21 December 1934, (AN: BB^{18} 2915, "Dorgères-Annexe"). The PAO's lists of meetings may underestimate the number of speeches, particularly in the early years.

29. Lépine, "Naissance," p. 74.

30. For example, "Roncevaux" (Boiscorjou d'Ollivier) in *Le Parisien libéré*, 2–4 September 1944.

31. Law of 30 April 1930. Farm workers' contributions were smaller, supplemented by a state contribution, and farmers were permitted to use already-existing rural mutual benefit plans instead of the national social security fund. It was voluntary for small, self-employed peasants until 1935.

32. According to the agricultural survey of 1929, French farms had 5,000,000 family workers but only 1,027,000 full-time salaried workers of French nationality, plus 814,000 seasonal workers of French nationality and 137,000 employees of foreign nationality. See *Statistique agricole de la France publiée pas le Ministre de l'Agriculture. Résultats généraux de l'enquête de 1929* (Paris: Imprimerie Nationale, 1936), p. 554.

33. The Communist party opposed the requirement of employee contributions in the French social security law of 1928.

34. Jean Moquay, "L'Evolution sociale en agriculture: la condition des ouvriers agricoles depuis 1936" (thèse, University of Bordeaux, Faculty of Law 1939), p. 90.

35. The Prefect of the Finistère to the Minister of the Interior, 27 March 1935 (AD Finistère: 1M 133).

36. Other grass-roots peasant movements prospered by opposing social security on the farm: for example, the Entente Paysanne, active in the Charentes and the southwest, and the Parti Agraire of Fleurant Agricola, particularly effective in the center and the Côte-d'Or. Dorgères dominated the movement in the west.

37. The Minister of the Interior to the Minister of Justice 21 December 1934. (AN: BB^{18} 2915).

38. Pierre Milza, *Les Fascismes français. Passé et présent* (Paris: Flammarion, 1987), p. 126. The Eure-et-Loir was never a Dorgériste stronghold, however. The leftwing Paysans Travailleurs were successful in the department, whereas the PAPF was dominant among conservatives. But Dorgères's media success was such that the PAPF actions in the Eure-et-Loir were recalled later as "Dorgériste."

39. Lépine, "Naissance," pp. 109ff.

40. The Prefect of the Ille-et-Vilaine to the Président du Conseil, Minister of the Interior, 1 February 1930, André Tardieu papers (AN: 324AP 64). The meeting's organizers, as usual, exaggerated the audience to 15,000 in the resolution *(ordre du jour)* they submitted to the prefect (who refused to accept it).

41. "Do we have to break windows before anyone pays attention to farmers' demands?" PAO, 5 February 1933.

42. The PCO (still a PAPF newspaper) of 15 June 1933 criticized Daladier's "fascist language."

43. PAO, 10 October 1937.

44. Ibid, 25 August 1935.

45. Dorgères's figures invite skepticism. His biggest claim was 30,000 at Pont-Château (Loire-Atlantique) on 11 October 1936. *Action paysanne* (Toulouse), 25 October 1936. The prefect, who probably wanted to prove how calm his department was, reported 15,000. Monthly Report, 5 November 1936 (AD Loire-Atlantique: 1M 611). Halving Dorgères's figures is probably a good rule of thumb.

46. Someone—Dorgères thought it was Flandin—leaked two of these letters to the press. Their publication in *Marianne* sealed Dorgères's reputation as a fascist. Emmanuel Berl, "'Minorités agissantes' et fascisme de prébendiers," *Marianne*, 8 May 1935. Berl neglected to inform his readers that the most incendiary letter, which spoke of castor oil and punitive expeditions that had worked for Mussolini and Hitler, was written *to* Dorgères, not *by* Dorgères. See the Public Prosecutor of Rouen to the Minister of Justice (Garde des Sceaux), 8 May 1935 (AN: BB^{18} 2914, "E"). These letters strained Dorgères's relations with the moderate wing of the Parti Agraire. See *La Voix de la terre,* 17 May 1935.

47. Letters of Henry Dorgères to Maurice Foissey, 22 August 1933, and to Georges Lambert, 2 February 1934 AN: BB^{18} 2914).

48. Judicial search of Dorgères's premises. (AN: BB^{18} 2914).

49. Hymn of the Jeunesses Paysannes; words by André Piot, music by Jean Vertès. See *Le Cri du sol,* 31 October 1936.

50. Henry Dorgères, *Haut les fourches* (Paris: Les Oeuvres françaises, 1935), pp. 177–78.

51. PAO, 16 December 1934.

52. PAO, 4 March 1934; Emile Lefèvre (Dorgères's "secretary"), "Loup garrou et fascisme," *La Voix du paysan,* April 1934, wrote that many in France want fascism, if that means "a spirit of defense of corporative, familial, and regional values" and "politicians *[politicards]* out of a job."

53. PAO, 8 December 1935, 14 April 1936.

54. Ibid., 11 November 1934, 30 December 1934.

55. Interview, 1972, in Fricot and Genaitay, *Dorgères,* p. 62.

56. PAO, 3 March 1935.

57. The police report indicates that Dorgères was quoting someone else as an example of how desparate the peasants, usually calm, had become (AN: BB^{18} 2914, "M").

58. Dorgères was also attacked in the courts by some individuals. A grain merchant successfully sued him for defamation in July 1935.

59. Dorgères's indictment hearings *(instruction)* were indeed suspended during the electoral campaign. The Public Prosecutor of Rouen to the Minister of Justice (Garde des Sceaux), 2 May 1935, Ministry of Justice (AN: BB^{18} 2914, "Dorgères—Annexe"). Dorgères himself said merely that he "reacted" to the indictment by running for parliament *(Haut les fourches,* p. 193).

60. During the Fourth Republic he was to serve as a deputy from Ille-et-Villaine from 1956 to 1958.

61. For example, a meeting of 400 at Neuchâtel-en-Bray (Seine-Maritime), 18 November 1934. The Ministry of the Interior (Direction-Générale de la Sûreté Nationale) to the Minister of Justice (Garde des Sceaux), No. 13.995, 30 November 1934. Ministry of Justice, Direction des Affaires Criminelles, No. 31 A34/26F, (AN: BB^{18} 2915, "Dorgères").

62. Commissaire spécial, Caen, No. 1419, 5 August 1935 (AD Calvados: M11323).

63. For the number and geographical distribution of Bilger's followers, see Christian Baechler, *Le Parti Catholique Alsacien, 1890–1939: du Reichsland à la République jacobine* (Paris: Editions Ophrys, 1982), pp. 629–35. Interviews suggest that the smaller *vignerons,* who usually also worked in the mines, were drawn to the Left, whereas the middling ones, who felt most vulnerable to decline, joined the Bauernbund, as well as some larger ones. Geneviève Herberich-Marx and Freddy Raphael, " 'Les Noirs' et 'les Rouges' au village," *Saisons d'Alsace* 92 (June 1986), 83–98.

64. PAO, 16 June 1935; *La Voix du paysan,* August 1935. Henry Dorgères, letter to Dominique Lerche, 4 May 1975 (personal archive). Ory, "Dorgères," pp. 156–58, notes some other precedents, such as the Entente Paysanne's Franc-Paysannerie.

65. PCO, 6 June 1935.

66. *Illustration,* 31 August 1935, gave big coverage to this rally, underscoring Dorgères's emergence as a national figure. But despite this meeting's size, the Dorgérist

movement never amounted to much in the traditionally republican territory around Toulouse.

67. PCO, 29 August 1935.

68. Ibid., 12 September 1935.

69. PAO, 6 October 1935; Commissariat spécial, Quimper, No. 4225, 8 October 1935 (AD Finistère: 1M 144).

70. The Procureur de la République (Seine) to the Procureur-Général, report on Les Jeunesses Paysannes, 24 September 1936 (AN: BB[18] 2914).

71. AD Eure: 3M 199. Dorgères, *Au XXe siècle,* p. 108, claims he lost by 300 votes. Modeste Legouez was a senator from the Eure after World War II.

72. PAO, 24 October 1935.

73. The motto of the Chemises Vertes was "Believe, Serve, Obey" *(Croire, Servir, Obéir).*

74. *L'Almanach 1936 des Chemises Vertes* (Paris: Dusserin, 1936), of which there is a copy in the Bibliothèque Nationale, is the fullest source for the ceremonies, uniforms, oaths, ranks, organization, and duties of the movement.

75. See Chapter 4.

76. The author Louis Forest (Louis Nathan), who worked for *Le Matin,* was Dorgères's main journalistic support in Paris until Forest's death in August 1933. As for *Le Jour,* the police believed that the Marquis de Vogüé introduced Dorgères to the editor, Léon Bailby, in early 1935, Note P-3196, 4 February 1935 (AN: CAC Fontainebleau, No. 1–8-2306, Carton 940451/28).

77. Jacques Dyssord, "Que veut, que peut la Défense paysanne?" *(Le Document,* 2nd year, No. 3 (Paris: Denoel and Steele, 1935); Louis-Gabriel Robinet, *Dorgères et le Front Paysan* (Paris: Plon, 1937).

78. *L'Illustration,* 31 August 1935, estimated the crowd at 10,000. Dorgères claimed 20,000 (PAO, 25 August 1935).

79. The Ministry of the Interior *(Direction générale de la Sûreté Nationale)* to the Minister of Justice (Garde des Sceaux), 11 April 1935 (AN: BB[18] 2915, "Dorgères-Annexe").

80. Ibid.

81. Cf. the Congrès de Défense Paysanne in the Calvados in July 1937, which claimed that seventy worker sections had been created. *Le Courrier du Bessin,* 9–16 July 1937.

82. PAO, 12 July 1936, 11 November 1938. Honoré Gautier, a Greenshirt active in the Loire-Inférieure in 1936–37, is described as a "son of a small farmer" (PAO, 19 September 1937).

83. The most thorough social analysis of Dorgérists finds that in lower Normandy, none of the subscribers to PAO who can be identified and about 9% of contributors to its appeals were salaried farm workers. Jean-Luc Allais, "Dorgères et ses hommes: la Défense paysanne en Basse-Normandie," Mémoire de maîtrise, Université de Caen, 1992–93, p. 169. Allais recognizes that there is no way to separate the sons of large farmers from the lifelong day laborers in his sample.

84. No charge was filed in October, but in December Dorgères was charged with "illicit pressure on a market" (article 419 of the penal code) and "provocation of illegal gatherings" (on the basis of a law passed in June 1848). The *Parquet de la Seine* decided not to prosecute. AN: BB[18] 2915, 31 A34/36 F.

CHAPTER 3

1. The 1931 census was the first in which the French urban population (defined as those living in communes of more than 2000 people) surpassed the rural population.

2. In Emile Guillaumin's classic 1904 memoir of peasant life, republished in English as *The Life of a Simple Man* (Hanover, N.H.: University Press of New England, 1983), the boy accompanies his father to market, where the father sells a calf, then gets drunk.

3. Yves-Marie Bercé, *Fête et révolte: des mentalités populaires du XVIᵉ au XVIIIᵉ siècle* (Paris: Hachette, 1976), p. 183; Jack Thomas, *Le Temps des foires: foires et marchés dans le midi toulousain de la fin de l'Ancien Régime à 1914* (Toulouse: Presses Universitaires de Mirail, 1993), p. 160.

4. I remember the hundreds of farmers who crowded my country town in Appalachia every Saturday in the late 1930s; now the town is deserted on Saturday morning.

5. AD Eure-et-Loir: 10M 26.

6. Gendarmerie Nationale, Section de Blois, Brigade Oucques, No. 4/4, 15 June 1937 (AD Loir-et-Cher: 4M 221.

7. Maurice Lévy-Leboyer, *Le Revenu agricole et la rente foncière en Basse-Normandie: étude de croissance régionale* (Paris: Klincksieck, 1972), pp. 46, 66. *Décret-loi* of 8 April 1933 and law of 2 July 1935. Dorgères supported these measures.

8. Vichy moved toward a *statut des fermiers* by providing indemnification of the renter for improvements and review of evictions by *commissions paritaires* (laws of 18 July 1942 and 4 September 1943). The Statut des Baux Ruraux of 13 April 1946 confirmed these rights and gave the renter first refusal at the time of renewal *(droit de préemption).*

9. *Humanité,* 27, 28, and 29 July 1936, portrays the beating as a deliberate Greenshirt ambush *(guet-apens).* PAO, 2 and 16 August 1936, takes pride in the vigor of the peasants' anticommunism and puts the blame on Renaud Jean for invading hostile turf. There is no disagreement about who beat whom. Yvetôt was the main railroad town of the Caux—a typical Communist beachhead for penetrating the rural population.

10. A note in *Les Travaux des chambres d'agriculture,* 10 January 1937, p. 69, announced the first session of Dorgères's course for orators in December 1936, taught by Rémy Goussault. Orators' schools were fairly widespread among conservatives, who were learning to use mass audiences in the 1930s; for example, see one organized in the Somme by the Républicains Nationaux et Ligue des Patriotes. The Commissaire Central of Amiens to the Prefect, 23 June 1934 (AD Somme: M104a).

11. For example, PAO, 19 September 1937, p. 568: Honoré Gautier, who practiced in small meetings, "overcoming his timidity." PAO, 26 September 1937, p. 583: maiden speech of "young Le Bihan," who lacks self-confidence but "goes ahead anyway because he has faith"; and the "real progress" of Forner.

12. The French is nearly untranslatable: "une belle violence et beaucoup de jovialité." PAO, 22 December 1935.

13. PCO, 29 August 1935.

14. AD Seine-Maritime: 1Z 6, "Pierre Supplice" *(sic).* The Subprefect of Dieppe to the Prefect, 22 January 1935, *Ibid.*

15. The PAO of 13 September 1936 describes Agriculture Minister Georges Monnet as frequenting night clubs with the African-American dancer Josephine Baker. Dorgères also bizarrely attributed riches to CGT leader Léon Jouhaux and a "superb limousine" to his main Socialist enemy in the Côtes-du-Nord, François Tanguy-Prigent.

16. *Le Pays d'Auge,* 23 October 1935 (AD Calvados: M11324).

17. "In a socialist fief, my face covered with blood, I force Monnet to decamp." Henry Dorgères, *Au XXᵉ siècle: dix ans de jacquerie* (Paris: Editions du Scorpion, 1959), p. 180.

18. "Nous ne sommes rien, nous voulons être quelque chose!" *La Voix du paysan,* 1st year, No. 1, 16 April 1933.

19. The *Larousse du XIXᵉ siècle* defines a peasant as "by extension, a coarse personnage"; the *Larousse du XXᵉ siècle* amends this to "by extension and wrongly."

20. *La Terre qui meurt* (1899). See Pierre Barral, *Les Agrariens français de Méline à Pisani,* Cahiers de la Fondation Nationale des Sciences Politics, No. 164 (Paris: A. Colin, 1968), p. 134.

21. Francis Duterte, "Le Progrès agricole d'Amiens, 1926–39," Mémoire de maîtrise, U.E.R. de Sciences Historiques et Géographiques d'Amiens, 1975. The Masse de Combat des Paysans was sponsored by Le Progrès agricole d' Amiens, an aggressive agrarian newspaper, from 1926 into the middle 1930s, when it was swallowed up by Dorgérism.

22. PAO, 3 July 1938, p. 422. The allegation that peasants pay lower taxes than other citizens and are "supported" by them always provoked anger among Dorgérists, who preferred to see farmers as victims. Resentment of this accusation pervades recent works like Michel Debatisse, *Le Projet paysan* (Paris: Seuil, 1983), pp. 13–14, 45, 112ff. One scholar concluded in the 1960s that "[French] farmers appear fiscally privileged," but "the fiscal privileges of agriculture mainly aid large units of cultivation." Suzanne Quiers-Valette, "Les Causes économiques du mécontentement des agriculteurs français en 1961," *Revue française de science politique,* XII, No. 3 (September 1962), 585–86.

23. See almost any issue of *Jeunesse agricole,* which began in 1930 as a monthly and grew to a biweekly on 1 October 1932.

24. Jacques Le Roy Ladurie, unpublished memoirs, II, Chap. 4.

25. Robert Fiche, interview, 1 July 1988.

26. See a letter in PCO, 22 March 1934, from a farmer in the Loir-et-Cher who was complaining of such a visit and threatening to repeat the tactics of Bray-sur-Somme, recounted in this section.

27. *Les Communistes défendent les paysans,* Les Publications révolutionnaires, n.d. (1935), pp. 10f, gave concrete advice about "how peasant can impede judicial sales" by gathering massive numbers of demonstrators. Philippe Gratton, *Les Paysans français contre l'agrarisme* (Paris: François Maspéro, 1972), p. 133, gives a list of Left manifestations against such sales. In the United States, reactions to sales for debt were more individualistic and more violent: at least one bank official was shot in the 1980s.

28. Left activists made up part of the crowd of demonstrators at Bray-sur-Somme since the local Communist party had issued a call to action. AN: F⁷ 13629; *L'Humanité,* 19 June 1933. One demonstration against a judicial sale was organized jointly by the

CGPT and the PAPF in the Côtes-du-Nord in June 1934. Cf. Weekly Prefect's Report, 25 June 1934 (AD Côtes-d'Armor 1M 264).

29. "Nous ne sommes vendus ni aux propriétaires ni aux communistes." PAO, 10 November 1935, 6 January 1935.

30. Gérard Belloin, *Renaud Jean: le tribun des paysans* (Paris: Editions de l'Atelier, 1993), p. 193. The case involved a sharecropper *(métayer),* and Jean's editorial was entitled "The Bourgeoisie Is Attacking! Peasants, Block the Seizure."

31. The Prefect of the Somme to the Minister of the Interior, 12 June 1933 (AN: F^7 13629, "Somme").

32. *L'Humanité,* 19 and 20 June 1933.

33. The Prefect of the Somme to the Minister of the Interior. 12 June 1933, (AN: F^7 13629, "Somme").

34. Ibid., also AD Somme: M128.

35. The Prefect of the Somme to the Minister of the Interior, 18 June 1933, (AN: F^7 13629. "Somme").

36. See James C. Scott, *Weapons of the Weak: Everyday Forms of Peasant Resistance* (New Haven, Conn.: Yale University Press, 1985).

37. I thank the archivists of the Somme for searching twice on my behalf. A full account of the events at Bray and the trial at Péronne may be found in Nicolas Varin, "Dorgères et le dorgérisme en Picardie," Mémoire de maîtrise, Université de Paris I, Panthéon-Sorbonne, 1993–94.

38. AN: F^7 13629, "Somme."

39. PAO, 8 September 1935. Although Pointier returned to obscurity after the war, he appeared on a speaker's platform with Dorgères in 1950. *La Gazette agricole,* 3 June 1950, p. 4.

40. Clément Lépine, "La Naissance du mouvement dorgériste (1926–30)," Mémoire de maîtrise, Université de Paris XIII, 1992–93, p. 133.

41. Pierre Coulomb et al., *Les Agriculteurs et la politique* (Paris: Presses de la Fondation Nationale des Sciences Politiques, 1990), p. 19.

42. *Mait' Jacques,* 21 May 1939.

43. Raymond Triboulet, *Un Gaulliste de la IVe* (Paris: Plon, 1985), p. 26. There are acute portraits here of Dorgères and many of his associates.

44. *Mait' Jacques,* 7 January 1934.

45. *Le Jour,* 4 June 1935; *Le Cri du sol,* 26 September 1936.

46. PAO, 25 September 1937.

47. Even Renaud Jean, the main Communust proponent of a program favorable to small farmers, praised Soviet collectivized agriculture following a visit to the USSR in 1936. Belloin, *Renaud Jean,* p. 246. After World War II, the Communist parties of western Europe were readier to work with declining small farmers, as with the Mouvement d'Orientation et de Défense des Exploitants Familiaux (MODEF) in France. Cf. Sidney G. Tarrow, *Peasant Communism in Southern Italy* (New Haven, Conn.: Yale University Press, 1967). By then, of course, there were almost no hired hands left to organize.

48. Philippe Gratton, *Les Luttes de classes dans les campagnes* (Paris: Editions Anthropos, 1971).

49. Ministry of the Interior, Note de renseignements sur le Parti Communiste, 11 February 1933 (AN: F^7 13628, "Agricoles, 1933").

50. A new study of rural communism in the Corrèze disputes the "Left tradition" explanation. Laird Boswell, "The French Rural Communist Electorate," *Journal of Interdisciplinary History,* Vol. 23, No. 4 (Spring 1993), 719–49.

51. The CNP published a weekly, *La Défense paysanne,* at Limoges, and another, *La Volonté paysanne,* in the Corrèze. See generally Gordon Wright, *Rural Revolution in France* (Stanford, Calif.: Stanford University Press, 1964), pp. 55–56, 63, 95–96, 219–220.

52. The Prefect of the Seine-Inférieure to the Minister of Agriculture, July 1936. (AD Seine-Maritime: 10M 380). This is a reply to a circular from Georges Monnet inquiring about the conditions of farm labor.

53. The Subprefect of Dreux to the Prefect of the Eure-et-Loir, 15 July 1936 (AD Eure-et-Loir: 10M 26). This responds to the same inquiry from the Minister of Agriculture.

54. Gratton, *Paysans français,* p. 130.

55. Pierre Fromont and Francis Bourgeois, "Les Grèves agricoles de Tremblay-les-Gonesse en 1936," *Revue d'économie politique,* 51st year, No. 5 (September–October 1937), 1413–51; Gratton, *Paysans français,* pp. 171–86.

56. Danièle Ponchelet, "Ouvriers nomades et patrons briards: les grandes exploitations agricoles dans la Brie, 1848–1938," Thèse de doctorat de 3e cycle, Université de Paris X, Nanterre, 1986, pp. 418–19.

57. Thus Gratton's survey of strikes of farm labor in *Paysans français* stops in 1935.

58. According to Ponchelet, "Ouvriers nomades," pp. 366–68, 69% of the strikers in the arrondissement of Melun were foreign, as were over 80% in many communes in the canton of Brie-Comte-Robert. Most of them were Polish.

59. Ministry of Justice (AN: BB^{18} 3064, "Paris"); *Le Seine-et-Marnais,* 3 August 1938. The farmer in question, Maurice Legras, did not lose prestige by his violent action; he was a local *syndic* of the Peasant Corporation from 1941 to 1944 (AN F^{10} 5037). Dorgères's reaction was, "Emprison Rius [farm workers' union leader, accused of carrying a pistol], free Legras!" PAO, 11 July 1937.

60. See Richard Cobb, *The Peoples' Armies: The Armées Révolutionnaires, Instrument of the Terror in the Departments, April 1793 to Floréal Year II* (New Haven, Conn.: Yale University Press, 1987).

61. An example of a prefect's reply is in AD Seine-et-Marne: 10M 380.

62. Paul Corner, *Fascism in Ferrara* (Oxford: Clarendon Press, 1976), is the most penetrating account of the development of rural fascism during labor conflicts on the big farms of the Po Valley. See also Anthony L. Cardoza, *Agrarian Elites and Italian Fascism: The Province of Bologna, 1901–1926* (Princeton, N.J.: Princeton University Press, 1982); Frank Snowden, *The Fascist Revolution in Tuscany* (Cambridge: Cambridge University Press, 1989); and Alice Kelikian, *Town and Country under Fascism: The Tranformation of Brescia, 1915–1926* (New York and Oxford: Oxford University Press, 1986).

63. *Le Courrier du Bessin,* 12–19 August 1937, and many others.

64. Commissaire spécial (de police) of Dieppe, No. 1698, 17 August 1936 (AD Seine-Maritime: 10M 380).

65. For example, *Havre-Eclair,* 24 July 1936, with a photo of Adolphe Pointier. This text appears in many rural newspapers. The Comité d'Action Paysanne is discussed in Chapter 4.

66. AD Seine-Maritime: 10M 380, "CDP."

67. Commissaire spécial, Aire-sur-la-Lys, 15 June 1937 (AD Pas-de-Calais: 4Z 807); ibid., 2 July 1937 (AD Pas-de-Calais: 4Z 791).

68. PAO, 13 June 1937.

69. *Le Cri du sol,* 17 June 1939.

70. For example, "numerous sympathizers" of the PSF went from the Châteaudun region of the Eure to the Seine-et-Marne in May 1937 "to help the farmers of this *département* where agricultural strikes are now going on." The Subprefect of Châteaudun to the Prefect of the Eure, 31 May 1937. (AD Eure: 1M 21).

71. Ponchelet, "Ouvriers nomades," p. 391.

72. Its appeal for volunteers is published in *Le Pays de Bray,* 21 July 1936.

73. *Le Courrier du Bessin,* 19–26 May 1938. This committee was headed by M. Thomas, secretary-general of the Fédération Générale Professionelle des Ouvriers Agricoles, probably a PSF union. *Le Cri du paysan,* August 1937, refers to a Comité National de Volontaires pour l'Agriculture, headed by M. Dolivier. Dorgères preferred to cite examples of rural mutual assistance rather than urban volunteers.

74. For example, the *Bulletin de la Société des Agriculteurs de l'Oise* of 7 July 1937 thanks the volunteers without mentioning any names.

75. The most thorough account is Ponchelet, "Ouvriers nomades," pp. 341–407. There is also a fascinating thesis written just after the strikes by someone close to the big planters, probably a son: Philippe de Chevigny, "Grèves et sociologie à la campagne," Thèse agricole, Institut Agricole de Beauvais: Section d'Enseignement Supérieur d'Agriculture de l'Institut Catholique de Paris, 20 May 1938. The case examined seems to be the farm where Maurice Legras shot the demonstrators.

76. Paul Caffin in the 1930s was president of the Confédération Nationale des Producteurs de Fruits et Légumes; of a similar organization for potato growers; and of a protectionist lobby, the Association Agricole Douanière; he became in 1941–44 the Peasant Corporation's regional chairman *(syndic)* for the Seine and Seine-et-Oise. We note in Chapter 4 his role in the Peasant Front in 1935.

77. See AD Seine-et-Oise: 13M 241. At Tremblay-les-Gonesse, "The farmers had summoned 150 colleagues to protect their workers who wanted to work; the police forces seemed to them insufficient to bring about that result." Capitaine de Gendarmerie de Montmorency, 15 June 1937 (AN: BB[18] 3064,"Poursuites contre Rius et Paquent").

78. Chevigny, "Greves et sociologie," pp. 53–54. Ponchelet, "Ouvriers nomades," does not mention Dorgères.

79. AD Aisne: 1M 22 contains the prefect's accounts of this action, in which he attempts to defend himself against the farmers' accusations. The prefect clearly had a low opinion of the big farmers' substandard working conditions and intransigence.

80. *Le Petit journal,* 19 August 1937.

81. PAO, 19 September 1937. Dorgères claimed to have led 3000 volunteers to the Aisne, a totally fanciful figure.

82. Ibid., 13 June and 18 October 1936. The ACEA's vice-president, however, Pierre Leclercq, was a militant Dorgériste and president of the CDP of the Pas-de-Calais.

83. Dorgères spoke in the Aisne in January 1936 and January 1939 (AD Aisne: 1M 19).

84. Michel Gervais et al., *La Fin de la France paysanne: de 1914 à nos jours,* Vol. IV, *Histoire de la France rurale,* sous la direction de Georges Duby and Armand Wallon (Paris: Seuil, 1977), p. 417, reprints a photograph from *Illustration* for 22 August 1936.

85. See Bernard Alexandre, *Le Horsain: vivre et survivre en pays de Caux* (Paris: Plon, 1988), the account by a parish priest of his failure to penetrate the society of his parishoners in the Caux.

86. AD Seine-Maritime: 1Z 723, "Bourg-Dun."

87. The Subprefect of Dieppe to the Prefect of the Seine-Inférieure, 26 July 1934 (AD Seine-Maritime: 1Z 6).

88. Ibid., 17 November 1934.

89. AN: F^{10} 5036.

90. AD Seine-Maritime: 1Z 6, "Parti Agraire."

91. The subprefect of Dieppe to the Prefect of the Seine-Inférieure, 22 January 1935 (AD Seine-Maritime: 1Z 6).

92. Ibid.

93. Ibid., 17 November 1934.

94. Ibid., 22 January 1935.

95. Ibid.

96. Ibid.

97. Ibid.; *Journal de Rouen,* 2 January 1935.

98. See Chapter 4 for fuller information about the *Comité d'action paysanne* and its petition and the "action order" intended to launch a tax strike, a purchasing strike, and a boycott of public officials in September 1935.

99. *Journal de Rouen,* 18 September 1935.

100. Inspecteur stagiaire de police spéciale Costerg to the Commissaire spécial, chef de service at Dieppe, No. 1925, 29 September 1935 (AD Seine-Maritime: 1Z 6).

101. AD Seine-Maritime: 1Z 6, "Réunions agricoles diverses."

102. Ibid., "Jeunesses Paysannes."

103. AD Seine Maritime: 10M 386.

104. AD Seine-Maritime: 10M 380.

105. AD Seine-Maritime: 1Z 16, "Grève des travailleurs agricoles."

106. Ibid.

107. The Subprefect of Dieppe to the Prefect of the Seine-Inférieur, 22 January 1935 (AD Seine-Maritime: 1Z 6).

108. Ibid., 16 November 1933.

109. AD Seine-Maritime: 10M 387,"Grèves, 1937."

110. The Lepicard brothers were influential farmers in the Seine-Infériere and rivals for the position of regional chairman *(syndic)* when the Peasant Corporation was set up in 1941–42. Jacques Lepicard would be president of the FNSEA in 1954–56.

111. The Prefect of the Seine-Inférieure to the Minister of the Interior, 16 June 1937 (AD Seine-Maritime: 10M 387).

112. Daily notes based on telephone reports from the subprefect of Dieppe concerning Suplice's activities in mid-June 1937 are found in AD Seine-Maritime: 1Z 16, "Grève des travailleurs agricoles."

113. AD Seine-Maritime: 2Z 94, "Grèves des ouvriers agricoles des Cantons d'Ourville et de Valmont" and "Grève des ouvriers agricoles de la région de Goderville."

114. PAO, 18 October 1936.

115. Senator Veyssière played a cautious waiting game that prevented the Peasant Corporation from being set in motion in the Seine-Inférieure for a long time, perhaps anticipating, correctly, that the Republic's interruption would be brief.

116. AD Eure-et-Loir: 10M 27, "Grève à la sucrerie de Toury, 1936."

117. François Mévellec, *Le Combat du paysan breton à son apogée* (Rennes: Imprimerie "Les Nouvelles," 1974), p. 338.

118. PAO, 14, 21, and 28 June 1936. Dorgères dissociated himself from "egotistical big industrialists" and supported more purchasing power for the workers, but he insisted that peasants not bear alone the price of the "struggle against the high cost of living."

119. See *L'Avenir du Bessin,* 6 May 1936. Colette got 29.5% of the vote, second only to the 34.6% he got in the commune of Lison. The Left could not prevent the election of the duc d'Harcourt on the first round, however.

120. In the Manche, where milk producers formed several cooperatives in 1929–32, the big companies tried to destroy them by refusing to pick up their members' milk. See Claude Letellier de Blanchard, "L'Evolution du syndicalisme agricole en Basse-Normandie de 1884 à nos jours," Thèse pour le doctorat en sciences politiques, Faculté de Droit et de Sciences Economiques, Université de Caen, 1968, p. 195. Around Lisieux (Calvados), the big buyers of milk—Lanquetit, Lepetit, Fermiers Réunies, Nestlé—formed a syndicate in 1934 and set milk prices a month in advance as a function of the market price for butter in the preceding month. When some farmers protested, the syndicate "quarantined" them and refused their milk. The Commissioner of the Police of Lisieux to the Prefect of the Calvados, 28 April 1934 (AD Calvados: M11274).

121. PAO, 14 June 1936.

122. Henri Babeur, head of the milk producers' cooperative in Isigny, as quoted in Letellier de Blanchard, "Evolution du syndicalism," p. 196.

123. The concept of interprofession had an important future. For the 1975 legislation authorizing such accords, see Pierre Coulomb et al., *Agriculteurs,* p. 190. An influential partisan of interprofessional organizations in the 1970s was FNSEA President Michel Debatisse. See his *Le Projet paysan* (Paris: Seuil, 1983), pp. 32, 144, 161n.

124. "Agriculture. Rapports sur la situation agricole" (AD Calvados: M11324).

125. Report of Gendarme Mauger, Lison, 26 July 1936 (AD Calvados: M11310).

126. Newspapers of both the Left and the Right report this accusation, but we are unable to find out the nationality of the manager or what he did to offend the work force.

127. See the union's account, reprinted in the *Journal de Bayeux,* 4 September 1936.

128. *Le Moniteur du Calvados,* No. 206, 4 September 1936.

129. Jean-Luc Allais, "Dorgères et ses hommes: la Défense Paysanne en Basse-Normandie," Mémoire de maîtrise, Université de Caen, 1992–93, pp. 110–11.

130. *Le Courrier du Bessin,* 24 September–1 October 1936.

131. "Front Paysan: manifestation du 27 septembre 1936 à Osmanville" (AD Calvados: 11324).

132. *Le Courrier du Bessin,* 1–8 October 1936.

133. *Mait' Jacques,* 4 October 1936.

134. AD Calvados: M11324; *L'Avenir du Bessin,* 30 September 1936.

135. *Journal de Bayeux,* 11 December 1936.

136. Ibid.

137. *L'Avenir du Bessin,* 16 December 1936.

138. The Commissaire spécial (de police) of Caen, No. 1386, 5 August 1937 (AD Calvados: M11392).

139. Ibid., No. 437, 5 March 1935.

140. AD Calvados: M8195.

141. The Commissaire spécial (de police) of Caen, No. 1178, 1 July 1935 (AD Calvados: M11323).

142. The Subprefect of Vire to the Prefect of the Calvados, 20 October 1936 (AD Calvados: M11323).

143. Allais, "Dorgères et ses hommes," shows that the energetic Boullot continued to create new sections and raise more money through 1938, only to lose momentum in 1939.

144. See *Corporation paysanne: feuille d'homologation* for the commune of Pleuven, 1941 (AN: F^{10} 4998).

145. The farm is still cultivated by his son, who now raises cattle, using machinery rather than hired hands—replicating the evolution of many small and medium French farms.

146. Tribunal Correctionnel of Rouen, "Jugement du 11 juillet 1935 contre Henry Dorgères et al., prévenus d'avoir, depuis la promulgation de la loi du 28 fevrier 1933, agi de concert pour organiser le refus collectif de l'impôt" (AN: BB^{18} 2915). We have Dorgères's version of the story but not the tax collector's.

147. *La Voix du paysan,* February 1934: "un dur et un chef."

148. PCO, 11 July 1935.

149. Tribunal Correctionnel of Rouen, "Jugement du 11 juillet 1935" (AN: BB^{18} 2915). The accused included Pierre Suplice; the agricultural school director, Le Floc'h; and two others.

150. The Public Prosecution of Rouen to the Minister of Justice (Garde des Sceaux), 29 August 1935 (AN: BB^{18} 2915). Dorgères's sentence of six months in prison was reduced, on appeal, to a suspended sentence. The Rouen trial was the occasion for sympathy meetings organized in the Somme, at Rouen, and elsewhere.

151. Interview, Joseph Argouarc'h, 30 June 1988.

152. Dorgères claimed that many hired hands became Greenshirts, thereby confirming the social solidarity of all levels of the peasantry. In Pleuven (and probably elsewhere), while most Greenshirts might technically be paid laborers, they were in fact sons of medium or large proprietors or renters who worked for pay on their fathers' farms.

153. Scott, *Weapons of the Weak.*

154. AN: BB^{18} 2914; AN: F^7 14819, "Robert Henri Bougeard"; PAO, 11 July 1937.

155. Henri Mendras and Yves Tavernier, "Les Manifestations de Juin 1961," *Revue française de science politique,* XII, No. 3 (September 1962), the fullest account, relate these demonstrations explicitly to the memory of Dorgérist direct action (p. 667).

156. The Prefect of the Finistère to the Ministry of the Interior, No. 1187, 5 June 1934 (AD Finistère: 1M 144).

157. Ibid., 5 July 1934.

158. Ibid., 1 April 1935 (AD Finistère: 1M 133).

159. PAO, 30 January 1938, announces a rally concerning peas at Le Trévoux that day, to be addressed by Divanac'h.

160. Renseignements généraux du Finistère, "Le Syndicalisme agraire dans le Finistère," unpublished, May–June 1964 (AD Finistère), pp. 13–14.

161. The militant Free Peasants' Movement, founded in the German Rhineland in 1919, experimented with "delivery strikes" *(Lieferstreike)* in 1920–22. See *Peasants and Lords in Modern Germany,* ed. Robert G. Moeller (Boston: Allen and Unwin, 1986), pp. 177ff. The militant Iowa farmers' leader, Milo Reno, tried to promote a "farmers' holiday," or producers' strike, in 1933.

162. The most frequent kind of farmers' production strike concerned milk. There are German examples from the 1920s and many French cases in the 1930s (such as Le Havre in 1937). These, too, were enforced by spoiling the milk of noncomplying farmers. The greatest success of this tactic in France came in the Breton milk strike of 1972. Coulomb et al., *Agriculteurs,* pp. 84, 539, describes this erroneously as a new tactic.

163. This account is based on several eye-witness reports, which were not in perfect accord and which no doubt suffered from the lapse of time.

164. The names of those sentenced appear in *Le Citoyen* of Quimper, 9 December 1938. The paper took a very dim view of such actions.

165. Renseignements généraux du Finistère, "Syndicalisme," p. 14.

166. PAO, 3 July 1938.

167. Mévellec, *Combat du paysan breton,* pp. 408, 460; Commissaire spécial (de police) of Brest, No. 1783, 16 October 1933 (AN: F^7 13529, "Finistère").

168. Claude Mesliand, *Paysans du Vaucluse (1860–1939)* (Aix-en-Provence: Publications de l'Université de Provence Aix-Marseille, 1989), No. 1, pp. 517–20. Resentment of amateur gardeners among industrial workers was also strong in the *maraîchers'* strikes in Paris.

169. Dorgères's obituary in *Le Monde* is mistaken: he did not organize peasants against the *maraîchers'* strike, but for it.

CHAPTER 4

1. He "triumphs from Brittany to Languedoc, from Flandres to Provence." *L'Action paysanne* (Toulouse), 4 August 1935.

2. The laborious process of setting up the local branches of the Peasant Corporation on solid local bases is documented in AN: F^{10} 4972–5046.

3. They were not "departmental" delegates because, in a few cases, their territories did not follow departmental lines (e.g., the Calvados had two, and the Finistère and the Côtes-du-Nord were joined). De Guébriant and Goussault liked to play at replacing the French Revolution's "artificial" geographical units, such as departments, with the "organic" units offered by regional *syndicats agricoles.*

4. Later a senator of the Fourth Republic.

5. Alphonse Guimbretière, *Histoire et cheminement des organisations agricoles de Maine-et-Loire* (Angers: Author, 1987), p. 55. In the spring of 1939, 2000 peasants gathered in front of the courthouse at Angers (Maine-et-Loire) to protest the trial of Macé and Dézé for violation of the law on family support payments. See *La Voix de la terre,* 28 April and 5 May 1939. Eugène Forget, *Le Serment de l'unité paysanne* (Paris:

Nouvelle Cité, 1982), p. 103, notes that Dézé was the first hands-on farmer to head agricultural associations in the Maine-et-Loire; he returned to activity in agricultural associations there after the war.

6. Four other regional delegates had supported Dorgères at times during the 1930s, but they were chosen primarily because of their leadership of other organizations: Pointier (Somme), Jacq (Finistère and Côtes-du-Nord), André Du Boullay (Pays d'Auge), and of course Jacques Le Roy Ladurie (Calvados).

7. Called Commissions Régionales d'Organisation Corporative (CROC) during the period when the Peasant Corporation was being set up; succeeded in 1942–43 (with few changes) by the definitive Unions Régionales Corporatives (URC).

8. Vice-president of the departmental *syndicat agricole* in 1946–47.

9. In 1950, Tellier was senator and a member of the Service d'Action Agricole of the Gaullist party, the Rassemblement du Peuple Français. See Charles De Gaulle, *Lettres, notes, et carnets,* (Paris: Plon, 1984), Vol. 6, pp. 438–40.

10. We can thus confirm the judgment of Ronald Hubscher, *L'Agriculture et la société rurale dans le Pas-de-Calais du milieu du XIXe siècle à 1914* (Arras: Mémoires de la Commission Départementale des Monuments Historiques du Pas-de-Calais, 1979–80), XX, Nos. 1–2, p. 613, that the Pas-de-Calais had the strongest Dorgériste movement in France in 1938, although it was a latecomer there.

11. Minutes, meeting of the committee that oversaw creation of the Peasant Corporation, the Comité d'Organisation Corporative (COC), 9 July 1941 (AN: F^{10} 4973).

12. AN: F^{10} 5036.

13. See Forget, *Serment de l'unité paysanne,* pp. 47–48. Forget concedes that Dorgérism was "colored by fascism," but he also admits his enthusiasm for it in the 1930s in the Maine-et-Loire. Forget was deeply admired by later farmers' leaders like Michel Debatisse, president of the FNSEA (1977–79) and secretary of state for agroindustrial enterprises under Prime Minister Raymond Barre (1979–81). See Michel Debatisse, *Le Projet paysan* (Paris: Seuil, 1983), pp. 34–35.

14. His memoirs, *Le Paysan révolté; entretiens avec Claire Touchard* (Paris: Mame, 1993), make no allusion to this association.

15. Albert Mitonneau took over an earlier movement, the Entente paysanne, and affiliated it with the CDP in December 1934.

16. *L'Illustration,* 31 August 1935, estimates the crowd at 10,000; PAO, 25 August 1935, claims 20,000.

17. Paul Bois, *Paysans de l'ouest* (Paris: Flammarion, 1971).

18. After the discredit of Edmond Jacquet, "Jan Printen," its new leader, Mitonneau, wound up as a Dorgériste.

19. Francis Duterte, "Le Progrès agricole d'Amiens," Mémoire de maîtrise, U.E.R. des Sciences Historiques et Géographiques d'Amiens, 1975, p. 148.

20. Manipulation by rural gentry *(hoberaux)* was the automatic interpretation of *L'Humanité* and *Le Populaire.*

21. The leading examples are Pierre Leclercq, vice-president in the late 1930s and president after 1942 of the sugar beet lobby (CGB), and Adolphe Pointier, president 1933–43 of the wheat lobby (AGPB).

22. For example, the duc d'Harcourt and the comte de Guébriant.

23. Dorgères claimed in PAO, 11 September 1937, that the Greenshirts were mostly workers; closer inspection shows that many of them were, in fact, sons of

proprietors or large renters *(fermiers)* who still worked on the family farm. Jacques Le Roy Ladurie, similarly, made an effort to give a few positions in the *syndicats agricoles* (SA) of the Calvados to salaried workers, for example, Arthur Guilbert. But their numbers were small.

24. At a rally in Neuchâtel-en-Bray (Seine-Maritime) on 17 November 1934, he drew a hostile reaction when he suggested that renters in arrears pay their rent in kind, with wheat. The Commissaire spécial of Dieppe to the Prefect, 18 November 1934 (AD Seine-Maritime: 1Z6, "Mouvement agricole").

25. *Le Cri du sol,* 12 September 1936: "We are not strike-breakers." See also PAO, 18 October 1936.

26. After their break, Dorgères and Le Roy Ladurie traded charges that the other defended the interests of big farmers. PAO, 10 October 1937; *Syndicats paysans,* 1 January 1938.

27. Cf. Balbigny, for example, in Jean Vercherand, *Un Siècle de syndicalisme: la vie locale et nationale à travers le cas du département de la Loire* (St. Etienne: Centre d'Etudes Foréziennes, 1994); the explicit connection between Dorgérisme and political polarization is mine, not Vercherand's.

28. Dorgères had no following in the Landes, for example, where poor sharecroppers had been organized by the Communist party for generations.

29. Jean-Michel Royer, "De Dorgères à Poujade," in Jacques Fauvet and Henri Mendras, *Les Paysans et la politique dans la France contemporaine,* Cahiers de la Fondation Nationale des Sciences Politiques, No. 94 (Paris: A. Colin, 1958), p. 204.

30. Jacques Chevalier, "Bouilleurs de cru et manifestations paysannes, 1934–36," *Le Pays Bas-Normand,* 73rd year, No. 3 (1980), 33.

31. Thomas, Jules, Inspecteur Principal de Police Mobile, to the Commissaire Divisionnaire-Chef of the Thirteenth Regional Brigade at Rennes (at the request of the Procureur de la République at Rennes), 11 August 1934 (AN: BB[18] 2915, No. 31 A34/26F, "Dorgères—Annexe").

32. PAO, 29 November 1936.

33. Ibid., 16 March 1937.

34. Ibid., 13 November 1938.

35. Ibid., 10 October 1937.

36. *La Provence paysanne,* No. 7, February 1939. During the war, when he was bidding for a larger role in the Peasant Corporation, he made less extravagant claims for his prewar membership: 450,000 (*Le Cri du sol,* 14 December 1940) and 420,000 (*Le Cri du sol,* 16 October 1943).

37. Dorgères claimed (probably with exaggeration) that he had gathered 20,000 people at Revel (near Toulouse) on 18 August and as many at Rouen a week later. PAO, 18 August 1935, 1 September 1935.

38. Ibid., 25 August 1935.

39. *Le Cri du sol,* 16 October 1943. Jean Bohuon said the same in a powerful letter, crudely typed, to de Guébriant in May 1941 (AN: FN[10] 5004). Dorgères's claim of 420,000 members was far below the 1,200,000 families claimed by the Union Nationale des Syndicats Agricoles. Moreover, "membership" meant something far looser in the CDP than did a member's card in a big *syndicat,* with its cooperatives, group purchases, and insurance policies.

40. AN: F[10] 4973.

41. Philippe Arnaud, secretary-general of the Coordination Rurale, expresses a similar disdain for numbers and for permanent local organization *(quadrillage du territoire):* "We are like the first resisters in 1940." *Le Monde,* 26 June 1993.

42. *L'Agriculteur du Sud-Est,* 21 April 1935, quoted in "Bilan d'une année de 'Front Paysan,' *Dossiers de l'action populaire,* No. 361 (10 April 1936), 799. The head of the Union du Sud-Est, Félix Garcin, said he agreed with Dorgères's aim but deplored his methods.

43. A good example is the creation of a vigorous new union in 1934 in the Loire-Atlantique, under Le Gouvello (with some Dorgériste associates), to compete with the old federation of SAs under J. de Camiran. The same failure to rejuvenate the slumbering federation of SAs under Senator Veyssière left room in the Seine-Maritime for a new federation under the Lepicard brothers and for Suplice's CDP.

44. John T. S. Keeler, *The Politics of Neo-corporatism in France: Farmers, the State, and Agricultural Policy-making in the Fifth Republic* (New York and Oxford: Oxford University Press, 1987).

45. Paul Brooker, *The Faces of Fraternalism* (Oxford: Clarendon Press, 1991), highlights the centrality of "mechanical solidarity" for Fascist Italy, Nazi Germany, and Imperial Japan.

46. The Left press tended to call all violent peasants' action from whatever source "Dorgériste" or "Greenshirt" and to lump it (quite erroneously) with monarchism and the Action Française.

47. PAO, 30 May 1937; quoted in Roger Fricot and Pierre Genaitay, "Dorgères et le mouvement paysan," Mémoire de maîtrise, Université de Rennes, 1972, p. 102.

48. PAO, 11 January 1931; quoted in Claude Letellier de Blanchard, "L'Evolution du syndicalisme agricole en Basse Normandie de 1884 à nos jours," Thèse pour le doctorat en sciences politiques, Faculté de Droit et de Sciences Economiques, Université de Caen, 1968, p. 244.

49. "La Vague rouge." PAO, 16 August 1936.

50. It sounds much better in French: "À droite les nouilles, à gauche les fripouilles." PAO, 14 February 1937. One will recognize in Bohuon's phrase a somewhat earthy way of saying "neither Left nor Right."

51. Germain Boullot, "Une manifestation paysanne," *Le Courrier du Bessin,* 17th year, No. 4, 27 January–3 February 1938, p. 2. Boullot was national head of the Greenshirts.

52. Gordon Wright, *Rural Revolution in France* (Stanford, Calif.: Stanford University Press, 1964), p. 219.

53. Félix Garcin, in *La France rurale,* 23 May 1935; quoted in "Le Bilan d'une année de 'Front Paysan,'" *Dossiers de l'action populaire,* No. 361 (10 April 1936), 798. But even Garcin felt compelled to appear on the platform with Dorgères in November 1936 at Bourg-en-Bresse. Vercherand, *Siècle de syndicalisme,* p. 66.

54. *Les Travaux des chambres d'agriculture,* August–September 1935, p. 475.

55. Reprinted in *Action paysanne* (Toulouse), No. 69, 29 November 1936.

56. Bertrand de Jouvenel, "Le Front Paysan," *Revue de Paris,* 1 December 1935, describes the Dorgères–Le Roy Ladurie "alliance" as the cement of the Peasant Front.

57. The Peasant Front was probably founded on 20 July 1934, though other dates are given (Fricot and Genaitay, "Dorgères," cite 19 June 1934).

58. See two full contemporary accounts: "Le Bilan d'une année du 'Front Paysan,'" *Dossiers de l'action populaire,* No. 359 (10 March 1936), 497–528; No. 360 (25 March 1936), 637–70; and No. 361 (10 April 1936), 797–820, is sympathetic to the familial and corporatist values of the front but warns its Christian-social readership against Dorgères's willingness to resort to illegal actions, polarization of a "peasant class" against the rest, and use of oaths of unquestioning obedience. Also well informed, and more sympathetic, is Bertrand de Jouvenel, "Le Front Paysan," *Revue de Paris,* 1 December 1935.

59. It became an official body, Assemblée Permanente des Présidents des Chambres d'Agriculture, on 30 October 1935, one of several measures by Laval to mollify agrarian notables.

60. Roger Grand farmed a property and headed farmers' organizations in the Morbihan, but he was also a scholar of medieval rural life and agriculture. A professor at the training school for archivists in Paris, the Ecole des Chartes, and a disciple of Le Play, he was one of several scholars in the 1930s who found medieval precedents for modern corporatism. Grand was also elected senator of the Morbihan for one term in 1927.

61. *Mait' Jacques,* No. 248, 27 May 1934.

62. Roger Grand had a long conversation with Mussolini in 1933. See "En Italie: l'economie dirigée: résumé d'une conférence de M. Roger Grand," *L'Agriculture française* (organ of the UNSA), April 1935, p. 6. He was still praising Salazar after the war, when Grand no longer had a role in farmers' organizations but was president of the Le Playist Société des Etudes Sociales and member of the French Academy of Moral and Political Sciences. See *Etudes sociales,* Nos. 23–24, December 1953.

63. *Mait' Jacques,* No. 306, 1 December 1935.

64. Comité Français des Relations Agricoles Internationales, 1938–39. (AN: F^{10} 2182). The Republican Joseph Faure was president of this committee.

65. PAO, 8 September 1934, quoting *Le Journal.*

66. "Le Bilan d'une année de 'Front Paysan,'" *Dossiers de l'action populaire,* No. 359 (10 March 1936), p. 511.

67. Dorgères urged a tax strike when he spoke at the PAPF rally at the Salle Wagram in Paris, in October 1932, and again in PAO, 25 December 1932.

68. François Mévellec, *Le Combat du paysan Breton à son apogée* (Rennes: Imprimerie "Les Nouvelles," 1974), p. 298.

69. *Journal de Rouen,* 18 September 1935.

70. Peasant Front leaders met in the office of Paul Caffin on 16 September 1935 to declare that the front's deadline had expired and to issue the "command for action." *La Voix de la terre,* 9th year, No. 345, 20 September 1935. Caffin subsequently played a role in the organization of big landowners of the Paris basin against the strikes of hired hands (see Chapter 3).

71. See Chapter 3, p. 91.

72. "Campagne tendant au refus du paiement de l'impôt." AD Calvados: M11324.

73. The Commissioner of Police of Lisieux to the Subprefect of Lisieux, 20 October 1935 (AD Calvados: M11324). See also *Le Pays d'Auge,* 23 October 1935. Du Boullay was acquitted a year later of carrying out an illegal subscription campaign. See Ministry of Justice, Cour d'Appel de Rennes, 31A 34/26 (AN: BB^{18} 2914, "Impôts, Protestations, Manifestations").

74. AD Calvados: M11324, "Agriculture—rapports sur la situation agricole."

75. The tax collector of Ouville-la-Rivière, quoted in the Ministry of the Interior (Direction-Générale de la Sûreté Nationale) letter to the Ministry of Justice (n.d., but August–September 1936) (AN: BB^{18} 2914).

76. Mévellec, *Combat du paysan Breton,* p. 303.

77. Suzanne Berger, *Peasants against Politics: Rural Organization in Brittany, 1911–67* (Cambridge, Mass.: Harvard University Press, 1972), p. 111 (quoting an interview with F. M. Jacq).

78. Ephraim Grenadou launched a tax strike in the Beauce but was left in the lurch when all his neighbors quietly paid up. See Ephraim Grenadou and Alain Prévost, *Grenadou, paysan français* (Paris: Seuil, 1966), p. 176.

79. These reached 10 francs a year at the end of 1936, which probably seemed a lot to many members. Dorgères exhorted them to pay by claiming that CGT members paid 60 francs a year. PAO, 6 December 1936.

80. See the account of Pleuven (Finistère), in Chapter 3. Local branches had to be self-sufficient: the CDP of the Seine-Maritime had to charge 5 francs a year to get through financial difficulties in 1936.

81. No big contributions by wealthy individuals are listed; Dorgères wanted to give an impression of modest peasants who were straining their resources to send a few francs or to collect several hundred in an act of village solidarity. Pascal Ory used these subscription lists to illustrate the fluctuating regional distribution of Dorgères's support. "Henry Dorgères et la 'Défense Paysanne' des origines à 1939," Mémoire de maîtrise, Faculté des Lettres et Sciences Humaines de Nanterre, 1970.

82. These varied from as little as 20 sous (PCO, 12 December 1935) to the more usual 1 or even 2 francs. A Communist heckler, Delannos, was expelled from a rally at Lillebonne (Seine-Maritime) in 1938 for complaining about an entry fee of 2 francs. The Commissaire of the Police of Lillebonne to the Subprefect, 15 June 1938 (AD Seine-Maritime: 2Z 134).

83. For 2 francs apiece (*La voix du paysan,* October 1935). Dorgères later claimed that he sold 600,000 of them. Meeting of the Peasant Corporation's Commission Nationale d'Organisation Corporative, 20 November 1941 (AN F^{10} 4947).

84. About fifty packets of photos of the demonstration at Salvaudon's farm on 18 June 1933 (discussed in Chapter 3), were sold for 10 francs apiece at a meeting in the Eure in July 1933. The Subprefect of Bernay to the Prefect (AD Eure: 1M 265).

85. One meeting collected 2000 francs from those present (PAO, 31 January 1936). Three collections were taken up during the July 1933 meeting in the Eure.

86. Note P.P., 5 February 1936, "Activité de M. D'Halluin, dit 'Dorgères,'" in Revillod papers (AN: 56AP 22). This report is a good example of the untrustworthy character of national police intelligence about Dorgères. He was probably not helping the Parti agraire's newspaper at this time, for example.

87. Fricot and Genaitay, "Dorgères," p. 43 and annex XXIII.

88. When Dorgères sent organizers into the Sologne in April 1937, they rented a Ford and bought another car "with M. Goury du Roslan as intermediary." The Commissaire spécial (of police) of Blois to the Prefect of the Loir-et-Cher, No. 57, 18 June 1937 (AD Loir-et-Cher: 4M 221).

89. *Le Cri du sol,* 14 December 1940, mentions the Alliance Rurale as a "parallel group." Dorgères calls it a group of "sympathizers" in *Au XXᵉ siècle: dix ans de jacquerie* (Paris: Editions du Scorpion, 1959), p. 111. He also spoke of it in 1972 to interviewers. Fricot and Genaitay, "Dorgères," pp. 52, 118–20.

90. Dorgères, *XXᵉ siècle,* pp. 90, 103; PAO, 28 March 1935; Rensignements généraux du Finistère, "Le Syndicalisme Agricole dans le Finistère," May–June 1964, p. 3.

91. Seventeen files were opened in a little over two years, May 1937–June 1939. Ministry of Justice, Direction des Affaires Criminelles. No. 31 A34/26f (AN: BB^{18} 2915, "Dorgères").

92. Three months of prison (Péronne, Somme, June 1933) for disrupting the sale of a farm for nonpayment of social security; six months of prison (Rouen, August 1935), suspended, for advocating nonpayment of taxes; fines for incitement to nonpayment of taxes (Rennes, February 1938), for opening a public subscription to pay the fine of one of his militants (Rennes, February 1936), and twice for advocating nonpayment of family allocations (see note 130). Dorgères was acquitted twice: of illegally opening a public subscription to pay his own judicial costs in 1935 (Lisieux, October 1936) and of charges arising from the strike of market gardeners he organized at Les Halles in the fall of 1936 (Paris, June 1938).

93. Handwritten note dated 3 May 1934, signed Chéron, on margin of a letter from the Public Prosecutor of Rennes, 30 April 1934. Ministry of Justice, Direction des Affaires Criminelles, No. 31 A34/26F (AN: B^{18} 2915, "Dorgères").

94. Note, 11 June 1934, annotated in the hand of Henri Chéron (AN: BB^{18} 2915, "Dorgères–Annexe").

95. Ibid.; the Minister of Justice (Garde des Sceaux) to the Public Prosecutor of the Appeals Court of Rouen, 17 April 1935.

96. Ministry of Justice (AN: BB^{18} 2915 passim).

97. *Les Travaux des chambres d'agriculture,* 10 December 1934, pp. 511–13; 10 January 1935, p. 46.

98. Ibid., 10 January 1935, p. 3

99. Dorgères was also taken to court by individuals. A grain merchant successfully prosecuted him for defamation in July 1935 (note 149).

100. The commissioner of police thought there were 500 (AD Calvados M11324); Le Roy Ladurie claimed 1500 (*Mait' Jacques,* 10 August 1935).

101. PAO, 8 September 1935.

102. Ibid.

103. The Public Prosecutor of Rouen to the Minister of Justice, Direction des Affaires Criminelles, No. 31 A34/26F, 26 August 1935 (AN: BB^{18} 2915, "Dorgères—Annexe"). Dorgères claimed 20,000 (1 September 1935).

104. Ibid., 20 July 1935.

105. The Procureur de la République, Paris, to the Procureur-Général, 23 October 1935 (AN: BB^{18} 2915, "Dorgères—Annexe").

106. In December 1936, Dorgères was being tailed by six agents of the Sûreté Nationale, as well as by agents of the Paris Prefecture of Police. See AN, CAC, Fontainebleau: No. 1-8-2694, Carton No. 940451/32.

107. AN: BB^{18} 1915, 31 A34/26F.

108. General Cambronne, summoned to surrender by the English at Waterloo, replied with the single word *merde,* which became legendary.

109. AN: BB[18] 2914, "Dorgères."

110. Jean-Luc Allais, "Dorgères et ses hommes: la Défense paysanne en Basse-Normandie," Mémoire de maîtrise, Université de Caen, 1992–93, p. 153.

111. The rally of 11 October 1936 at Pontchâteau (Loire-Atlantique).

112. He claimed 15,000 at the Congress of Peasant Unity in Paris in September 1937, an inflated figure. About five rallies after 1936 exceeded 5,000, two in the Pas-de-Calais and one each in the Loir-et-Cher, the Loire-Atlantique, and the Loire.

113. These public reasons seem compelling enough, though more personal ones have been advanced. Le Roy Ladurie complained that Dorgères had begun calling his (Dorgères's) groups *syndicats,* though that step had been taken in the spring of 1936. Dorgères was disillusioned that Le Roy Ladurie had chosen a deputy, Gaston Bergery, to defend him after his arrest at Castres and had became close to Bergery, but that seems trivial. Jean-Luc Allais, "Dorgères et ses hommes," using the papers of Germain Boullot who was close to both men, is not certain who began the quarrel or why.

114. AD Calvados: M11324, "Front Paysan. Manifestation du 27 septembre 1936 à Osmanville."

115. *Le Courrier du Bessin,* 9–16 December 1937.

116. Jacques Le Roy Ladurie, "Silence aux incapables," *Mait' Jacques,* No. 346, 17 September 1937. The "incapables" are unnamed.

117. Chantérac, who had wide influence in the southwest, also broke publicly with Dorgères in his newspaper, *L'Effort paysan,* in January–February 1939. See Ferdinand Carmé et al., *Alain de Chantérac: un maineteur et un constructeur paysan,* Preface by Jacques Le Roy Ladurie (Aurillac: Imprimerie Moderne, 1954), pp. 22–23.

118. *Mait' Jacques,* No. 386, 21 May 1939.

119. Law of 11 March 1932.

120. Decree of 5 August 1936.

121. Decree-law of 31 May 1938, covering family members over twenty-one and sharecropppers *(métayers);* decree-law of 14 June 1938, covering independent farmers *(chefs d'exploitation),* voluntary for small ones. See Jean Moquay, "L'Evolution sociale en agriculture. La condition des ouvriers agricoles depuis juin 1936," Thèse, Faculté de droit, Université de Bordeaux, 1939, Chap. IV; André Kettenmayer, "Les Allocations familiales en agriculture," Thèse pour le doctorat, Faculté de droit, Université de Paris, 1943.

122. The prefect reported to the minister of the interior on 1 March 1938 that a speech by Dorgères before 3000 persons near Romorantin had "borne fruit"; whereas three-fourths of those concerned had accepted the new law, now there were "a thousand irreducible recalcitrants." The following August the *comice* of Neung-sur-Beurron was interrupted by protests against the family support program *(Allocations familiales)* in the presence of "une centaine de chemises vertes" (AD Loir-et-Cher: 1M 59. Cf. also the spring 1939 demonstrations in the Maine-et-Loire (note 5).

123. *La Voix de la terre,* 28 April and 5 May 1939.

124. The leaders of the Syndicat Agricole of the Loir-et-Cher "became partisans [of family support payment for farm families] as soon as they learned that they were the ones who would organize the office *[la caisse]*." Letter of "a farmer" to M. De-

cault, president of the Chambre d'Agriculture of the Loir-et-Cher, received 7 December 1937 (AD Loir-et-Cher: 4M 221).

125. PAO, 3 October 1937.

126. Isabel Boussard, "Le pacifisme paysan," in René Rémond and Janine Bourdin, *La France et les français en 1939–45* (Paris: Presses de la Fondation Nationale des Sciences Politiques, 1978), pp. 59–72; Pierre Barral, "Mémoires paysannes de la grande guerre," in *Mémoires de la grande guerre,* ed. Pierre Conini (Nancy: Presses Universitaires, 1989).

127. PAO, 20 September 1936; *Syndicats paysans,* 1 April 1938.

128. The Minister of Agriculture to the Minister of Justice, (Garde des Sceaux) 11 April 1938 (AN: BB^{18} 2915, A34 F26, "VI").

129. "Résumé des affaires Dorgères contenues dans le présent dossier (mai 1937– juin 1939)," (AN: BB^{18} 2915, A34 F26, "Dorgères–Impôts").

130. Ibid. Dorgères was fined 50 francs by the Tribunal Correctionnel of Rennes on 9 September 1938 for an article in the PAO that urged peasants to "make the decree-laws [on family support payments] fail, as we made the law [on social security] fail," and 100 francs by the same court on 15 February 1939 for another article that urged nonpayment of *cotisations* for family support.

131. Ibid.

132. Philippe Pétain, speech at Pau to the peasants, 20 April 1941, in *Discours aux français: 17 juin 1940–20 août 1944,* ed. Jean-Claude Barbas (Paris: Albin Michel, 1989), pp. 123–127.

133. Isabel Boussard, *La Corporation paysanne* (Paris: Hachette, 1973), p. 27; AN: Z^5 127.

134. Ibid. The new regime was experimenting with new forms of contact with citizens. Having decided against a single party, it was turning to war veterans, organized in the Légion Française des Combattants.

135. Report of Inspecteur Regerat, Division de la Police Judiciaire, Préfecture de Police, 10 October 1945. AN: Z^5 127 No. 5815.

136. The basic scholarly work on the Peasant Corporation is Boussard, *La Corporation paysanne.* See also Boussard's *Vichy et la Corporation paysanne: documents réunis et présentés par Isabel Boussard* (Paris: Presses de la Fondation Nationale des Sciences Politiques, 1980). Mévellec, *Combat du paysan Breton,* though partisan, draws on important material concerning the corporation from the unpublished memoirs of Count Hervé Budes de Guébriant.

137. Rémy Goussault had been secretary-general of the Association des Producteurs de Fruits à Cidre and in the early 1930s a farmers' representative at the commodities exchange (Bourse de Commerce) in Paris, where he had been aggressively suspicious of the grain merchants. He spoke often at publicmeetings with Dorgères.

138. *Journal officiel de l'etat français,* 22 January 1941, Lois et décrets, Arrêté du 21 janvier 1941: members of the Commission d'Organisation Corporative Paysanne.

139. AN: F^{10} 4973.

140. He tried, and apparently failed, to increase his reprentation in the Pays d'Auge and to be represented in the Deux-Sèvres and the Lot-et-Garonne. Pointier and Goussault helped him obtain one representative in the Oise.

141. AN: F^{10} 4945–51.

142. AN: F^{10} 4947.

143. Ibid. De Guébriant objected to the Francisque, saying one must look to the long term, beyond Pétain: "You know how I feel about the Marshal, but enough is enough *[mais enfin]!*"

144. Session of 27 April 1942 (AN: F^{10} 4948).

145. Session of 4 August 1942 (AN: F^{10} 4950).

146. Session of 27 April–1 May 1942 (AN: F^{10} 4948).

147. Session of 6 August 1942 (AN: F^{10} 4950).

148. Session of 27 April–1 May 1942 (AN: F^{10} 4948).

149. Sessions of 19 and 20 November 1941 (AN: F^{10} 4947). Dorgères was not entirely accurate here. He was sued for defamation by a grain merchant whom he accused in the pages of the PAO of fraud, on 15 July 1935 (AN: BB^{18} 2914: "Dorgères: Poursuite en diffamation: requête Frémont et Jacqueline à Pont L'Evêque").

150. Sessions of 20 November 1941 (AN: FN^{10} 4947) and 27 April 1942 (AN: F^{10} 4948).

151. (AN: F^{10} 5046. Pays d'Auge, "Correspondance"). Du Boullay had in fact distanced himself from Dorgères in 1937–38, at the same time as Le Roy Ladurie.

152. The more or less forced unification of the cooperative and mutual credit associations during Vichy was the end of the separate network affiliated with the boulevard de Saint-Germain, although the Société d'Encouragement was revived and had a shadowy existance for a time after Liberation.

153. Dorgères seems to have remained a *chargé de mission* in the spring of 1943, though he denied it in his trial.

154. "Letter to my friends," September 1943 (AN: F^{10} 5004, Ille-et-Vilaine, "Constitution U.R.C.").

155. For example, issue of 7 September 1940: "Today we must agitate the country again, keep it from sleeping, keep it from believing that the defeat is just a passing incident that will work out in the end" (AN: Z^5 127, No. 5815, "Cri du sol").

156. Testimony of Paul Marion, 25 April 1945, Cour de Justice de la Seine, AN: Z^5 127 No. 5815.

157. "Letter to my friends." Cf. also "Défense Paysanne pas morte," *Le Cri du sol,* 16 October 1943.

158. The texts are in AN: F^5 127 No. 5815.

159. *Le Cri du sol,* fall 1940; quoted in *Parquet* of the Cour de Justice of the Department of the Seine, "Exposé: Affaire D'Halluin, Henri, dit Dorgères, 2 March 1946 (AN: Z^5 127 No. 5815). This passage seems to have been censored.

160. *Le Cri du sol,* 4 January 1941.

161. Ibid., 23 August 1940, 21 December 1940.

162. Dorgères attacked these "holdovers from the Old Regime" *(ci-devants)* in *Le cri du sol,* 5 July 1941. Anti-Semitic remarks were common in this newspaper without being an obsessively central theme.

163. Ibid., 26 April 1941.

164. Ibid., 8 March 1941.

165. Ibid., 11 July 1942.

166. Ibid., 14 November 1942.

167. Ibid., 17 June 1944. Jean Bohuon wrote him a letter on 20 June, using the same terms AN: Z^5 127 No. 5815.

168. Ibid., 16 October 1943. Jacques Le Roy Ladurie, secretary-general of the UNSA, seems to have felt that the corporation "stole" corporatism from the UNSA *(mémoires inédites)*. A look at the personnel of the departmental organizations suggests that Dorgères's version, for once, is the more accurate one.

169. Ibid., 11 September 1943.

170. *Le Cri du sol,* 16 January 1943, 17 July 1943, tried to deny the "myth" of peasants' profiteering as "starvers" of the city.

171. Ibid., 16 October 1943.

172. Dorgères's reports to Pétain, April and October 1943 AN: Z^5 127, No. 5815. He wanted to form a special militia, Gardes Messiers, to protect crops from pillage by the Resistance.

173. Several of Dorgères's followers were active in the Resistance, including Jacques Eynaud in the Sarthe and Jean Nobilet, head in 1938 of the Comité de Défense Paysanne of the Ille-et-Vilaine, who died in a concentration camp for participating, with his two sons, in the reception of parachuted arms during the occupation.

174. *Le Cri du sol,* February and March 1944. Believing Pétain would remain in power after the war, Dorgères urged him to promise that agricultural protectionism would continue.

CHAPTER 5

1. He would have arrived just in time for Marshal Pétain's forced departure on 20 August, with his German guards, for Metz.

2. Much of what follows is based on Dorgères's dossier in the archives of the Cour de Justice de la Seine, AN: Z^5 127 No. 5815.

3. AN: BB^{18} 7128, "Cri du sol."

4. The Minister of Agriculture to the Minister of Justice, (Garde des Sceaux), 12 April 1945 (AN: BB^{18} 7128); see also AN: Z^5 127 No. 5815.

5. *Indignité nationale* was a new penalty created at the Liberation for collaboration cases too minor for treason charges but sufficiently grave to be punished.

6. AN: BB^{18} 7128.

7. Jean-Luc Allais, "Dorgères et ses hommes: la Défense Paysanne en Basse Normandie," Mémoire de maîtrise, Université de Caen, 1992–93, p. 186.

8. PP: 92.412, "D'Halluin, Henry, dit Dorgères."

9. The Commissaire aux Renseignements Généraux to the Procureur de la République of the Mayenne, 14 December 1948 (AN: BB^{18} 7128).

10. Philippe Gratton, *Les Paysans contre l'agrarisme* (Paris: François Maspéro, 1972), p. 215.

11. Dorgères was also sued successfully for defamation during this period by an agricultural official and by the PCF newspaper, *La Terre.* PP: 92.412, "D'Halluin, Henry, dit Dorgères."

12. Pierre Alphandéry, *Trente ans de syndicalisme gestionnaire dans le Calvados* (Paris: INRA/CORDES, 1977), pp. 85–87. See also Jean-Michel Royer, "De Dorgères à Poujade," in Jacques Fauvet and Henri Mendras, *Les Paysans et la politique dans la France contemporaine,* Cahiers de la Fondation Nationale des Sciences Politiques No. 94 (Paris: A. Colin, 1958), p. 170. Voivenel demonstrated against social security as early as 1929 and wrote in the PAO in the 1930s.

13. Françoise Mandersheid, *Une autre sécurité sociale: la Mutualité Sociale Agricole* (Paris: l'Harmattan, 1991), pp. 51–52. Dorgères managed to gather 2000 people to block a sale in the Vacher incident.

14. Régis Fricot and Pierre Genaitay, "Dorgères et le mouvement paysan," Mémoire de maîtrise, Rennes, 1972, pp. 194–95; Royer, "Dorgères à Poujade," pp. 170–79. Dorgères's postwar clientele was more narrowly concentrated among the poor and backward than in the 1930s.

15. Dorgères was arrested, along with French Algeria militant Georges Sauge, but not prosecuted (PP: 92.412). Newspaper accounts revived prewar errors, calling Dorgères a "vicomte." See "Des Chemises Vertes aux comités civiques: Dorgères a derrière lui une longue carrière de fasciste," *Libération,* 13 February 1960; also *Le Monde,* 13 February 1960.

16. Henri Mendras and Yves Tavernier, "Les manifestations de juin 1961," *Revue française de science politique,* XIII, No. 3 (September 1962), 647–71.

17. Old sympathizers now active in the FNSEA either ignored him (Forget) or renounced him publicly (Bohuon). Unsigned note, 29 May 1947, Archives Michel Cépède, OURS, "Dorgères."

18. Robert Fiche, private archives.

19. "If the countryside had uniformly refused it, France . . . would not have become republican." Maurice Agulhon, *La République au village* (Paris: Plon, 1970), p. 13.

20. PAO, 15 October 1933.

21. Ibid., 4 March 1934; quoted in Pascal Ory, "Institution et discours d'une colère paysanne (1929–39)," *Revue d'histoire moderne et contemporaine,* XXII, No. 2 (April–June 1975), 185. Ory says that Dorgères considered himself a "cisalpine Mussolini" up to mid-1934 (p. 187).

22. PAO, 15 October 1933. I have found no positive references to Nazi Germany in PAO later than this.

23. Ibid., 4 March 1934 (he was referring to Mussolini only). See also *La Défense paysanne* (Aurillac), No. 19, 13 May 1934: "Without fascism, we would have Russian chaos and misery at our door."

24. Ernest Lefèvre, "Loup-garou et fascisme," *La Voix du paysan,* April 1934. Lefèvre was Dorgères's secretary.

25. PAO, 14 June 1936.

26. Ibid., 2 May 1937.

27. Ibid., 23 March 1937.

28. Ibid., 14 June 1936, 2 May 1937.

29. Gabriel Arnaubec, "République? Dictature?" *La Provence paysanne,* June 1939. Unlike his ally Jacques Le Roy Ladurie, Dorgères had no contact with monarchists after he left the Nouvelliste de Bretagne in 1926.

30. "La 3e Fête paysanne allemande—Goslar, 14/17 novembre 1935," communication faite par M. Goussault au Comité français de relations agricoles internationales. Mimeographed text in Augé-Laribé papers, Ministry of Agriculture, Paris, "La Corporation Paysanne, 1935–49."

31. *Mait' Jacques* praised the Nazis' family policy (1 April 1934, 19 March 1939), but criticized both Hitler and Stalin for overindustrialization at the expense of the

peasantry (17 September 1939). *Mait' Jacques* recognized the Nazis as "our possible adversaries" on 6 August 1939.

32. I have borrowed this illuminating phrase from Philippe Burrin, "La France dans le 'champ magnétique' des fascismes," *Le Débat*, No. 32 (November 1984).

33. He attacked the "bicots et métèques," whom he blamed for the fight between North African sugar refinery workers and farmers at Toury (PAO, 1 November 1936), and he expressed alarm over the proposed use of "bicots" as farm workers in case of war (*Le Cri du sol*, 17 June 1939).

34. Dorgères had the crowd take an oath to follow the "command for action" in a mass meeting in Rouen on 25 August 1953 (PAO, 1 September 1935). The Greenshirts swore an oath but used no form of salute.

35. I approach fascism in this way in "The Five Phases of Fascism," *Journal of Modern History*, forthcoming.

36. Marc Bloch, "Pourquoi je suis républicain," *Les Cahiers politiques* (organ of the Comité Général d'Études de la Résistance), No. 2, July 1943, one of the "clandestine writings" *(écrits clandestins)* published in *Etrange défaite* (Paris: Gallimard, 1993), p. 215.

37. The crucial distinction between fascism and authoritarianism is best analyzed by Juan Linz, "An Authoritarian Regime: Spain," in Erik Allardt and Stein Rokkan, *Mass Politics: Studies in Political Sociology* (New York: Free Press, 1970).

38. Paul Brooker, *The Faces of Fraternalism* (Oxford: Clarendon Press, 1991), applies Durkheimian concepts of solidarity fruitfully in his study of obligatory unity under fascism.

39. The essential works on this point are Martin Broszat, *The Hitler State* (London: Longman, 1981), and the "polyocratic" interpretation of Hans Mommsen, in *National-sozialismus und die deutsche Gesellschaft* (Reinbek: Rohwohlt, 1991) and elsewhere.

40. Bilger's Bauernbund adopted fascist-like rhetoric in the 1930s but allied itself politically with any groups willing to support its peasant agenda: sometimes French nationalist, sometimes autonomist, and pro-German only after 1938. Bilger fought in the French army in 1939–40 and, upon his return from a German POW camp in October 1940, served the Nazi occupation as a propaganda officer and as a member of Gauleiter Bürckel's council in Lorraine. In 1942, however, objecting to Nazi reset-tlement of Lorrainers in Germany, he ceased working with the occupation authorities. After the war, he was sentenced to ten years of hard labor. In the 1960s, he returned to activism as an official of the MP-13 group that defended French Algeria. See Léon Strauss, "Les Organisations paysannes Alsaciennes de 1890 à 1939: notables et contestataires," in *Histoire de l'Alsace rurale* (Strasbourg and Paris: Librairie Istra, 1983); Strauss, "Joseph-Théodore Bilger," in *Nouveau dictionnaire de biographie alsacienne* (Stras-bourg: Fédération des Sociétés d'Histoire et d'Archéologie d'Alsace, 1983), III, p. 224; and Bernard Reimeringer, "Un Mouvement paysan extrémiste des années trente: les chemises vertes," *Revue d'Alsace*, No. 106 (1980), 113–33. Joseph Bilger's son Fran-çois, professor at the University of Strasbourg, has vehemently challenged this ver-sion, portraying his father as primarily a victim of the Nazis. See François Bilger, "Droit de réponse," *Saisons d'Alsace*, 96 (June 1987), 104; and his "Reimeringer, Lerch et Strauss ou comment certains 'historiens' écrivent l'histoire de l'Alsace et des Alsa-ciens," *Elan: Cahiers des ICS*, Vol. 24, Nos. 5–6 (May–June 1980), 9–11. See also Chapter 2, note 63.

41. Dorgères held one joint meeting with Doriot during the market gardeners' strike in December 1936 but generally felt nervous enough about these rival movements to exclude any militant who associated with them.

42. For example, Jules Radulphe, the new agrarian deputy from Vire (Calvados).

43. This is how Zeev Sternhell got into trouble with French reviewers and courts with his *Ni Droite, ni gauche: l'idéologie fasciste en France* (Paris: Seuil, 1983).

44. Paul Corner, *Fascism in Ferrara* (Oxford: Clarendon Press, 1976), p. x.

45. Adrian Lyttelton, *The Seizure of Power: Fascism in Italy, 1919–29,* 2nd ed. (Princeton N.J.: Princeton University Press, 1987).

46. Thomas Childers, *The Nazi Voter* (Chapel Hill: University of North Carolina Press, 1983), pp. 58, 61.

47. Ibid., pp. 157–59, 223–24.

48. Serge Berstein, "La France des années 1930 allergique au fascisme. A propos de Zeev Sternhell," *Vingtième siècle,* No. 2 (April 1984).

49. Corner, *Fascism in Ferrara,* passim.

50. Maurice Agulhon, *La République au village,* 2nd ed. (Paris: Seuil, 1979), dated the transformation of the Var from conservative to republican to the 1820s–40s. Tony Judt, *Socialism in Provence* (Cambridge: Cambridge University Press, 1979), found that socialism grew strong rural roots in the Var in the 1880s.

51. Maurice Agulhon, Gabriel Désert, and Robert Speckler, *Apogée et crise de la civilisation paysanne,* tome 3: *Histoire de la France rurale* (Paris: Seuil, 1976), pp. 80, 499.

52. Michel Gervais, Claude Servolin, and Jean Weil, *Une France sans paysans* (Paris: Editions du Seuil, 1965), pp. 10–12.

53. Ibid., p. 34.

54. Phyllis Deane and W. A. Cole, *British Economic Growth, 1688–1959,* 2nd ed. (Cambridge: Cambridge University Press, 1980), p. 142.

55. *Historical Statistics of the United States* (Washington, D.C.: Bureau of the Census, 1975), p. D11–23.

56. Philippe Ariès, *Histoire des populations françaises et de leurs attitudes devant la vie depuis le XVIIIe siècle* (Paris: Seuil, 1970), p. 296.

57. Farmers of the Midi were probably better integrated with the surrounding towns than those of the rest of France during the Third Republic.

58. Bertrand Hervieu, *Ouvriers ruraux du Perche* (Nanterre: Université de Paris X, 1976), Chap. II: "La désindustrialisation des campagnes et la constitution du ghetto paysan."

59. See the strained visit by city cousins in Emile Guillaumin, *The Life of a Simple Man* (Hanover, N.H.: University Press of New England, 1983), Chap. XLVIII.

60. Gilles Postel-Vinay, "L'Agriculture dans l'économie française: crise et réinsertion," in *Entre l'état et le marché: l'économie française des années 1880 à nos jours,* ed. Maurice Lévy-Leboyer (Paris: Gallimard, 1991), pp. 68–73.

61. Jacques Le Roy Ladurie, "Vers une politique paysanne," in Union Nationale des Syndicats Agricoles, *Congrès syndical paysan, 5–6 mai 1937* (Paris: Flammarion, 1937), p. 43.

62. The 150,000 or so agricultural wage laborers remaining today work mostly on southern fruit and vegetable farms.

63. The title of Dorgères's postwar memoirs, *Au XXe siécle 10 ans de jacquerie* (Paris: Editions du Scorpion, 1959), may be the idea of his son, who worked for its publisher.

64. Ted W. Margadant, *French Peasants in Revolt: The Insurrection of 1851* (Princeton, N.J.: Princeton University Press, 1979).

65. Charles Tilly, Louise Tilly, and Richard Tilly, *The Rebellious Century, 1830–1930* (Cambridge, Mass.: Harvard University Press, 1975).

66. Luc Raveleau, "Royalisme et nationalismes en Vendée, 1919–39," Mémoire de maîtrise, Université Catholique de l'Ouest, Angers, December 1986, p. 180.

67. PAO, 25 August 1935.

68. *Le Cri du paysan,* May 1937. The Confédération Générale du Travail (CGT) is the principal labor union of France.

69. This is the version used in the CAP program. Cf. *L'Action paysanne,* No. 13, 27 October 1935.

70. Farm revenues fell 25% in the decade following the "turning point" of 1974. Pierre Alphandéry, Pierre Bitoun, and Yves Dupont, *Les Champs du départ: une France rurale sans paysans* (Paris: Découverte, 1989), pp. 50, 65.

71. Decrees of 18 September and 10 October 1957.

72. Ordinance of 28 December 1958.

73. On 9 August 1995, following peasant demonstrations, Agriculture Minister Philippe Vasseur announced reduced taxes and social costs for southern fruit and vegetable producers, damaged by the devaluation of the lira and the peseta. *Le Monde,* 11 August 1995, p. 5.

74. Postel-Vinay, "L'Agriculture dans l'économie francaise," p. 69.

75. *Mait' Jacques,* 18 January–1 February 1942 (AN: F^{10} 4986).

76. Socialist governments in 1981–86 and 1988–93 infringed on *cogestion* slightly by trying to bring additional agricultural associations, such as the Confédération Paysanne, the FFA, and the MODEF, into official functions. See John T. S. Keeler, *The Politics of Neocorporatism in France: Farmers, the State, amd Agricultural Policy-making in the Fifth Republic* (New York and Oxford: Oxford University Press, 1987), pp. 213–40.

77. Letter from Yves Houitte de La Chesnais to Adolphe Pointier, 2 October 1943, Adolphe Pointier papers, "Syndic National et U.R.C.A., 5: Ille-et-Vilaine" (AN: F^{10} 5104).

78. Letters and telegrams exchanged among Bohuon, Pointier, and de La Bourdonnay are found in the archives of the Corporation Nationale Paysanne, Adolphe Pointier papers (AN: F^{10} 5104) and "Organisation syndicale: Ille-et-Vilaine" (AN: F10 5004).

79. Jean Bohuon, letter "Aux Syndics d'Ille-et-Villaine," 19 September 1943 (AN: F^{10} 5004). Bohuon still spoke of himself as a *cultivateur-cultivant,* as in his youthful days with the Abbé Mancel.

80. Letter from de La Chesnais.

81. Ibid.; see also the letter from de Guébriant to Bohuon, 16 May 1941, replying in these terms to Bohuon's complaints that the CDPs were underrepresented in the corporation.

82. Henry Dorgères, "Lettre à mes amis dans tous les départements," 28 September 1943 (AN: F^{10} 5004). Dorgères was referring explicitly to Bohuon's elevation at the same time to the national council of the CNP.

83. Mme. Christiane Lambert was president of the CNJA, 1994–95.

84. "Où va l'agriculture française?" Interview with Emmanuel Le Roy Ladurie, *Le Débat,* No. 28 (January 1984). Guillaume was still at that point president of the

FNSEA. Michel Debatisse had already served as under-secretary for agro-alimentary industries in the Raymond Barre cabinet (1978–79).

85. Ibid.

86. An angry delegate of the Ile-de-France at the Forty-seventh Congress of FNSEA called French farmers "victimes d'un génocide voulu et organisé." *Le Monde,* 25–26 April 1994.

87. The creators of the Coordination rurale are from the Gers, a department where Dorgères was never active. Its secretary-general, Philippe Arnaud, did not reply to my letter asking him whether he knew about Dorgères.

88. For example, the FNSEA/CNJA's "national day of action" on 30 June 1992, after 3the Coordination Rurale had blockaded Paris. *Le Monde,* 3 July 1992.

89. The election by proportional representation of representatives of the *chambres d'agriculture* in January 1995 showed that The Coordination Rurale was strongest in areas of "large-scale cultivation of wheat, soybeans and colza," such as the Loire Valley, the Beauce, the Oise, the Seine-et-Marne, the Calvados, and so on. See *Le Monde,* 10 Febuary 1995.

90. Article 1, *Loi d'Orientation Agricole* of 5 August 1960.

91. "Vers l'état paysan," PAO, 14 July 1935.

92. "Pour un ordre paysan: organisation corporative ou marxisme?" (Paris: Comité d'Action Paysanne, July 1936), p. 4. This is the second brochure published by the CAP, the first being its program (September 1935).

93. Jacques Le Roy Ladurie, *Mait' Jacques,* 15 February 1942.

94. Dedication by Marshal Pétain on 11 November 1935 of the *monument aux morts* of the smallest rural commune in France, Capoulet-Junac (Ariège). Agrarians often quoted this speech, for example, Jacques Le Roy Ladurie's *Syndicats paysans,* 15 December 1939.

95. PAO, 12 November 1933.

96. Dorgères, as quoted in *Journal de Neufchâtel,* 14 February 1939. (AD Seine-Maritime: 1Z 9).

97. Jacques Le Roy Ladurie, "L'Heure de la paysannerie," *Mait' Jacques,* 20 June 1937.

98. Marshal Pétain, speech, 30 June 1939, quoted in *Mait' Jacques,* 16 July 1939.

99. René Dumont, *Misère ou prospérité paysanne?* (Paris: Editions Fustier, 1936), Preface by Jacques Duboin. Dumont was to participate in postwar agricultural planning and then embark on a long life of criticism of the impact of Western agricultural success on the Third World.

100. Richard F. Kuisel, *Capitalism and the State in Modern France* (Cambridge: Cambridge University Press, 1981), pp. 155–56.

101. Marc Bloch, *Strange Defeat* (New York: Norton, 1968), p. 149: for example, "our dear dead towns," and the refusal to replace a donkey cart by a motor car.

102. "Collaboration," *Le Cri du sol,* 8 March 1941. This was Dorgères's only mention of collaboration, and he urged his readers, "before reacting upon seeing the title of this article," to heed Pétain's "language of a leader" on 30 October 1940—the speech explaining his recent handshake with Hitler at Montoire.

103. République française, Présidence du gouvernement, Commissariat général du Plan de Modernisation et d'Equipement, *Rapport général sur le premier plan de modernisa-*

tion et d'équipement, Deuxième session du conseil du plan, November 1946, pp. 19, 27, 56–57, 144–53.

104. Alphandéry et al., *Champs du départ,* pp. 147–50.

105. Loi d'Orientation Agricole of 5 August 1960; Loi Complémentaire of 26 July 1962.

106. *Sociétés d'intérêt collectif agricole* (SICA); *groupements agricoles d'exploitation en commun* (GAEC). Contrary to official expectations, GAECs were used principally within families to facilitate a gradual passing of the responsibilities and the property from father to son.

107. All farmland put up for sale must be offered first to the regional *société d'aménagement foncier et d'établissement rural* (SAFER), which assembles efficient plots and makes them available at reasonable prices only to farmers (preferably young ones starting up). The SAFERs prohibit any residential or industrial construction on farmland, so that the French countryside has almost none of the roadside trailer camps, factories in open fields, scattered home sites, and subdivisions that have disfigured the American landscape.

108. Hélène Delorme, "La Politique agricole dans l'internationalisation des échanges," in Pierre Coulomb et al., *Les Agriculteurs et la politique* (Paris: Presses de la Fondation Nationale des Sciences Politiques, 1990), pp. 33, 51. France alone accounted for about a quarter of the entire EC agricultural production.

109. The GATT ruled at the end of 1992 that France had subsidized unduly the export of colza, soybean, and sunflower products and authorized the United States to institute counterprotection measures against French wine, cognac, and milk products.

110. *Le Monde,* 23 February 1993.

111. According to the *Economist* (19 September 1992), French farmers "use up to five times as much fertilizer and 50 times more chemical pesticides than their American rivals."

112. Alphandéry et al., *Champs du départ,* p. 15.

113. Ninety percent of farm labor is now familial. Ibid., p. 16.

114. French farmers are not perfectly homogeneous, of course. There are two tiers: larger or more specialized farmers who are surviving, and the marginal ones who are failing or barely surviving with the aid of second jobs or tourism. The second group has fueled the growth of farmers' opposition organizations, which claim that the FNSEA has sold out to the government and the EC: the Mouvement de Défense des Exploitations Agricoles Familiales (MODEF), founded in 1959, which is close to the Communist party; Fédération Française de l'Agriculture (FFA), founded in 1968, which is rightwing and free market, with some old Dorgérists, and is now close to Le Pen's National Front; Confédération Paysanne, founded in 1977, which is non-Communist communitarian Left; and Coordination Rurale, in 1991, which is close to Le Pen's National Front and opposed to reductions in EC farm support programs. The FNSEA/CNJA won only 60% of the *chambres d'agriculture* seats in the January 1995 elections (by proportional representation), followed by the Confédération Paysanne (20%) and the Coordination Rurale, now including the FFA (12%). See *Le Monde,* 10 February 1995.

115. With e-mail, the electronic integration of the countryside into a new society without urban-rural distinctions has already advanced even further than Henri Mendras foresaw in *Voyage au pays de l'utopie rustique* (Paris: Actes Sud, 1992).

116. Bernard Kayser, *Naissance de nouvelles campagnes* (Paris: Editions de l'Aube, 1993).

117. Emile Guillaumin, *Life of a Simple Man,* Chap. XLVIII.

118. In 1929, 218,487 French farm workers were housed in spaces "not intended for habitation," such as stables and barns. *Statistique agricole de la France publiée par le Ministre de l'Agriculture. Résultats de l'enquête de 1929* (Paris: Imprimerie nationale, 1936), p. 637.

119. In 1992, 6.8% of the active French population was employed in agriculture. This percentage was below Italy (9.9%) and Japan (7.9%) and above Denmark (5.8%), Canada (4.5%), Germany (4.5%), the United States (2.9%), and Britain (2.3%). *La Tribune de l'expansion,* 22 April 1992.

120. *La Croix,* 21 January 1995.

121. *Le Figaro,* 10 June 1993. The minister was announcing a concession by the EC to France whereby some land taken out of wheat cultivation can be used for industrial crops, such as soybeans or colza.

122. Agriculture Minister Jean Puech in *La Croix,* 18 May 1994.

123. *L'Humanité,* 6 October 1992: "desertification intended by Brussels and the United States."

124. Simon Schama recalls this distinction in *Landscape and Memory* (New York: Knopf, 1995), p. 570. It was made earlier in Leo Marx's classic, *The Machine in the Garden* (New York: Oxford University Press, 1964), p. 64.

125. *La Croix—L'Evénement,* 18 May 1994.

126. In fact, 42% of farms are part-time occupations. Alphandéry et al., *Champs du départ,* p. 21.

127. The seven regions with the biggest farms receive 50.8% of government aid to agriculture. Ibid., pp. 89–90.

128. The Compagnie Nouvelle des Sucreries Réunies, with offices in Paris, sued the French state for failing to prevent a strike on its sugar beet farms in the Aisne in July 1937. (AD Aisne M11404.)

129. Marie-Joseph Durupt, *Les Mouvements d'Action Catholique: facteurs d'évolution du monde rural* (Paris: Hachette, 1973).

130. *Le Figaro—Economie,* 30 May 1995.

131. France had a net gain from CAP until 1989, when it became a net cost for France, as it already was for the other members of the EC—a significant turning point. See Henry Nallet, "Pour une nouvelle agriculture," *Le Monde,* 2 June 1992.

132. Jean-Paul Mulot, "Les Questions que se posent les français (30): faut-il continuer de subventioner l'agriculture?" *Le Figaro,* 30 March 1995. Supporters of the future President Chirac were the most favorable (80%).

BIBLIOGRAPHICAL ESSAY

Very little had been written about Henry Dorgères and his Greenshirts when I undertook this study. Those interested in a closer look should begin with Dorgères's own editorials in his two provincial weekly newspapers, *Le Progrès agricole de l'Ouest* (Rennes) and *Le Paysan du Centre-Ouest,* published in the Loire Valley; his Paris weekly *Le Cri du sol;* and the monthly *La Voix du paysan,* called *Le Cri du Paysan* after 1937. One must use with caution the three versions of his autobiography: *Haut les fourches* (Paris: Oeuvres Françaises, 1935), *Au XXe siécle 10 ans de jacquerie* (Paris: Editions du Scorpion, 1959), and *Au Temps des fourches* (Paris: Editions France-Empire, 1975).

Contemporary accounts by authors who took Dorgères seriously are Louis-Gabriel Robinet, *Dorgères et le Front Paysan* (Paris: Plon, 1937); Jacques Dyssord, "Que veut? que peut? . . . la Défense paysanne," *Le Document,* 2nd year, No. 3 (Paris: Denoel and Steele, 1935); "Le Bilan d'une année du 'Front Paysan,'" *Dossiers de l'action populaire,* No. 359 (10 March 1936), 497–528; No. 360 (25 March 1936), 637–70; and No. 361 (10 April 1936), 797–820; and Bertrand de Jouvenel, "Le Front Paysan," *Revue de Paris,* 42nd year, No. 23 (1 December 1935), 652–63. These relatively favorable observers are less inaccurate than Dorgères's opponents on the Left, who consider the Greenshirts mere tools of a capitalist conspiracy. See, for example, Victor Picard and Marceau Pivert, *L'Armée prétorienne des trusts: Croix de feu, Front national, Front paysan* (Paris: Librairie populaire, Editions du parti socialiste SFIO, 1936).

Scholarly work on Dorgères began with Pascal Ory in the 1960s, using newspapers since archives were still closed: "Henry Dorgères et la 'Défense Paysanne' des origines à 1939," Mémoire de maîtrise, Faculté des Lettres et Sciences Humaines de Nanterre, 1970; and "Institution et discours d'une colère paysanne (1929–39)," *Revue d'histoire moderne et contemporaine,* XXII, No. 2 (April–June 1975).

Several French *mémoires de maîtrise* (MA theses) are very helpful. Roger Fricot and Pierre Genaitay, "Dorgères et le mouvement paysan," Université de Rennes, 1972, interviewed Dorgères himself. Also useful are Clément Lépine, "La Naissance du mouvement dorgériste (1926–30)," Université de Paris XIII, 1992–93, and two enterprising local case studies: Nicolas Varin, "Dorgères et le dorgérisme en Picardie," Université de Paris I, Panthéon-Sorbonne, 1993–94; and Jean-Luc Allais, "Dorgères et ses hommes: la Défense Paysanne en Basse-Normandie," Université de Caen, 1992–93.

Dorgères's movement apparently left no archives, but one may follow its activities in police and prefectoral records. These are surprisingly incomplete for the late 1930s. The Ministry of the Interior files (series F^7 in the Archives Nationales) contain many gaps after 1935, largely because of destruction in 1940. No minister of agriculture left archives until after World War II; see Isabelle de Richefort, "Les Archives du Ministère de l'Agriculture," Institut d'histoire du temps présent, *Bulletin trimestriel,* No. 23 (May 1986), 17. At the Centre des Archives Contemporaines, the repository of the Archives Nationales at Fontainebleau devoted to recent documents, the Ministry of Finance records contain material concerning agriculture. The most important source for me there was the archives of the Sûreté Nationale, seized in Paris by the Germans in 1940 and then, in Germany in 1945, by Soviet troops, and in 1996 beginning to be returned from Moscow to French custody. These confiscations explain why the Prefecture of Police in Paris has no file on Dorgères' activities between the wars, although it does have a postwar file. Another essential source for Dorgères's career is the Ministry of Justice files of his several trials, before and after the war (Series BB^{18} in the Archives Nationales).

The study of Dorgérism at the grass roots must depend on departmental archives, which wartime destructions and bureaucratic shortcomings have made far less informative than I expected when I began this project. These inadequacies make the local press more important for this sort of research than I first imagined. Although local newspapers often slanted the news to favor the owner (more often than not the local deputy or senator), they can be vivid and informative.

While works devoted directly to Dorgères are scarce, a library could be filled with general works on the French peasantry in the twentieth century. The suggestions that follow make no pretense of being exhaustive. They direct the reader to the most enduring classics or to some particularly authoritative recent studies, many of which contain full bibliographies.

First, a certain number of classics remain indispensable:

1. Michel Augé-Laribé, *La Politique agricole de la France de 1880 à 1940* (Paris: Presses Universitaires de France, 1950). The point of view of the principal agricultural expert of Republican sympathies of the late Third and early Fourth Republics.

2. Pierre Barral, *Les Agrariens français de Méline à Pisani,* Cahiers de la Fondation Nationale des Sciences Politiques, No. 164 (Paris: Armand Colin, 1968). A rich survey of the politics of agriculture under the Third, Fourth, and Fifth Republics, with informative annexes and bibliography.

3. Gordon Wright, *Rural Revolution in France: The Peasantry in the Twentieth Century* (Stanford, Calif.: Stanford University Press, 1964). An authoritative work on the modernization of French agriculture and its political impact.

4. Volumes 3 and 4 of the superbly illustrated *Histoire de la France rurale,* ed. George Duby and Armand Wallon: Maurice Agulhon, Gabriel Désert, and Robert Speckler, *Apogée et crise de la civilisation paysanne* (Paris: Seuil, 1976); and Michel Gervais, Marcel Jollivet, and Yves Tavernier, *La Fin de la France paysanne: de 1914 à nos hours* (Paris: Seuil, 1977).

A series of conferences held at the Institut d'Etudes Politiques in Paris has provided state of the art scholarly assessments of contemporary peasant politics and rural society in France at regular intervals since the 1950s: Jacques Fauvet and Hervien Mendras, *Les Paysans et la politique dans la France contemporaine,* Cahiers de la Fondation Nationale des Sciences Politiques, No. 94 (Paris: A. Colin, 1958); Yves Tavernier, Michel Gervais, and Claude Servolin, *L'Univers politique des paysans dans la France contemporaine,* Cahiers de la Fondation Nationale des Sciences Politiques, No. 184 (Paris: A. Colin, 1972); and *Les Agriculteurs et la politique,* ed. Pierre Coulomb, Hélène Delorme, Bertrand Hervieu, Marcel Jollivet, and Philippe Lacombe, (Paris: Presses de la Fondation Nationale des Sciences Politiques, 1990). Less theoretically inclined and more uneven, yet full of interesting detail, is Philippe Chalmin and André Gueslin, *Un siècle d'histoire agricole française,* Special Issues No. 184–186 of *Economie rurale,* March–August 1988.

Authentic peasants have spoken for themselves in two classic works. Emile Guillaumin (1873–1951) was a modest sharecropper *(métayer)* in the Bourbonnais region of central France. Guillaumin was awakened to books and writing by the local primary school teacher but elected to remain a peasant. He divided his life between farming and campaigns for peasant self-respect, self-help, and tenants' rights, including editing a local newspaper and organizing local peasant associations. His best-known book was a semifictional autobiography of a nineteenth-century peasant, originally published in 1904. It is available in English as *The Life of a Simple Man,* ed. Eugen Weber, rev. trans. Margaret Crosland (Hanover, N.H.: University Press of New England, 1983). Ephraim Grenadou, *Grenadou, paysan français,* with Alain Prévost (Paris: Editions du Seuil, 1966) was a prosperous middling owner-cultivator on the Beauce plain near Chartres, a man of remarkably sunny temperament and enterprising nature whose recollections of the two wars and the Great Depression are incomparably graphic. Although Guillaumin amd Grenadou, men of exceptional energy and intelligence, can hardly be considered typical, they are the most authentic French peasant autobiographies we have. Both lived in areas where Dorgères had no influence, but Grenadou (though he always considered himself a man of the Left) was drawn momentarily to militant actions with the Parti Agraire.

An excellent recent survey of the history of French farmers' organizations, with a particularly full bibliography, is Mark C. Cleary, *Peasants, Politicians, and Producers: The Organization of Agriculture in France since 1918* (Cambridge: Cambridge University Press, 1989). See also Paul Houée, *Coopération et organisations agricoles françaises—bibliographie* (Paris: Editions Cujas, 1970); Louis Prugnaud, *Les Etapes du syndicalisme agricole en France* (Paris: Editions de l'épi, 1963); and Henri Mendras, "Les Organisations agricoles," in *Les Paysans et la politique dans la France contemporaine,* ed. Jacques Fauvet et Henri Mendras (Paris: A. Colin, 1958), pp. 231–51.

Interwar French peasant leaders have been little studied. One catches a glimpse of Henry Queuille, country doctor, Radical politician, and ten times minister of agriculture before the war in Isabel Boussard, "Henri Queuille et la France rurale," in *Henri Queuille et la République,* ed., Pierre Delivet and Gilles Le Béguec (Limoges: TRAMES, 1987), pp. 69–136. The rather pedestrian memoirs of Joseph Faure were published in a special issue of *Chambres d'agriculture,* March 1975. The much racier memoirs of Jacques Le Roy Ladurie, *Souvenirs, 1902–1945* (Paris: Flammarion, 1997), unfortunately say almost nothing about his years of militancy alongside Dorgères in the 1930s.

A comparative perspective, all too rare in agrarian history, informs *Europäische Bauernparteien im 20. Jahrhundert,* ed., Heinz Gollwitzer, (Stuttgart and New York: Gustav Fischer Verlag, 1977). French farmers' political organizations are compared to others in that book by Hans-Jürgen Puhle, "Warum gibt es in Westeuropa keine Bauernparteien?" (pp. 603–67), and by the same author in *Politische Agrarbewegungen in kapitalistische Industriegesellschaften: Deutschland, U.S.A., und Frankreich im 20. Jahrhundert* (Göttingen: Vandenhoeck and Ruprecht, 1975). For a recent treatment of agrarian politics in Germany, see *Peasants and Lords in Modern Germany,* ed., Robert G. Moeller, (Boston: Allen and Unwin, 1986).

The classic work on peasant fascism in Germany is Rudolf Heberle, *Landbevölkerung und Nationalsozialismus: Eine soziologische Untersuchung der politischen Willensbildung in Schleswig-Holstein 1918–1932* (Stuttgart: Deutsche Verlags-Anstalt, 1963), based on research completed in 1932. In exile, the author published a much abridged English version, *From Democracy to Nazism* (New York: Grosset and Dunlap, 1970). Italian rural fascism is explored deeply in a setting of labor conflict in the big farms of the Po Valley by Paul Corner, *Fascism in Ferrara* (Oxford: Clarendon Press, 1976). See also Anthony L. Cardoza, *Agrarian Elites and Italian Fascism: The Province of Bologna, 1901–1926* (Princeton, N.J.: Princeton University Press, 1982); Frank Snowden, *The Fascist Revolution in Tuscany* (Cambridge: Cambridge University Press, 1989); and Alice Kelikian, *Town and Country under Fascism: the Tranformation of Brescia, 1915–1926* (New York and Oxford: Oxford University Press, 1986).

Some of the most enlightening works about French farmers' organizations and aspirations are local studies. A penetrating comparison of different strategic options chosen by farmers in two regions of Brittany is Suzanne Berger, *Peasants against Politics: Rural Organization in Brittany, 1911–1967* (Cambridge, Mass.: Harvard University Press, 1972). Ronald Hubscher, *L'Agriculture et la société rurale dans le Pas-de-Calais du milieu du XIX*e *siècle à 1914,* Mémoires de la Commission Départementale des Monuments Historiques du Pas-de-Calais, XX, Nos. 1–2, Arras, 1979–80, is the most thorough case study of the crises of ecomomic globalization that began to affect French farmers in the 1880s and their various responses. Other local studies include Claude Mesliand, *Paysans du Vaucluse (1860–1939)* (Aix-en-Provence: Publications de l'Université de Provence Aix-Marseille, 1989), No. 1; Jean Vercherand, *Un Siècle de syndicalisme: la vie locale et nationale à travers le cas du département de la Loire* (St. Etienne: Centre d'Etudes Foréziennes, 1994); Pierre Alphandéry, *Trente ans de syndicalisme gestionnaire dans le Calvados* (Paris: INRA/CORDES, 1977); Bertrand Hervieu, *Ouvriers ruraux du Perche* (Nanterre: Université de Paris X, 1976); Claude Letellier de Blanchard, "L'Evolution du syndicalisme agricole en Basse-Normandie de 1884 à nos jours," thèse pour le doctorat en sciences politiques, Faculté de Droit et de Sciences Economiques, Université de Caen, 1968; Alphonse Guimbretière, *Histoire et cheminements des organisations agricoles de Maine-et-Loire* (Angers: chez Author, 1987); and Gabriel Lantin, *Cent ans d'histoire des organisations agricoles de la Sarthe* (Le Mans: Union des Organisations Agricoles de la Sarthe, 1982).

For the Vichy Peasant Corporation, the fundamental work is Isabel Boussard, *La Corporation paysanne* (Paris: Presses de la Fondation Nationale des Sciences Politiques, 1980). See also *Vichy et la Corporation Paysanne: documents réunis et présentés par Isabel Boussard* (Paris: Presses de la Fondation Nationale des Sciences Politiques, 1980).

The economic conditions of French agriculture have been most profoundly analyzed by Gilles Postel-Vinay, mostly in article form. A good place to start is his "L'Agriculture dans l'économie française," in *Entre l'etat et le marché: l'économie française des années 1880 à nos jours,* ed. Maurice Lévy Leboyer (Paris: Gallimard, 1991). Also important is the work of Maurice Lévy-Leboyer, such as *Le Revenu agricole et la rente foncière en Basse-Normandie: étude de croissance régionale* (Paris: Klincksieck, 1972).

The impact of World War I on the agrarian economies of the world is surveyed by Avner Offer, *The First World War: An Agrarian Interpretation* (Cambridge: Cambridge University Press, 1989).

Eugen Weber, *Peasants into Frenchmen: The Modernization of Rural France* (Stanford, Calif.: Stanford University Press, 1976), and Roger Thabault, *Education and Change in a Village Community: Mazières-en-Gâtine, 1848–1914* (New York: Schocken, 1971), are two classic accounts of the slow and incomplete integration of peasants into the French national community in the late nineteenth century.

The shrinkage of the French rural population and peasant culture since the 1880s, gradual at first and then cataclysmic since the 1960s, has concerned many French people passionately. The most influential work in this vein is by the indefatigable rural sociologist Henri Mendras, *La Fin des paysans,* 2nd ed. (Paris: Actes-Sud, 1984). The subject is brought up to date by Pierre Alphandéry, Pierre Bitoun, and Yves Dupont, *Les Champs du départ: une France rurale sans paysans* (Paris: Découverte, 1989). Michel Gervais, Claude Servolin, and Jean Weil, *Une France sans paysans* (Paris: Editions du Seuil, 1965), is still interesting.

Specialized works on social and financial institutions affecting farmers include André Gueslin, *Histoire des Crédits agricoles,* 2 vols. (Paris: Economica, 1984); Jean Moquay, "L'Evolution sociale en agriculture: la condition des ouvriers agricoles depuis 1936" thèse, University of Bordeaux, Faculty of Law 1939; André Kettenmayer, "Les Allocations familiales en Agriculture," Thèse pour le doctorat, Faculté de droit, Université de Paris, 1943; and Françoise Manderscheid, *Une autre Sécurité Sociale: la Mutualité Sociale Agricole* (Paris: l'Harmattan, 1991).

A tendentious but intimately informed account of rightwing farmers' politics in Brittany is François Mévellec, *Le Combat paysan Breton à travers les siècles* and *Le Combat du paysan Breton à son apogée* (Rennes: Imprimerie "Les Nouvelles," 1973–1974).

Useful studies of the activities of the Left among farmers in the twentieth century include Philippe Gratton, *Les Luttes de classes dans les campagnes*

(Paris: Editions Anthropos, 1971); Philippe Gratton, *Les Paysans français contre l'agrarisme* (Paris: Maspéro, 1972); Gérard Belloin, *Renaud Jean: le tribun des paysans* (Paris: Editions de l'Atelier, 1993); Laird Boswell, "The French Rural Communist Electorate," *Journal of Interdisciplinary History,* Vol. 23, No. 4 (Spring 1993), 719–49; and Laura Frader, *Peasants and Protest: Workers, Politics, and Unions in the Aude, 1850–1914* (Berkeley: University of California Press, 1991).

The great farm workers' strikes of 1936–37 have been little studied. Two contemporary accounts are informative: Pierre Fromont and Francis Bourgeois, "Les Grèves agricoles de Tremblay-les-Gonesse en 1936," *Revue d'économie politique,* 51st year, No. 5 (September–October 1937), 1413–51; and Philippe de Chevigny, "Grèves et sociologie à la campagne," Thèse agricole, Institut Agricole de Beauvais: Section d'Enseignement supérieur d'Agriculture de l'Institut Catholique de Paris, 20 May 1938. The most thorough recent scholarly account is Danièle Ponchelet, "Ouvriers nomades et patrons briards: les grandes exploitations agricoles dans la Brie, 1848–1938," Thèse de doctorat de 3e cycle, Université de Paris X, Nanterre, 1986.

The most penetrating analysis of the Fifth Republic's way of dealing with agriculture is John T. S. Keeler, *The Politics of Neo-corporatism in France: Farmers, the State, and Agricultural Policy-making in the Fifth Republic* (New York and Oxford: Oxford University Press, 1987). See also the special issue of *La Revue française de science politique,* XII, No. 3 (September 1962), devoted to the peasantry and politics under the Fifth Republic. Particularly useful are Henri Mendras and Yves Tavernier, "Les Manifestations de Juin 1961," and Suzanne Quiers-Valette, "Les Causes économiques de mécontentement paysan."

The historiography of rural violence in France is brilliantly introduced by Alain Corbin, "Histoire de la violence dans les campagnes françaises au XIXe siècle: esquisse d'un bilan," *Ethnologie française,* XXI, No. 3 (July–September 1991), 224–35.

INDEX